D1365060

# All I Never Knowed

## Mental Illness, a Mother's Love, and a Broken System

Stephanie Giese

ISBN: 978-1-7372068-0-4

*To Nicholas, because you asked and I promised I would try.*

# Contents

# Prologue

My laptop sits open on the oblong oak dining table, next to scattered Play-Doh crumbs and unfinished coloring pages. I'm trying to meet the Friday deadline for the education article I have been assigned by our local parenting magazine. I need to submit a thousand words on college savings options to my editor, but finding financial experts willing to be interviewed on short notice is proving trickier than anticipated. The girls, having abandoned their crayons, are now standing on the stone fireplace hearth, using it as a stage to take turns belting Disney ballads. I think I saw Donny take a miniature screwdriver into his bedroom after lunch. He's probably tinkering with last year's Pinewood Derby cars again. Nicholas sits across from me, piecing together tiny bricks. He's been working there for three hours.

"Mommy," Penny runs up to me, still in her mismatched pajamas at 3pm. "Ana keeps singing the wrong words on purpose even though me and Abby told her to stop."

"I said not to tell Ms. Stephanie," Ana yells from the living room.

"Abby and I," I correct my six-year-old. "And don't tattle. You can work it out. Mommy needs to write." I wave her back to the living room, where she sits arms-crossed on the overstuffed leather loveseat, deflated with the disappointment of being unsuccessful in her attempt to get her foster sister into trouble.

"Mom, one day will you write a book about me?" Nicholas doesn't bother looking up from the LEGO helicopter he's putting together on the other end of the table. We don't have a helicopter set, he's working from his memory of a Google image he asked me to look up yesterday. I have to admit, what he's put together so far is impressive, not just "impressive for a fifth grader," actually impressive. Much better than anything I could do. It's realistic and to-scale, and it looks like something LEGO could actually market and sell.

"Would you like that? Do you like when I write about you?" I pause and fold the top of my computer down in order to look at his face while I speak to him. His glasses are smudged and his fingernails are filthy. I think he wore that same Star Wars shirt yesterday.

"Yeah, people like to listen to my stories." He furrows his dark, bushy eyebrows behind the glasses. His freckles have faded from months of being indoors and his skin is so translucent it almost seems blue. The harsh Pennsylvania winter hasn't helped, but of course there are other reasons.

"Your story is a very important one." I try to convey with my tone and my facial expression just how solemnly true this is, but it doesn't matter because he isn't watching. When he finally looks at me, he's holding a long, flat brick between two fingers.

"What would the book be about?" I ask.

"You know, how brains can get sick and stuff."

"I would like to do that one day. I wish there were more people talking about that." This is not the first time we've had this conversation. Last week he told me the same thing. I wish more books like that did exist, as I haven't been able to find them when I need them. It might help to know how other people cope.

"Uh-huh. Have you seen the other grey piece that matches this one?"

"No, I haven't seen that. Do they have to match? Can you use that yellow piece right there?"

"I want the grey one. I need the grey one. Yellow isn't grey," he stands and shouts. His chair crashes behind him while he turns to throw the helicopter at the wall. It shatters into hundreds of separate pieces.

Ana scrambles off the fireplace and joins Penny on the sofa, where she curls into a ball and rocks while she screams in that high-pitched wail that pierces through my patience. Penny gently pats a small hand on Ana's head and whispers that it is going to be okay in a few minutes.

"Ana, stop, it's just Nick being Nick. Ignore him. Come sing with me," Abigail tries to coax her, which only makes her scream louder. Donny appears in the doorway, holding the tiny screwdriver like a weapon and glaring at Nick.

"Pick it all up," I tell Nicholas, mostly for the pretense of attempting to seem in charge, even though I know perfectly well the only person cleaning any of this mess is going to be me.

***

There are three things I know for sure. The first is that real love is unconditional, and the second is true beauty is found in brokenness. The third is that our stories are our most powerful assets. They are the basis for how we understand the world, form human connections, and find meaning and worth.

My son asked me to tell this story. It is his story. He will happily tell it himself, should you ever meet him in person, but he wanted me to be the one to write it down. I still don't know if that is the right thing to do, but I will do my best to honor his request to the best of my ability. I know that in order to do his story any kind of justice it needs to be told with the kind of raw, uncomfortable honesty that only a mother owns. I also know that if I'm going to be authentic, then I have to use the lens of my own experiences. So, this is my story as much as it is his. It is the story of the unbreakable, beautiful love between a mother and her son, as well as a husband and his wife. It is a story of family, trauma, treatment, and education, and my hope is that it may also be a commentary on the many ways we can all be better to each other. May it serve as a love letter to each family struggling through mental illness, each child battling the scars of trauma, and each mother questioning her worth.

Every part of this story is rooted in truth, although subject to the error of human memory. A few names of people and places have been changed to protect individual privacy. The dialogue has been recreated from memory, reviews of social media posts, journals, emails, and text messages to friends and family, with some artistic license taken. I also recorded several interviews with my children and my husband, a few of which are transcribed at the end of the book. Some specific dates have been confirmed through medical records, academic testing, and court documents. Where they could not be confirmed, others are estimations. In some cases, scenes have been condensed in order to convey events that occurred over the course of several months. One written encounter with police, social workers, or educators may contain events that actually occurred over several separate occasions, for example.

There are people represented within these pages who have been invaluable in carrying us through more tumultuous times, and still so many others I wish I could have included, but unfortunately one book only has enough space to hold so many stories and characters. To everyone who sees themselves represented in these words, and also to those who don't but are no less important in our story: we have seen and felt your love through your actions, and we are grateful. Occasionally within these pages, one person represents a compilation of many. Pastor Bob is a real person, and I did attend several counselling sessions with him. In the context of this book, for the purposes of continuity and simplicity, he stands in to represent sessions with several different professionals. Certain other characters were built in a similar way.

I feel it is important to say that Nicholas was consulted throughout the entire process of writing of this book, and his input regarding sensitive subjects like toileting, puberty, adoption, and therapy was always respected. At the time of this writing he is a teenager, and while I want to highlight the reality facing families like ours who parent children with mental illness and special health or neurological needs, I will not publish content that compromises my relationship with my son. He is aware of the graphic nature of some of the later scenes in this book, and he has always been willing to share those details publicly. Nicholas hopes that there will be other children who understand the way he feels and that sharing our story might help their parents find the resources they need.

The reader should be aware that this book contains strong language and graphic descriptions of domestic violence, childhood trauma, sexual assault, mental illness, attempted suicide, and self-harm. It is not a substitute for professional advice and counseling. Please consult a healthcare professional, therapist, guidance counselor, or trusted adult if you are in a similar situation. In a life-threatening emergency, dial 911. Information about further resources is also provided at the back of this book.

My intention is to allow our family to be seen as we are: imperfect people who love deeply and desperately seek change. I want to wish you enjoyment as you read these pages, but I can't because that would be disingenuous when the truth is that I hope certain aspects of our story make you very uncomfortable and that discomfort opens eyes and hearts. However, before we begin I do want to remind us all that it should never be my son or his disabilities and illness that make us angry or uncomfortable. Nicholas is only one boy, doing the best he can in impossible circumstances.

Those feelings should be directed where they belong: toward a system failing to deliver on its promise to serve families, leaving children like Nicholas and so many others to suffer.

I hope you fall in love with my son just as hard as I have and that love just might inspire some of the changes our country and its children so desperately need.

Thank you for giving us a space to share our story and your willingness to receive it. I hope you will allow it to change you, if only a fraction of the way in which it has changed me.

*"I never knowed I could make a family."*

-Nicholas, age 6

# Chapter 1

*York, Pennsylvania 2013*

We have to drive across town to take Nicholas to school, but at least this time they agreed to let him back into class. There are three children in the backseat of my Nissan minivan, but his silence is the most suspicious. Rarely, if ever, is our son this quiet.

"Mom? One day will I get married like the song man?" he finally asks.

"Huh?" I voice my confusion, and he starts to hum. I have to turn the radio dial up further. I hadn't noticed anything was playing, but once I hear the melody I recognize Kip Moore's *Hey Pretty Girl*. We've heard this song at least a dozen times before.

"Sure, Bubba, if you want to." I shrug. He takes a deeper, shaky breath.

My eyes connect with his in the rearview mirror, which is when I notice that there are tears falling down his cheeks. The familiar tightening starts to creep into my chest as I ask him what is the matter, but he insists nothing is wrong.

"I'm not sad, Mom. It's just this song," he nods toward the radio. "It is making my heart feel something."

His head sways back and forth with eyes closed for a minute, brown hair simultaneously flopping down into his face and also poking out in all directions because I didn't bother to put any gel into his miniature Mohawk this morning. The guitar hums as Mr. Moore tells us how he and his wife build their home and family together. When the song is over, Nicholas looks out the window and speaks in the high-pitched tone of a kindergartener. He has the slightest lisp, due to the absent front teeth.

"Sometimes people cry even when they're not sad," he tells me with solemn six-year-old wisdom. I have to acknowledge that it's true, though I've never been a happy occasion crier myself. I pride myself on my ability to get through an entire Hallmark movie or sappy commercial unscathed. Sadness, though, is another story.

I blink into the mirror. "What is your heart feeling now?" I ask him. He is quiet for a long stretch of time, remembering the lyrics and looking for an answer that seems just beyond his reach. On the surface the song is simply about a man falling in love and spending his life with a woman.

"I can get married. And then I would really have my own family? A real family?"

Oof. There it is.

I hate that word, real. That one stings the worst. It feels like he's trying to tell me, as best he can, that he will always feel a little bit out of place in my arms, and neither one of us knows if there is anything we can do about that. My son is entitled to feel however he feels about being adopted, but it's such a heavy weight on the shoulders of a child and I won't ever be able to make it go away. But I can continue to offer support carefully packaged inside of platitudes.

"Nicholas, we will always be your real family. It's my job to be your mom. Forever. But, yes, if it's what you want, then one day you can get married and have biological babies like the man in this song."

More tears start to fall from his face and he wipes them away with his entire open palm, leaving small streaks of dirt between his freckles.

"I never knowed I could make a family," he muses. I suppose growing up and getting married is not the sort of thing little boys tend to spend very much time thinking about.

"Sure, Bubba. When we grow up, we all get to make our own families. When Dad and I grew up, we made sure you were part of ours. We picked each other and we chose you, and one day you can pick someone too."

"I just never knowed that before." He smiles and swings his feet from the booster seat as we pull into the school drop-off lane. When our turn comes to park along the curb I cringe with embarrassment as I press the button to slide open his door and reveal the pile of trash, crushed Goldfish crackers, and week-old sippy cups covering the floor of my car.

"Bye, Mom." He doesn't look back as he mounts the blue L.L. Bean backpack onto his body. It hangs almost down to his knees and bounces when he runs inside the glass doors and up the stairs toward his classroom.

The principal, standing a few feet away on the sidewalk as he's observing the morning routine, holds up a finger to signal me to wait. He waves the car behind me around and knocks lightly on my window with bent knuckles. I roll it down and say good morning.

"Hello, Mrs. Giese. I just wanted to let you know I'll be calling you later today. We'd like to schedule some more testing and another meeting for Nicholas."

"Sure, Dr. Walker. I'll be available in the afternoon."

He pats the roof of my van to signal our brief conversation is over, and I pull away to take the girls to their own school.

Once the kids are accounted for, I have an appointment of my own this morning. Today is my first meeting with Pastor Bob, the leader of our church. It seemed like it would be a good idea to finally talk to someone about everything, but I've been holding it in for so long that I don't have any idea where to begin. I've been taking children to therapy for years, but I've never gone myself. Does pastoral counseling even count as therapy?

When I arrive at the church, I walk into the detached office building and sit down in the foyer.

"Stephanie," Kathy, the receptionist smiles and greets me. I had no idea she knew my name. "Nice to see you. Did you have an appointment?"

"Um, yeah. I have a meeting with Pastor Bob. For counseling?" The last part squeaks out in a cracked whisper, and I have no idea why it feels as embarrassing as it does. I believe in therapy. My own mother is a therapist. There is nothing wrong with this. This is a good thing. It's good. At least that's the mantra I will repeat to myself while I close my eyes and wait on the upholstered maroon chair, which must be older than I am.

"Great. He should be with you any minute. If he doesn't come out by 9:30, just knock on his door. It's that one right there," she points before she turns back to her paperwork.

Barely five minutes go by before his office door opens and Pastor Bob emerges. He is small and unintimidating in stature, but he stands straight and confident. "Well, hello, young lady. I'm glad to see you today. Come on in."

I stand to follow him and he closes the door gently behind me.

He doesn't have a couch in his office, as I'd imagined. Instead we sit in new leather chairs, just he and I, a large round table filling the space between us. Rows of paperbacks are stacked from floor to ceiling in the built-in shelves. The table is brown like our chairs and the bookshelves and everything else. The clock is behind me, and it would be rude to take out my phone. I don't know how long I've been here, but I know I need to leave by 10:45 if I'm going to pick Abby up on time. I have to concentrate to maintain eye contact. I can see my own reflection in his glasses, and I have to look past myself to see him.

"I'm glad you decided to come in today." His tone is warm and patient, fatherly. Pastor Bob leans back in his chair and folds his hands, resting them on top of the beige sweater vest that is covering his stomach. "Why don't you tell me a little bit about why you wanted to talk?"

I guess we're getting right to it. "Well, the last few years have been," there really aren't any words to describe how they have been, so I let the sentence hang. He waits. "Stressful."

"How so?" he asks and I freeze. How can two words be both so simple and so loaded that the memories rush back to me, buzzing and stinging inside my head like a swarm of hornets? When they threaten to escape through my tear ducts, I have to pinch the bridge of my nose to push them back.

"I don't know how familiar you are with our story?" I raise the last word like the question it is and wait for his response.

"A bit. Your family has been coming here for a few years now. But I'd like to hear your version, in your own words. I would like to know more about your story, specifically the parts about you. You are a storyteller, correct? That's all we are trying to do here."

"That is actually something I've been struggling with. I don't know how to separate my story from his. I'm really not sure which parts are mine to tell, and what only belongs to him."

Shouldn't it be my job to respect that? Protect Nicholas? I don't know how much I'm allowed to share of someone else's story.

"Hmm. You know, sometimes our stories do overlap and intertwine with each other. They should, if we are doing this right."

"This?"

"Life."

The silence that follows is not unpleasant. He is giving

6

me the space I need to think. When I open my mouth to speak again there is only one thing that I know to be true.

"I don't even know where to start."

He nods and leans forward. "We have time. Why don't you start from the beginning?"

"If you say so."

I raise my eyes again to look across the table at the pastor patiently waiting for me to speak, and I start to tell him our story. The version that starts with Nicholas.

# Chapter 2

*Tampa, 2008*

"Are you ready?" Eddie pulls into the McDonald's parking lot and we sit, fidgeting, wondering if they are here.

"Not at all. You?"

My husband shakes his head in repose to my question. I pass the camera between my hands, bouncing it on my knee. Eventually we are going to have to work up the courage to go inside. I should have worn something different, brighter. I'm regretting the black shirt and skirt combination I picked out for work this morning. It makes me look like I am dressed for a funeral, but this is a happy occasion. Probably. Although I didn't bring a present. Is that bad? Should we have flowers? What am I supposed to say to him? To her? To them? We only got the phone call yesterday.

I hadn't been expecting it. This was not supposed to be a special day. Then again, the ones we tend to remember rarely are. Twenty-four hours ago, I was in the car driving to a meeting after school. All of the Hillsborough County elementary science department chairs had another professional development training at Busch Gardens. I thought seeing the owls would be the best part of this Thursday. I was wrong.

Somewhere along Linebaugh Avenue my cell phone rang and I saw Christy's number. I thought she was going to ask me a question about our paperwork or maybe tell us about another match event coming up next month. I had no idea answering that call was going to change everything. The conversation will forever be etched into my memory the same way I sit and recall every detail now.

"Hi, Christy."

"Hey, Stephanie." Christy's voice always sounds like it is smiling. Her thick southern accent makes it seem like my name ends with three extra e's.

"Would you mind if I called you back in a little while? I'm driving."

"Actually, this is pretty important. I'm going to need you to answer fast."

"Okay?" There is only one place she could be going with this.

"There is a little boy who has come up. His name is Nicholas. He's Caucasian and he is thirteen months old. He has been in state custody for eleven months. He is legally free for adoption." She's reciting his profile, trying hard to sound professional and appropriately robotic, keep the emotion out of it. This is the part where we are only allowed to deal with facts. It's hard for both of us because neither one of us was made that way.

"When is the match meeting?" I put on my teacher voice

to match her social worker one.

Eddie and I have already had our home study presented to the committee and have been rejected twice. We're young, too young, and we have no experience parenting any children at all, much less children dealing with trauma. The youngest foster children almost always go to families who are more seasoned. It's been less than two years since we graduated from college, we don't feel comfortable parenting teens. It's been difficult to place us with any of the available kids.

I'm still wondering who was good enough to be matched with the little girl who could have been our daughter if the team had chosen us last month. Her name is Dana. She's four-years-old and has Hispanic heritage. That's all I will ever know about her because it is the only information they told us on the phone. Now I wonder how it is that this new baby, maybe our baby, came to be in custody. I do the math in my head and realize that according to what Christy just told me, Nicholas was only eight weeks old when he entered the system.

"That's the thing," she pauses. "This is a very strange situation. Our agency has been working with kids in foster care for quite a while, and this really doesn't happen." Christy is buying time, trying to figure out how she wants to word what she is about to say. "This one is going to have to be a private adoption. He doesn't meet our criteria."

"I don't understand." I know there are certain criteria children need to meet in order to qualify as having "special needs" in foster care. They are different than the special needs I see as an educator. It's a broader category meant to encompass any child in care. These needs include things like their race, age, and if they have any siblings, in addition to any medical issues there may be. I have never heard of a foster child not meeting the definition.

Christy goes on, "If you decide to move forward, the whole process might be a little different than we expected. There is no match meeting. You've already been selected." They picked us? "But Nicholas is very young, he is not a minority, he is healthy, and he doesn't have siblings. He just doesn't meet the special needs criteria for a state-sponsored adoption. I can still help you, but if you choose to proceed you will need to do your adoption through a private attorney."

She takes a breath, then continues, "He will not receive any of the benefits typically granted to former foster children. It is important that you understand that. And it might get expensive." There it is. He can be ours, but only if we can afford him. He will remain a ward of the state until she finds a family who can buy his freedom. We're the first name on her list.

"How expensive?" I stop at a red light.

"I really don't know. Again, this just does not happen. I have never seen it before. But I asked a colleague with a bit more experience and she's been through it once. She said to estimate between five and ten thousand dollars." I'm a little bit relieved. It's significantly less than I expected her to say. Only a fraction of what I know most private adoptions cost. I've seen families try to raise three times that much to cover international adoption fees. Still, it's odd that we are even having this conversation. He's been in foster care for a year.

Christy is still talking. "So, I'm sorry, but before I continue here, I have to ask you, do you have access to that much money?" Adoption out of foster care is supposed to be free. She's uncomfortable asking if we have the means to purchase a child from the state of Florida, as if we are real estate developers buying a piece of land. There is no time to be uncomfortable, so I just answer.

"We do." After a few years of saving, there is about $11,000 in our account. I guess I could write her a check if she needs one. For all I know, that's what she is asking. Christy breathes an audible sigh of relief.

"Great. Then I get to ask one of my favorite questions. Would you like to meet him? His foster mother is willing to meet with the prospective parents tomorrow." Apparently, that's us.

"What?" I think I might have gone into shock. The light changes to green and I forget what that means until the car behind me beeps. I start driving again, too slowly, while Christy moves on with the conversation.

"He has been living with Debbie, do you remember her? She was the foster mother who spoke at your training. Her home has been his only placement while in custody. That's fortunate," she notes before continuing, "Debbie's one of our best. She is willing to meet with you tomorrow and introduce him, if you'd like. Why don't you call Eddie and y'all call me back as soon as you can. I'll be in the office for another hour. In the meantime, I will email you a few pictures. Talk to you soon."

With only one hour and three pictures I can't access from a flip phone, she's asking us to make the biggest decision of our lives. We're not prepared for a baby. We don't even have a crib. A month ago, they told us that there was no chance we would ever be matched with a child under the age of six. Now she's telling me that by this time tomorrow I might be changing diapers. It occurs to me that I don't have any diapers.

There are too many thoughts in my head to process. I need to talk to my husband right away, but he is not answering his phone, and now I'm here at Busch Gardens and I need to get into the stupid science meeting because I'm the only representative for our school. For a moment I consider signing in with my employee number and then just leaving, or saying I got sick. But I'm supposed to go back and report on whatever happens here to the entire faculty, and if I am going to be a mother at twenty-three, I guess I also need to practice how to be responsible. I call Eddie five or six times and leave several messages before he finally calls me back, just before we all start filing in to the large conference room.

"Wait. What? Tomorrow? Like the day that starts eight hours from now? And they already chose us before even telling us about him? How do you do a private adoption out of state care? Isn't that an oxymoron?"

He's confused. It's not supposed to happen this way and the engineer in him has a hard time deviating from a set plan.

"I don't know. That's what Christy says." My stomach is a ball of knots, I'm talking too fast and I'm not explaining it well enough, but I try my best to tell him that all I know is I'm standing in a lobby at Busch Gardens, and I only have a minute, and I need to know if he wants to meet this little boy tomorrow.

"I mean, yeah. Of course." He doesn't hesitate. "It sounds great, it just doesn't make a lot of sense, though."

For the first time since the phone rang in the car, I can breathe. I tell him to call Christy because she can explain it all better anyway and I need to go to my meeting. It's the longest hour and a half of my life and I don't remember a single thing that happened. By now I should know better than to get my hopes up. We've been doing this for a year and a half, and this part of the adoption process has knocked us down before. But it's hard not to let myself get too excited when there are pictures waiting for me at home on the computer, and those pictures are of a little boy who just might be our son.

# Chapter 3

Only one day has passed, and now an eight-by-eleven-inch piece of paper sits between us on the center console. The photos from Christy's email stare up at me in black and white. One shows a bath towel wrapped around a small head with a wide toothless grin, the other the same face poking out of a polo shirt probably handed down from an older foster sibling, because it's at least two sizes too big.

Eddie looks in the rearview mirror and combs his fingers through his own black hair, although the pomade has already left it stiff. A few more deep breaths and it's time to open the doors to the Nissan minivan we bought a year ago because we knew eventually this day would come. Although, we didn't ever dream our family would start here, in a McDonald's parking lot, with empty gum wrappers on the ground and the smell of hot oil in the air. I stand and tug on my skirt to straighten it then move my hands up to my shoulders, brushing off stray pieces of dog hair that might just be in my imagination. Eddie walks around the van to meet me and puts his hand on the small of my back as we walk inside together.

Debbie is already there, situated in a booth in the Playplace. We recognize her right away from the speeches she gave to our preparation class. Today she brought her oldest daughter to help her wrangle the seven youngest children she has in her care at the moment. There are more at home. Only a few of them are biologically related, she explains as she briefly introduces everyone. She's not really supposed to have that many placed with her at once, it's against the guidelines, but Hillsborough County has over two thousand foster children and only a few hundred licensed homes. Where else are they going to go?

She is all broad shoulders and big smiles, sitting in a booth and balancing a toddler who is chewing on a french fry. This is Nicholas. The same face from the photographs stares up at me, now in three dimensions. I make a mental note that if he were mine, when he is mine, he would not be eating fast food, but I smile pleasantly and do my best to ignore my nerves and engage in the small talk.

"So, do your kids play any sports?" I ask, tentatively, prompted by a Tampa Bay Rays t-shirt passing by.

Debbie is friendly and outgoing and makes easy conversation. She talks about the baseball league of her oldest son as well as the little boy she is holding and all of his developmental milestones.

"He's been walking for a few months now, and he can say 'ball' and 'outside' and 'Mason.' That's his foster brother's name," she tells us. Nicholas has filled out some more since taking the pictures that were in my email. His cheeks are round and dimpled, and he cannot stop chewing and drooling, drooling and chewing. He's teething.

An eight-year-old girl runs up to us, her ponytail bouncing. "Are you going to adopt Casper?" his foster sister asks. I wish I knew.

"Casper?" I tilt my head.

Debbie explains, "Our family has taken to calling him Casper because he is so pale and so bald that even this Florida sun can't seem to give him any color."

I smile. Half of the children Debbie has with her don't know who we mean when we call him Nicholas. I know better than to make any promises.

"I hope so." The best I can offer is honesty in response to her question. The girl takes it as a cue to head back to the slide and let the grown-ups keep talking. There's so much we need to say, only half of it can be put into words. The rest are emotions that rise to thicken the air and overwhelm the moment. They sit at the forefront in hearts and heads and throats. We're walking a tightrope because we all want this day to be a cause for celebration, but we don't know yet if we can trust each other, and we really only have an hour and a few cold french fries to share between us in order to find out.

Debbie continues, "This one here likes to eat. He sleeps all night too." She is giving us a sales pitch, as if we would need convincing. I have wanted to adopt a child from America's foster care system since my freshman year of college when I read Dave Pelzer's book *A Child Called It*. It took a bit more convincing to get my husband on board, but now he's as invested as I am.

Eddie and I have spent the entire first year and a half of our marriage in trainings preparing for this moment. As far as we're concerned, we are here to sell ourselves to her. If we say something wrong, if she goes back and tells Christy we are not the right fit, or if she decides she wants to adopt Nicholas herself, then this is going to fall through. I don't know if I can handle another rejection.

I thought they said they needed loving homes in order to place the waiting children, but for reasons unbeknownst to me they keep passing on ours. The classes, the home study, and the background checks are finished. We've done everything they told us to do. Now we need Debbie on our side. It's the closest I've ever been to being a mother, and the decision is not mine to make. It's a hell of a job interview.

"He looks very healthy. All the kids do. I have no idea how you are so calm. I'm a little overwhelmed right now," I confide to her.

There are a lot of big and small people here in the Playplace whom I need to convince to like me. Will they think we are good enough? I feel reserved and awkward awaiting her approval, but Debbie doesn't seem to notice. She hops seamlessly from one topic to the next.

"Tell me about your families," and then "What do you do at work?" she asks while she turns around to break up an argument or make sure someone comes back to finish their chicken nuggets. We tell her how Eddie designs highways and I teach math and science to academically gifted kids. Before my current job, I taught first grade in a much poorer school district, just outside of Washington, D.C. We moved to Tampa on a whim about two years ago when Eddie got a job offer. I don't know how Debbie is keeping track of who has eaten how much of what. She talks about her oldest son's baseball season and the other kids she has fostered through the years.

"Must be about thirty-five or forty of them by now, but you gotta remember some of them just came for a day or two." She laments that she cannot be the one to adopt Casper, but the timing did not work out. She has just taken in a sibling group of four and she needs to focus on them right now.

"I knew it would be easy to find a good home for a baby," she says. "It's the older ones that are real tough to place." She talks with passion about the Foster Angels and her work as one of their coordinators.

"We use Foster Angels to give birthday and Christmas gifts to every child in foster care in Hillsborough. Working on a website." She's thrilled with the donations that have come in so far this year. Her goal is to make sure all foster children have their own bicycle. I always envy women who are so comfortable with themselves and their passions that their enthusiasm becomes contagious. Debbie is at home here, in her own skin, talking about the one thing she loves most in the world: taking in other people's children and making them her own.

Sitting across from her, watching and listening, it is impossible not to be astounded. She is about to take the baby on her lap, this child she has raised for a year, and hand him over to us—to me—in the same way that she has done with dozens of children and dozens of forever families before us. Under the small talk about first words and baseball games, what I'm really doing is asking her to trust blindly that I will work just as hard and love just as fiercely as she does every day. It's the same silent promise she must have made to his birth mother. All the birth mothers. Looking into her eyes, I'm struck by the notion that I have no idea how I am ever going to be able to compare. All of the confidence I managed to build for this moment disappears. Unlike Debbie, I've never done this before, and I don't know what I'm doing. I don't know why anyone would have chosen me to be Nicholas' third and final mom. Christy must be insane to think we can do this.

But that doesn't seem to stop anything. Debbie likes us, and so does Christy.

As we gather ourselves to leave, Debbie assures me, "I'm going to call the agency tonight and give you both my recommendation." Her words carry weight. It means he's almost ready to come home, which is as terrifying as it is exciting. We take our first family photo sitting in the sticky booth.

We've just met our son in a McDonald's. I'll never look at a BigMac the same way again.

# Chapter 4

Nicholas won't keep his clothes on. It's Florida and it's August, so he doesn't have to. I used all of my sick days as maternity leave when he moved into our house in May, and by the time I ran out school was closed for summer break, so I have been home with Nicholas for three months. I can't remember the last time I needed to dress him in more than a diaper. Our ninety-day trial period should be over by now, but we still don't have a date to appear before the judge to finalize the adoption, which is why I'm stuck making call after call, trying to figure out how the health care is supposed to work.

"Oh my God, are you serious?" I ask the computerized robotic tone on the other end of the receiver. "Operator? Representative?" I try pressing zero a few times in succession, but it is useless.

Eddie works half days on Fridays and is outside mowing the lawn again. The grass needs to be cut twice a week this time of year. Nicholas stays inside with me, in the air conditioning, but he runs around the house from window to window trying to see out. His bare feet make a hollow slapping sound as they hit the laminate wood floors. Lucy, our beagle, chases him. Her ears flop and her tail wags as her paws slide to a stop at his side. Nicholas is just tall enough now to see over the marble ledge, and he's obsessed with the lawnmower. His legs are bowed, and there is a rash starting to form on his chest from either the drool or the heat, I'm not sure. He bounces up and down, diaper sagging, as he bangs on the windowsill.

"Dada, mow mower. Mow Mower!"

"Yes, baby. Daddy is using the lawnmower."

"Mow Mower. Mow mower outside." He continues to bang, trying to get me to see how important it is that we get out there immediately and lay eyes upon such a magnificent thing. I take a bib from the drawer in the kitchen and snap it around his neck, hoping it will absorb some of the spit. He takes it off immediately and throws it on the floor. I don't even bother to stop Lucy when she grabs it and runs down the hall. The phone resting on my shoulder is still taunting me with elevator music. I wish I had remembered to look at the clock when they put me on hold. I'm not sure how long it's been now, but it sure feels like forever.

"We'll go outside later," I promise. "Mommy is still on the phone."

I have to take Nicholas to the doctor, but it's proving impossible to get an appointment. He needs a check-up and most likely some shots if we want to put him in day care. I'm supposed to go back to work this month, but we are still in limbo because he doesn't technically belong to anyone at the moment. He's still a foster child, we think, but I'm not a foster mother. I'm a permanent placement, his adoptive mother. Except I'm not yet, I can't be until there is an adoption. He might not actually be a foster child anymore, since this has transitioned to a private case. But he was under the guardianship of the state, so no one knows how that works. How do you have a child who is simultaneously a ward of the state but also not a foster child?

No one gave me a Medicaid card for him, and they told me he wouldn't qualify for benefits once it had been decided that he didn't meet the special needs criteria. Half of the people I have spoken to seem to think he doesn't qualify now that he is in our home. His name has disappeared from some of the computer databases, but it still shows up in others. Several caseworkers believe he should still have Medicaid access until the court date is finalized, but they don't seem to know how to get me an updated card for him because of his unique circumstance.

We are his guardians, but by law not his adoptive parents yet. We are fortunate enough not to need help buying food or diapers, so I haven't bothered looking into WIC, the government benefits that cover basic needs for children from low-income or foster families but are separate from healthcare coverage. I do want to take him to the doctor. I cannot add him to our private insurance until we go to court, but I can't seem to get him covered under any kind of state insurance either. According to the last three people on the phone, the state wants to say they have passed his care onto us, but they haven't actually granted us legal custody in writing anywhere that I can find.

It's not just me. No one who works for the state or our agency can find it either. Since he doesn't really seem to belong to anyone, no one knows how to claim him. No doctors want to see him. I've spent all day on the phone. Finally, after three more calls, someone suggests taking him back to whatever doctor Debbie had him seeing. They should have his information on file. Let them think you are his latest foster mom, or even that it's still Debbie, they tell me. Maybe even see if she'd be willing to take him. I don't want to lie. Is that a lie? I don't know anymore. It can't be Medicaid fraud if half the people working for the state think he is still on Medicaid. I hang up for what I assume is the last time today, just thankful to have some sort of plan.

When the phone rings again I want to throw it, but thankfully, it's Christy.

"Howdy. I have good news for ya. We've got a date. Looks like it'll be two more months yet, but, hey, we have our court date." I write it on the whiteboard calendar in our kitchen with lots of exclamation points, thank her, and hang up again. Then I look in the pantry for something to give Nicholas for lunch. We seem to be out of most of his favorites. Now that I think about it, I also wanted to grab some shaving cream and that one other thing. The August heat has me feeling dizzy and nauseated. I probably just need to eat. I walk over to the window, now covered with wet and sticky handprints, and pick him up. I blow raspberries on his belly and make him laugh.

"Come on, Bubba. Let's get you dressed. You're coming with me. We have a few places to go."

I'm finally learning how to venture out of the house by myself with an entire extra person. Nicholas and I have spent the afternoon running errands and having lunch, and he is exhausted, asleep in his stroller as I stand in line at Target for the last few things we need to get today. The woman checking out in front of us is overly friendly. The sun has bleached both her hair and her skin, and there are faded pastel versions of tropical flowers printed all over her shirt. She points to him with both hands and lifts her shoulders so that she smiles with her entire body.

"Aw, is he yours?" she asks, and I freeze. Maybe she thinks I'm the nanny. I smile back at her, a more reserved kind of smile, and hope that the look all women have perfected to protect themselves from strangers will serve as an adequate answer. She seems nice enough. I can't hold it against her. She couldn't know that with three words she has managed to unlock the question I've been afraid to ask myself.

Yes, I am the one waking up at night, filling bottles, and kissing boo boos. But no. I can't take him to visit my parents in Baltimore without permission, and there are appointments on my calendar for a trained professional to come to my house and observe our interactions. Eddie and I haven't gone out to dinner alone in three months because I can't hire a babysitter who hasn't been fingerprinted and approved, and I'm still waiting to stand before a judge.

This is a test drive. Ninety days at a minimum where Christy is terrified that we will decide to hand him back and she will have to start looking at new prospects. Three months that have now stretched into five before we'll be in court, and we are equally concerned that if we do something wrong she can decide to take him away from us. I'm afraid to let him call me Mama, but I still do. It's the first test in my life no one told me how to pass, and until I get the elusive stamp of approval, I guess I'm only half a mother.

He's belonged to two women before me, and they both loved him enough to let go. I don't know if I'm ever going to be that strong. Is he mine? I don't know. She is still looking at me, expecting an answer. I don't have one to give her. I can only offer, "This is Nicholas."

"Oh, look at him sleeping there. He's so handsome. And he looks just like his mother. And look at all that hair." Nicholas' hair has grown into a floppy brown mop that falls into his eyes. She is bobbing her head from him to me and back down again. She thinks it's a compliment, yet I feel like she punched me. I plaster the smile of protection back on my face and force myself to thank her. I've just met her. She has no idea that when she is talking about the mother who gave him his genes, she isn't talking about me. She waves one last time as she takes her bags from the young cashier.

It's our turn now. "Will that be everything?" The cashier turns her attention to me.

"Actually, I think I changed my mind about this one," I say, handing a box of blonde hair dye across the counter.

Maybe it's my fault for letting it hurt. I'm going to need to find tougher skin, but that's not exactly something we can pick up here at Target. He does have blue eyes and pale skin and freckles. He does look like me, he even shares my natural hair color. Maybe he looks like her too, the woman his genes are actually from. Maybe we all look like each other. We're family now, all of us. Or we will be. For a minute it makes me feel guilty. Do I want him to look like me? If I do, is that bad? This is nothing, really. How can I stand here and complain about an old lady who was only trying to be nice? How many other awkward conversations in parking lots are going to be avoided just because we are raising a little boy white enough to earn the nickname Casper? What about all of the families, adoptive and biological, who never get to have this conversation? No one would have said that to me about Dana. What would people have said instead?

At home I let Eddie take over with Nicholas and walk into the bathroom with our bag from the store. I set the shaving cream on the counter and take out the small pink box. I need to take a pregnancy test.

# Chapter 5

*October 2008*

Our court date is the first day of October. Christy has asked us to make our final choices about his name because she needs to get the correct spelling to the right people in order for a new birth certificate to be issued. I never knew adopted children received brand new birth certificates with different parents listed.

Eddie doesn't want to have this conversation. Neither do I.

"There is nothing to talk about," he's insisting. "We already made this decision."

"That was when everything was still hypothetical, and we thought we were talking about a six-year-old. Nicholas is a baby. He won't remember. I just want you to be sure. This is permanent."

It's a question they must have asked a dozen times in our trainings. Once we were matched with a child, would we keep his name? It always seemed odd to me that they even give you the opportunity to change it. We said we wouldn't, unless it was at the request of the child. We didn't want to erase anyone's history, unless an older child might happen to ask for a slate wiped clean. At the time we thought we were talking about an elementary school student with a first name that might represent a culture different than our own. We thought it wouldn't be our place to delete someone's heritage. We had no way to know he was going to come to us with the one name in the world we would never have chosen for our son.

Eddie is adamant, "I am sure. And I know he won't remember. That's exactly why we need to let him keep it. That's the name she chose. It's the one gift he has from his birth mom."

Well, there is that whole Gift of Life thing, but it doesn't seem like the best time to bring that up. Eddie's on a roll, and he is being much more mature about this than I am.

"I'm not going to be the one to take that away from them. Not because of him." Fresh salt in old wounds. Fine. I deserve it. "It could be a family name for them for all we know. Maybe he's named after his grandfather or an uncle."

"Or Santa Claus. Or Nick Nolte," I offer.

"You're not funny."

No, I'm really not, and it's my fault we are here. It's also my fault I am this worried about what people are going to think. Will our friends think I wanted to name our son after him? Is *he* going to think I named our son after him? The one and only ex-lover I have, if I can even call him that. How was I supposed to know those few weeks Eddie and I "took a break" in college would come back to haunt us for the rest of our lives? Eddie and I have managed to avoid this name for three years, but now there is a little boy in our house who shares it. I swear to call my son by his full name for as long as I live just to differentiate the two of them. I'm forgetting that babies grow into little boys, and then bigger boys, and then men with their own opinions and personalities. It is not a promise I'm going to be able to keep.

"We are already giving him my last name. After we go to court, all three of us will have my name." It's true. Eddie is right about that. Our last name will tie us together as a family. Way back then, I picked Eddie. We have our own Nicholas. We picked him, too. Eddie is mostly talking to himself. "It's fine. It's plenty. It's enough."

It has to be.

Fate has given us a son named Nicholas. And a new beginning. And right now, that new beginning is standing a few feet away from us in the living room playing with the plastic t-ball set one of my friends from college gave him when she and her husband came to visit last week. His toy comes up to his chest and talks to him in pre-recorded monosyllables. There is a small, rounded bat he can use to hit the ball that is attached to the tee, and it will go around in circles. He loves it, and it is fun to watch him laugh and clap at himself when he makes the ball go all the way around. He comes running up to us, holding the bat high above his head. My conversation with Eddie is over. My husband turns his attention to the baby.

"Yes. Bat. That's a bat. Can you say 'bat?' You're a bat boy."

Nicholas' lip starts to quiver and his eyes look to me. His

whole face turns red as he starts to cry harder than we have ever seen from him. Eddie doesn't understand, "What's the matter? Did he hurt himself? He was just standing there."

"No. He thought you said 'bad.' He thinks he's in trouble." Nicholas hates being in trouble. "Come here, honey. This is a bat. Baseball bat. You are a good boy. Such a good boy," I scoop him up and try to soothe him, bouncing and rubbing his back. "Daddy wouldn't say that." Eddie would never call any child a bad child in front of me, especially not Nicholas. My mother would never allow that in her house, and there is no way I would allow it in mine.

Every mother has a mantra. Sometimes we stumble on them ourselves, and sometimes they are just our own mother's words in her voice repeated in our heads. My mother is not touchy-feely, but she is kind and she is fair. She is careful with her words because she knows that words leave wounds that scar, and she will never let anyone tell a child that they are bad. Instead, she would repeat phrases to us when we were in trouble. I don't know if she made them up or if she read them in some dime store 1980's self-help book, but either way they have started to come back to me in the classroom when I'm dealing with difficult students, and now here at home with Nicholas.

"*There is no such thing as a bad child, there are only bad behaviors.*"

"*You are not bad, what you did was bad.*"

We don't need to worry about it today, though, because he wasn't even doing anything wrong.

"I'm sorry, buddy. Here let me take him." Eddie reaches out and takes Nicholas and walks over to the sofa, continuing to talk to him. "Hey, guess what? On October first, it's going to be a special day. It's going to be your Adoption Day, and it'll be here sooner than you think."

He turns his attention back to me, "What did Debbie say about the doctor?"

"She gave me his name. I made an appointment. I'm just not supposed to tell them he's been moved to a new placement and then everyone thinks it will be fine."

Eddie is right. October first comes, somehow faster than we ever thought it would, even though we seemed to be drowning in the waiting for so long. Nicholas is eighteen months old. We have dressed him in a three-piece suit and dressed ourselves to match, and we're headed downtown to the courthouse. As Eddie pulls into a parking space, I realize we forgot to bring a camera. We are not late, but there is no spare time to go to a store or back to the house to get one. It's not the type of oversight a new mother gets past easily.

"I can't believe we didn't bring it. What is the matter with us? We are going to be the worst parents ever. This is the most important day of his life so far, and we can't even remember to bring the stupid camera?" My new hormones are exaggerating my failure, and I feel suffocated.

Eddie is doing his best to comfort me, but it isn't working. He is nervous and he doesn't really have the patience required to deal with me in addition to appearing before a judge. "Babe. Relax. Let's just try to focus on getting through what we need to do and then having a great day. Maybe they'll have a gift shop or something where we can buy one."

"A gift shop? In the courthouse? For all of the people

who want to commemorate their parking tickets and custody disputes?" Sarcasm is the lowest form of wit, or at least that's what I think I heard on *Dr. Phil* once. It's also my default setting under stress.

"Right. I don't know. Maybe Debbie or Christy will have one. I'm sure they will take some pictures for you."

"That's not the point." It is the point, but I can't think about it right now. It will only hurt worse to admit that there are other women here who already know so much more about this than I do. There are people who actually have their lives together. Who can be trusted not to forget the camera. Who are better at all of it. I know full well I'm acting like a spoiled child stomping in a parking lot, but now is not the time to tell him that I'm angry because it's not supposed to hurt. Adoption does that, I'm learning. To every party involved. It presents these moments that sneak up and slap you with emotions you never expected, but sometimes as the adult you have to push down the pain because it's not entirely about you. Or even really about you at all.

This day is about Nicholas. I know that. It's a happy day, and that is what I want it to be. This is the day that he joins a forever family, our family, and we are supposed to be celebrating, so that's what I'm going to do. There are tears pooling, unwelcome, in the corners of my eyes, threatening my mascara, so I dab them with my index fingers and inhale deeply to reset myself. Then I look at the little boy standing between us and smile.

His brown hair has grown in shaggy and his grass-stained tennis shoes are peeking out from under the too-long legs of his creased suit pants, and a tiny button-down vest rounds out his courthouse ensemble. His arms are stretched as high as they can reach as he holds each of our hands in one of his. I know he doesn't care about the camera. I make my voice cheery again and vow I will keep it that way for the rest of the day. "Okay, let's do this."

I expected to be taken directly to a courtroom, but instead we are asked to sit around a long, rectangular conference table in another part of the building. The judge wants to talk to us privately first. Is this what being "in chambers" means? I notice Debbie and Christy in the hallway and wave. They come join us around the table.

"Hey, did either of you guys happen to bring a camera? We forgot." Eddie asks.

"No, sorry," Christy shakes her head.

"Yep, I always bring one to the adoptions," Debbie pats the side of her purse, then reaches in and pulls out a Polaroid. "No worries, you have a lot of other stuff on your minds today. I'll send you home with some photos."

"Awesome, thank you so much." Eddie leans back in his chair as he looks at me and turns his palms upward to indicate the problem has been solved. Just then the judge enters, donned in a flowing black robe. I'm surprised she is a woman and equally irritated with myself for being surprised.

"Well, hello," Judge Esrig greets us. "I heard we have an adoption today. That's exciting. Before we head into the courtroom, I just want to ask a few basic questions so we can make sure we are making the best decisions we can."

We are relieved that her questions are easy. Are we who we say we are? Yes. Why do we want to adopt Nicholas?

Because we have grown to love him and we believe strongly that all children deserve to grow up in a home where they are loved. Do we swear to treat this child the same as we would a biological one? We do.

"Okay then, let's head on over and make it official," Judge Esrig smiles and we are directed to a more formal courtroom. She sits behind the raised wooden bench. A few caseworkers from our adoption agency and our lawyer have also come to join us, but we still barely fill a single row of seats. Or should I call them pews, even if this isn't a church? That's what they are. It feels like an episode of Court TV when we raise our right hands and swear to tell the truth. She repeats a few of the same questions she asked a few minutes ago, then the gavel goes down and I feel exactly the same, but in an hour everything has changed.

Debbie takes out the bulky grey cube from her handbag and Christy asks Judge Esrig if she is willing to stay for a photo. We pose and smile a few times with the judge and a few more without. Debbie clicks away and gives us a few Polaroids so that we can commemorate this day, and she keeps one for herself. As she puts the camera away, she sheepishly pulls something else out of her purse and hands it to me. The gift is a small rectangle covered in blue pinstriped paper, wrinkled from its time inside her bag. I pull back the paper to reveal a silver-plated four-by-six-inch photo album where she has collected all the pictures she took of Nicholas' time in her home. There are only ten pictures.

"I'm sorry there aren't very many, but I try to take at least a few pictures of all the kids who stay with me. Now you can add the ones from today. I figured I was just getting you started, you'll have plenty soon enough." Debbie says.

"Thank you, so much. It's very thoughtful." I hug the book to my chest. "Oh, we almost forgot to tell you our news. Guess what? We are expecting. The baby is due in April." Part of me thought she and Christy would be upset with us for not giving Nicholas enough time with us alone to bond. To the contrary, they are thrilled. Looking down at the photos, everyone is smiling, including me. It's possible to feel so many things at once.

The social worker who hands me the manila envelope is not Christy, but another woman from the agency who must have been silently observing the ceremony. In the packet of paperwork she gives us, most things are redacted with thick black lines to comply with confidentiality regulations. Ours is supposed to be a closed adoption. His birth mother has chosen for it to be this way. We are not supposed to be given any information about her.

The caseworker nudges me as she whispers, "I'm not saying that anyone did this for Nicholas, but I am just saying that occasionally people accidentally make mistakes. Human error and whatnot." I look at her quizzically and she nods toward the thick stack of paper in my hands.

"If that happened to occur on page 23, in the section of the form where his birth parents' information is located, then you should probably just take a marker and black it out. Although, sometimes adoptive parents are able to look up birth parents on the computer and print a picture for their child to keep first." She winks at me and smiles before she adds, "Oh, and completely unrelated of course, but were you aware that the Hillsborough County Sherriff's office has an online record of arrests? Anyone who has been arrested recently in our county has their photo printed online, you just have to search their name. Isn't that interesting?" She points to the album in my hand. "That was a lovely present. Photos are so important, don't you think? So many of the kids we see wish they had early photos of themselves or pictures of birth parents." She smiles and gathers her belongings to leave. She knows what a precious gift she has just bestowed upon our family. We have their names now. And access to their photos. It also means she trusts me enough to know that I would never try to contact Nicholas' birth parents until my son makes that decision for himself. It occurs to me that he's my first child, but I'm his third mom, and I will always have to share him. I need to learn how to be at peace with that.

Back in the church office, sitting across the lacquered brown table, Pastor Bob tilts his head and looks at me curiously.

"You've been talking about that as a day you were looking forward to, but once it came, it didn't go completely as you expected?"

"You could say that." I shrug.

"What would you say?" He's not going to let it go.

I never told anyone how much it hurt. I guess I should have known better than to have expectations, but I couldn't help it. Of course, I was excited that he was finally ours, officially and forever. I hope that goes without saying. But it was not the first day of motherhood I imagined. It was hard to reconcile the day in my imagination with the day in my reality, and even harder to feel the weight of the guilt for having those feelings when there are half a million children in foster care living a life that is vastly different than the one they imagined. I didn't expect to grieve for his birth mother, and for Debbie, and for all of the older children who aren't adorable little babies with higher chances of being chosen. I also didn't expect to feel abandoned by our own friends and family.

How could I dare stand in their spotlight, on the one day they look forward to, the day that for many never comes, and complain because it didn't happen to be up to my standards? Debbie was there, and I tried to hold onto that. Debbie was there to mother our son, and to mother us, because our mothers were not. No one from either of our families came. None of our friends. No one. I'm not sure I actually invited them, I didn't know what to expect or who was allowed, but it had gone differently in my head. Nicholas was to be the first grandchild for both my parents and Eddie's. I thought there would be a much bigger cause for celebration. I had imagined, at the very least, one or two of them would be there in the courtroom with us. Instead there was silence, and I wasn't prepared for how painful that silence could be. Or maybe it was like the camera. Maybe I just didn't realize it was my responsibility to invite them until it was too late.

There are no social norms for dealing with adoption and every family handles it differently. It made me angry. And sad. And disappointed in myself for feeling angry and sad when I thought I was supposed to be feeling nothing but happy.

There was a biological baby in my belly, and I knew the day I went into the hospital to deliver that child I would be surrounded by family showering us with love (and I was right, I was), but that was not the day or the way I became a mother for the first time. This was, standing in a courtroom, swearing before a judge. I wasn't prepared for it to feel isolating, but that's exactly what it was. It was the first stark realization that our journey was going to be much different than I thought it would be and probably different than everybody else's.

Finally, I lock eyes with Pastor Bob and offer, "I would say it was lonelier."

"The Adoption Day?"

"Becoming a mother."

"How did you handle that loneliness?"

Admittedly, not well.

I fall backward into the memories.

# Chapter 6

*November 2008*

"A hundred grand, Steph." Eddie's eyes are wide as he raises his chin toward the ceiling.

"I know. It's a lot," I concede.

"No, I don't think you do." He swings his head down to face me. "We're never going to recover from that, especially if we get up there and you can't find a job. You're four months pregnant and we have a one-year-old. This is not the time to make a move like this. The entire economy is turning upside down. We both have steady work here." Eddie is trying to sway me with logic, and I can't seem to make him understand that sometimes the right decision isn't necessarily the rational one.

Also, what he's saying is not true, at least for me. I was one of the last teachers hired, I have the least amount of experience, and I'm not tenured. I will definitely be one of the first they let go if public schools do start making the cutbacks the news has been predicting for months.

"It's not ideal. I know that." I'm trying to stay calm, but it is irritating that he thinks I am not capable of thinking these things through myself.

"Do you? Seriously, do you?" he raises his voice.

"Don't you dare yell at me," I lecture. "Let me remind you that you are the reason we are here. Florida was all you, and I supported that. I was the *only* one who supported that. I sold my house, and I quit my doctorate program, and I followed you down here. I would have a PhD by now, but instead I dumped all of *my* money at *your* feet to follow *your* dream. Invested everything I had in this." I wave my hand back and forth in the space between us before poking my finger into his chest.

"You came into this marriage with nothing but student loans and pipe dreams." I continue. "Don't you even try to tell me I don't know what it feels like to be losing money. How do you think it feels to know that I'm willing to do all of that for you, but now you won't do it for me?"

"That's," he pauses to censor himself and gently moves my finger away, "not fair."

"No, you're right." I make no effort of my own to slow down. "It's not fair. Because this time you are also keeping your children a thousand miles away from their grandparents. How much is that worth to you?"

I want to go home, and I'm going to fight dirty to get there. He's right, I'm pregnant and we have a one-year-old. I also miss my mother, and my sister, and my grandmothers, and my aunts, and my friends. I need my women right now. Plus, my little brother is only twelve years old. I want to see him grow up. I don't know what possessed us to come to

Florida in the first place. Eddie made the decision to apply to jobs in Tampa on a whim after a spring break trip our senior year of college, but I can't really say I regret it now that we know our son was here waiting. Only now that our little family is about to be complete, I need to get the hell off of this peninsula and back to any city within two or three hours of Baltimore where they can actually make a decent pizza.

Eddie is thriving here. He loves his job, and he is good at it. So good that they offered to let him transfer to their Pennsylvania office even though there is no work for him to do there. He could work remotely for Florida, keep doing exactly what he's doing now, and we could be close to family. I wouldn't have to feel so alone. There is no question that I want him to do it, but he's resistant. He has made dozens of friends here, and he is playing a different sport almost every day of the week. He has joined two different volleyball leagues, flag football, the company softball team, and he loves being able to golf year-round. My husband has convinced himself we live in paradise. Maybe we do, just not mine.

I'm done with Tampa. We've been here two and a half years now, and while I have started to form new relationships with a few of my colleagues, I still can't figure out how to make friends with anyone my own age.

We are the youngest homeowners in our neighborhood. I've tried to get to know the neighbors, but I don't fit in with The Stepford Wives. I cringe thinking of the time one of them invited me to her Botox party. That didn't go well. I'm twenty-three. They hate me on the principle of collagen.

I've taken Nicholas to a few classes at the library, but I can't seem to click with anyone there either. We tried church a few times, but the closest one of our denomination is forty minutes away, and no one there was friendly. I am open to the possibility that maybe I am part of the problem, I understand that I'm shy and standoffish until I get to know someone well, but in my defense it's hard to have a good attitude when this is the kind of neighborhood where the Homeowner's Association issued us a letter last week scolding us and threating a fine because we need to wash our mailbox. Who polices the dirt on other people's mailboxes? Florida, apparently. I want out. I need to get out. It's time.

But getting out is going to cost us. A lot. Since we bought this home two years ago, the housing bubble burst and Florida was one of the states hit the fastest and the hardest. Everybody started selling their vacation homes when money got tight, and the housing prices have fallen dramatically. There are already five houses for sale on our street at prices we would not have believed when we were looking to move here, and none of them is selling. The economy is tanking and we just took a vote at our last faculty meeting about whether we would rather take significant pay cuts or start to lay off teachers.

We've spent the majority of our savings on legal fees for the adoption. Furniture, car seats, diapers, and strollers cost money, too. The small mutual fund my father set up for me as a graduation gift is gone, thanks to a rush-hour collision that totaled Eddie's car last year. The profit I made from selling my first house has been reinvested in this one.

Stephanie Giese

There's no money left. In hindsight, we wish nothing more than that we would have just rented for these first few years of our marriage. Then we could have avoided this entire mess.

"Look," I offer, "We couldn't have predicted the real estate bubble would burst as hard and as fast as it did. When we bought this house, it seemed like a sound investment. Geez, it appraised for $40,000 more than we paid for it at the time. We thought we were being smart."

It's true. We really did. But today there was a realtor sitting in the living room telling us that if we sell this year we are going to be out at least one hundred thousand dollars, assuming we can sell for our asking price, which is unlikely. Is that money we are prepared to lose? And do we realize that when we sell, if we can sell, we are going to need to come to the settlement with tens of thousands more in cash? We are going to need shell out my entire take home pay for the year just to be able to move.

I don't care how much it costs, I just want to get my babies home. I can't do this here.

"I'm calling my father."

"Don't." Eddie's voice is firm. I can't tell if it's a command or a challenge, but he must know me well enough to understand that I'm calling either way. There is nothing Eddie hates more than when I call my father about money. My husband believes strongly in hard work without handouts, especially handouts from his father-in-law. Eddie and I come from starkly different upbringings. He worked five summer jobs our junior year of college and drove a car that was held together with duct tape. I grew up down the street from the owner of an NFL football team. My family has the means to help us, and I intend to let them, even if it bruises my husband's ego a bit.

"Do you have a better idea?" I ask him darkly.

"Staying in Florida? Refinancing?"

"Until when? How long do you think it is going to take for housing prices to go back up as much as we need them to? A decade? Two? Are these kids supposed to go off to college having only seen their family once or twice a year for their entire lives? Your grandfather just died. How many memories with him would you be willing to give back if it meant a little extra padding in your parents' bank account?"

That hurt him. Good. Maybe now he will wake up.

"What is the matter with you?"

What does he think? "I want to go home."

"You are standing in your home."

"This will never be my home," I scream at him before I stomp away into our bedroom, slamming the door behind me, and grabbing the phone.

# Chapter 7

*December 2008*

The setting sun is making the Patapsco River glow underneath a purple sky, and there are snow flurries clinging to the windshield with their icy fingers. The trees we are driving by are mostly empty branches. I bet if I rolled down the window, I could see my breath. This is the way December is supposed to feel, like mittens and hot chocolate and roaring fireplaces. It won't be long until we can let Florida drift into a memory.

We left yesterday and drove through the night in our tiny caravan. Eddie, Nicholas, and I in our minivan, Eddie's parents in the U-Haul towing our furniture, and his brother, Bobby, and my sister, Charlotte, driving Eddie's dilapidated Ford Explorer. Our family flew to Florida to help us load our belongings and bring us back.

"Bridge. Bridge." I twist in my seat and see Nicholas pointing to the road in front of us. We are about to cross the Francis Scott Key Bridge and head into Baltimore. He has

been such a trooper and hardly fussed for the entire drive.
There is still an hour to go before we reach the Pennsylvania
line, but Baltimore is where our family lives. We grew up
here. It's where we met, fell in love, and got married.
Looking out over the water, it finally feels like home. Eddie
keeps his eyes forward but nods as the van starts to drive
under the huge metal trusses.

"Yep. This is a bridge, little man. Do you see those
shapes up there? Those are triangles. Engineers like Daddy
build lots of bridges like this with triangles." Eddie points
up at the hunks of metal holding the bridge together.

"Why is that?" I ask him, only mildly interested. It was
only supposed to take seventeen hours to drive from
Tampa, but it has already been twenty-two. The Explorer
got a flat tire before we hit the Georgia line, and there wasn't
a spare. We lost a good bit of time waiting for roadside
assistance. My eyelids are heavy, and my ankles are swollen.
I really couldn't care less about a geometry lecture. Eddie
knows that and takes his right hand off the steering wheel
to lay it on my knee, a silent thank you that I am still willing
to pretend for him. When he smiles at me, the bags under
his eyes temporarily disappear. He must be exhausted too,
but he's not complaining. He hasn't asked me to drive at all.
His eyes are green today, reflecting the color of his jacket. In
an hour, when the sun is down, they'll be brown again.
Either way, they are bloodshot from the lack of sleep.

He squeezes my knee and returns his hand to the wheel.
"Because they are the strongest shape. Well, actually circles
are the strongest shape," he corrects himself and my eyes
catch the glint of the sun hitting my wedding ring. "It's just

not usually very practical to build something like the trusses for a bridge or the roof of a house out of circles."

"So, triangles are better?" I yawn.

"There's kind of a debate about it. I think circles are better. That's why you will see a lot of arch shapes in construction. Triangles are the next best thing. They only have three sides, but they do have weak points. The more sides and angles you start adding, the weaker something is going to get. A rectangle is even weaker than a triangle, for example." I nod at him and yawn again, but I'm listening. Sort of. He's talking about engineering stuff now, and this could go on for a while. "Circles don't have that," he continues. "If you put pressure on a circle it will distribute evenly. That's why most water tanks you'll see are cylinders. A circle can take the pressure."

My husband knows how to build things that are meant to withstand a ridiculous amount of pressure. The thought should be comforting. I rest my hand on my belly, which is protruding like a bowling ball from under my purple Disney sweatshirt. The seatbelt is digging into my ribcage from the outside while the baby kicks me from within, and I squirm because I can't get comfortable. While I'm wriggling, I can't help but continue to stare down at the ring resting on top of my stomach. Every time you add another point it weakens your original shape. Can that be true?

I turn once more to look back at Nicholas. He has fallen asleep again. His head is titled backward in a position that can't possibly be comfortable, and he is drooling. A bottle of apple juice has tipped over in his lap, and I stretch just far enough to reach it and take it away before it can leak onto his clothes. Here in the minivan, the three of us are sitting in a makeshift triangle. It won't be long until we add a second car seat to the captain's chair behind me and our family becomes rectangular.

Facing the road in front of us again, I arch my back and shake my feet to try to get the feeling back. I can't complain. This trip was my idea. I won. We're moving. By some miracle, our house was one of the few in the neighborhood that sold and we had to get out because the new owners wanted to be in their new home for the holidays. We left immediately after I taught the last half-day scheduled before winter break. A sweet parent volunteer threw me a small baby shower during the final few hours of class in conjunction with our winter party. A few of the gift bags are still sitting at my feet. My exhausted father-in law is driving the moving van behind us, and Bobby is taking a turn driving our Explorer. Looking in the rearview mirror, I can see Charlotte asleep in the passenger seat.

They want us closer to home as much as I want to be there, and it feels good to be supported. They were loading the moving van all day yesterday while I was at work. No one expected me to help since I'm not allowed to lift anything. We tried to time it so that we did the majority of our driving overnight, while Nicholas was asleep. I'm the only adult in our caravan who isn't allowed to have very much caffeine, and I've reached a point well beyond exhaustion, but I'm happy. Stressed, but happy. Now if we could only figure out what in the world we are going to do about the money.

Our bank accounts are empty, and I don't have a job

lined up. Pregnancy is a pre-existing condition, which means we have no idea if Eddie's health insurance is going to choose to cover my medical expenses now that I've left my job and switched from my own coverage to his. We are praying that the baby is healthy, but even delivering a healthy baby has the potential to put us in a mountain of debt, beyond the student loans we are already carrying.

We couldn't find a traditional bank willing to give us a mortgage, so my father bought the house we chose in Pennsylvania. It's not unusual for him to invest in real estate, but this arrangement is different. His asset management company is holding our new mortgage. We will write our check every month to his company until we pay him back. He's not charging us interest. Eddie hates this arrangement, but the terms we have worked out with my dad make it cheaper than renting a smaller place, and we still get to own. It's better for tax purposes and as a long-term investment, probably, and he knows it. We tried to apply the lesson we learned in Florida. We cut our housing budget in half. We chose a house that we can afford on one salary if we have to.

The "new" house is almost forty years older than the one we are leaving, and it needs a lot of renovating before it will even be safe for the children, but I fell in love with the neighborhood when we visited because it was the only one in our new much-lower-price-range with sidewalks on both sides of the street. I will be able to push a stroller around the block, and the kids can grow up riding their bikes without worrying about cars. The brown wood paneling peeling off the walls, old shag carpet, and disintegrating cabinets are just cosmetic changes. Those iron bars on the stair rail wide enough for a toddler to stick his head through are something that we can change eventually. I hope.

There could be asbestos in the flooring or lead in the paint, but we'll just have to cross our fingers and hope there isn't. There definitely is a gigantic burn mark on the gold-speckled laminate kitchen countertop because at some point over the past four decades someone left a hot pot on top of it, and the only full bathroom is completely tiled in powder blue ceramic squares that are cracked and falling off the walls. There is probably water damage behind those walls. The electricity is not up to code. There aren't any GFCI outlets in the entire house, so I'm probably going to get electrocuted drying my hair. Whatever. At least this house has a new roof and a big back yard. We'll be there soon.

Everyone is so exhausted that we stop to sleep at Eddie's parents' house and decide to drive the last hour in the morning. My mom, my dad and his new girlfriend, and a few cousins are planning to meet us at our new house tomorrow, bring lunch, and help unload the truck. We aren't even there yet, and already I feel more like a family than I have in years.

# Chapter 8

*May 2009*

We named the baby Abigail. It means "father's joy." I wanted a name that stood on its own without being derived from an older male version, and it was the only one we could agree on. She's only a few weeks old, but she is already over ten pounds and has a lot of opinions. I guess she takes after her mother. Eddie is sitting at the new-to-us dining room table, leaning over a calculator. My father is getting remarried, and he and Helen are redecorating their house. They passed the large oval oak table along to replace the flimsy build-it-from-a-box set we had been using. These sturdier chairs are much less likely to topple on the kids.

"We need to cut back some more." Eddie shakes his head. We already cancelled the cable bill, and my cell phone, and we've stopped eating out at all. I scaled the grocery budget down to around fifty dollars a week, which doesn't stretch very far when you're trying to feed an entire family and have two children in diapers. I haven't made a lasagna in almost six months because we can't afford a container of ricotta. I don't shop. I'm exchanging outgrown children's clothing with other women. I'm only going to a library playgroup or the park to entertain the kids. I did join a Mom N Me group at a local church, but the fee for the entire year was only thirteen dollars. I'm trying to schedule all of my appointments and errands in one day so I can save gas. When we were invited to that last birthday party, we built the present out of wood we already had in the garage. I'm not really sure what he means by "cut back." What else can we do?

"I'll put in a few more applications, and I'll email the principals," I offer.

"You can try, but I don't know how much good it is going to do, even if you find something. Every way I run the numbers, it works out to be about the same whether you go back to work or not." He lets out a heavy sigh. "Honestly, if it's only going to net us around a hundred bucks in the long run, I'd rather have the kids with you. Nick was in that daycare in Tampa for twelve hours a day. Abby's just an infant. Is that what you want?" No. Yes. Maybe. I don't know. "I'll put some ads on Craigslist. There's some stuff around here we can sell. And I can always design a few websites or cut lawns or something for extra cash," he says.

He shouldn't have to do that. I have been looking, but no districts here are hiring, not that any principal would have wanted to take on a teacher who was nine months pregnant, then immediately out on maternity leave at the end of the school year anyway. They don't seem to pay as much in Pennsylvania as they did in Florida. Maybe it's because we left an affluent suburb, and now we are in a more rural area. We sat down and did the math, and it was bleak. Daycare costs for two kids mean it might not be worth it for me to go back for a few years. Maybe I should listen to Eddie and wait until they are both in school.

I flop down into the chair next to my husband, trying to conceal my irritation that we aren't even going to discuss the option of maybe having him be the one who stays home. Why would we? It's my own fault for choosing a career path that is notoriously underpaid as well as child-focused. I'm the one with all the kid-related experience. It makes sense for me to be with the babies. He's an engineer. They make more money than teachers do. He has more earning potential. Potential being the key word. At the moment, he is still an Engineer in Training. It's similar to being a doctor in residency. He is finished with school and is a qualified engineer, but he can't sign and seal any plans until he passes his Professional Engineering Exam, which he isn't even eligible to take for at least two more years. Until he becomes a P.E. and earns his own stamp, he isn't earning much more money than I did as a teacher. If I go back now and he stays home our income will stay about the same, so it feels unfair and sexist to me to end my career without a fight.

But I'm not stupid, I know that would pause his career trajectory and teachers' earnings don't increase at the same rate as engineers' do. Once Eddie does pass his P.E. exam and gains a few more years of experience, he will make three times what I could ever earn teaching. He also has better job security in this recession. The government almost always pours money into transportation when the economy is bad, and he is a highway engineer. It's still true here in Pennsylvania that a young gifted-specialist or untenured new classroom teacher would be among the first positions fired when schools start making cutbacks, even if I can find a job. I suppose I could change my career path, but that doesn't make any sense either because I would be starting from the bottom at any other job, if I could even find one, whereas he already has a degree and experience in his field. It's much better for our future if he is the one who continues to work.

It's not personal, it's just economics. So, I guess it's been decided. My teaching career is over. Suddenly, the kitchen feels much smaller than it did ten minutes ago. I'll be home indefinitely now, completely reliant on my husband and his salary and his insurance, which, thank God, did at least say they will pay the majority of my hospital bill for the delivery.

"Mommy," Nicholas calls from his bedroom. "New shirt. PJ's too itchy." Everything is always too something. Earlier the toothpaste was too spicy, and last week the ice cream was too cold, so he wouldn't eat it. I get up and toss him a different shirt from the basket in the hall, where the three loads of laundry I did yesterday still sit, unfolded.

"No. Too itchy," he whines. "Halloween shirt?"

"I don't know where that is, probably packed away with the Halloween stuff? Please just go to bed."

"I like Halloween shirt. No PJs," he yells, then slams his closet door, shutting himself inside, then opening the door to slam it again and banging his fists.

Nicholas is not sleeping. It's normal for toddlers to get up a few times throughout the night, but this is different.

He doesn't sleep at all. He stays up until three or four o'clock in the morning just screaming and slamming his closet doors. He's ripped his bedroom door clean off its hinges twice, so we have to keep it down, and we have replaced it with a baby gate. I didn't think a two-year-old had the strength to do that. He's so tiny, but he gets so angry so quickly. Eddie calls him Bruce Banner. At first, I thought Nicholas was just adjusting to the move and the new baby. I thought he might be a little jealous. I bought him a doll so he could hold it while I held Abby. He held the doll by the feet and slammed her head against the floor, screaming that he hated babies.

Or maybe it's just an adjustment period. They warned us about this in our pre-adoption parenting classes. Debbie spoke about it. I think that's understandable, all things considered. He has been through a lot in his two years here on Earth: we're his third family. He spent a year in foster care, and he's had to transition through three mothers and at least four different houses that I know of. New family, new state, new weather, new sister. There have been so many changes for him in such a short time. That has to be hard for a young mind to comprehend. I can understand why he would act out a bit. But lately, he's been getting worse. I started keeping a journal and writing it all down.

The rage bubbles up and gives him strength far beyond what should be considered normal for his size. I can't have him around the baby any longer. He hits and bites her. I even have to take Abby into the bathroom with me now because two weeks ago when I took thirty seconds to pee, he climbed into her crib. I found him sitting on top of her legs. I didn't see what he did. I only heard her scream. I've been strapping her into her car seat and leaving her on the bathroom floor while I shower ever since. Sometimes she is balanced on my knees while I'm on the toilet. I'm afraid to let her of my sight. But Nicholas is also my son, and he's only two years old. What am I supposed to do with him?

It might be the transitions causing this behavior, but more importantly, what can I do to make it stop? I have to wonder if it's something I am doing wrong. I just want someone to tell me so I can fix it. Is it me? I hope it's me. If it's me, I can change it. I can start to do things differently. Maybe if I change my behavior, he will change his response. That's how all the parenting books say this is supposed to work. If it's him, then this might be something bigger than I am equipped to handle, and I'm not really sure what that means for us. It's too scary to let my mind go any further down that path.

I hesitate to open the marble notebook I bought from the school supply aisle at the grocery store. I put a can of baked beans back on the shelf so the notebook would fit in our budget this week. I don't know if I want to read over what I've written. It feels like maybe if I ignore it, it will go away. Not that it ever works that way. That strategy isn't going to work with the stack of bills piled on the kitchen counter, and it isn't going to work with Nicholas either. I know that his history won't change if I ignore it. I know I need to read the words, and maybe other people will need to see them too before they believe me.

So far, it's been hard to convince anyone else that I'm not exaggerating. Someone needs to look and try to see the patterns. If Christy were here, she would be trying to look at the facts in addition to the emotions. That is my job now. Maybe this is how we figure out what is wrong and who can help. So, even though I don't want to see what it says, I sit down and read the words I already know. I wrote everything in the third person because I was trying to maintain some distance and objectivity. It doesn't matter how objective I'm trying to be, there is no denying that his behavior is getting dangerous.

**Monday-** *Biting (mom and sister), hitting, spitting, during nap time when mom went downstairs to do laundry Nicholas climbed over his baby gate, emptied four tubes of toothpaste onto a hairbrush, and "painted" the bathroom. Did not sleep well at night. Aggressive.*

**Tuesday-** *Attempted children's class at the local library. Nicholas would not stay in the circle. He refused to participate in the activities, ran around the room, threw toys at children, and screamed when held or touched or placed in time out. Left early as not to distract other families. Fecal smearing in living room. Did not sleep or nap well. Did sit on mother's lap to watch portion of* Cars *movie.*

I don't need to read past Wednesday, when he climbed over the baby gate I had in the doorway of his room, pulled the television out of the entertainment center, and took a marker to the sofa while I was in the bathroom with the baby. It's just more of the same. What I should do is think about what I would tell a friend to do if she came to me in this situation and asked for advice. I need to do the same thing I would tell her to do, which is call the pediatrician. So that's what I'm going to do. Nicholas needs to go to the doctor soon anyway. He has another birthday coming up, and there are preschool registration papers staring at me from the kitchen counter.

At least it has been so much easier to get Nicholas into school in Pennsylvania. The first three preschools I tried in Tampa all had waitlists at least a year long. Here, they simply told me which day I had to show up for registration, and we walked into the school that morning and put his name on the list. We even got to choose between the morning or afternoon class. It seemed like it was going so smoothly. Of course, it couldn't be that easy. They need his vaccination records, which is a completely normal thing for a school to request. He will need them to start kindergarten anyway. But I don't have them. I called Debbie and she says she doesn't have them either. The doctor in Florida does, the one we told Nick was still living with Debbie. She sent me the number to his office, and I passed it along to our pediatrician last week. Now I'm here at Nicholas' three-year wellness exam, and there seems to be a problem.

The exam hasn't even started yet, and we are waiting for the nurse to come in and tell me about his shots. When she walks into the room, her lips are pursed and she isn't holding any needles.

"Hmm. This is a bit odd. Nicholas probably will need shots today, so go ahead and stay right here. It's just that at the moment we don't know which ones he needs. The paperwork hasn't come through yet."

"I'm sorry?" I turn to face her, but I'm distracted by the baby, who is chewing on my shoulder, leaving a dark, wet spot on my oversized t-shirt.

"We can't seem to obtain his previous medical records, ma'am. We've called your Florida doctor several times. He doesn't seem to remember you."

That's not a surprise. "He wouldn't know me. I only met that doctor once. He would know Nicholas by a different last name. I wrote it on the paperwork."

Just then there is a knock on the door and the frail, dark-haired receptionist I remember from when we checked in says she is sorry to interrupt. "Could I borrow Mrs. Giese for a minute, please?" I pull a pacifier out of my purse and blow on it before I stick it in Abby's mouth. I mount her higher on my hip and take Nicholas by the hand so we can follow this lady down the hall to her desk, where an engraved rectangle exists to tell me that her name is Ellen. When we reach our destination, Ellen lowers herself into her rolling leather chair and asks me if it is all right to offer Nicholas some candy. He's jumping up and down and digging through her open desk drawer before I have a chance to answer.

"Is there a problem?" I don't understand what is going on.

"Well, actually, kind of," she stares at her computer and clicks the mouse a few times. "The doctor's office in Florida is not being very forthcoming with information." I stare at the back of her computer blankly because I don't know what I'm supposed to do about that, and she continues, "They are refusing to release Nicholas' medical records."

"Why?"

"They don't seem to have any record of a Nicholas Giese." Well, clearly, he exists because he's standing right next to her. I clench my teeth behind the smile I'm forcing and raise my eyebrows. The breath I take in through my nose is so deep that it almost whistles as I shift Abby to the other hip.

"I know. He's adopted. We changed his last name after that doctor saw him," I try to explain.

"I understand. But that is just the first problem. You also aren't listed as a parent or emergency contact on any of the forms they have on record in their office." I wouldn't be. I was never officially his foster mother. I lied and let them think he was still living with Debbie so they would treat him. "They are claiming they cannot release information to us on your behalf. They think, based on the information given to them by his legal guardians while he was their patient, it would be a HIPAA violation. I personally don't agree, but my hands are tied."

"But I'm his mother. I have the adoption records and the new birth certificate and everything." Except I wasn't his mother for the first entire year of his life, and that is when he had most of his shots. Now when I need to prove it, I can't.

"I understand. I'm sorry."

Oh, for crying out loud. Is Debbie still listed as the contact? "What if I have his foster mother get the records? Could she send them to you?" Like Debbie doesn't have a million other things on her plate, but I guess I could ask her.

"They really do need to be verified by the physician, unfortunately. I would love to be able to tell you to do that because it would be easy, but we can't establish the practice of taking unverified records that could be tampered with.

Not that we don't trust you in this case. It's just not something we do." I guess I get that. Then anyone could just make up whatever kind of fake records they wanted.

"So, then what?"

"Well, it's entirely up to you. If you'd like, we can revaccinate him here."

"What? Why? He already had all the shots."

She pushes the blank school form back to me. "Just be aware that in the state of Pennsylvania immunizations are mandatory before starting school, and he will not be able to start kindergarten in a few years without a record of these shots."

I squeeze my eyes together and shake my head. It doesn't feel like we have much of a choice, so I ask if we can please see the doctor now. She says of course and leads me back into the same room we were in five minutes ago, the one with the puppies on the wallpaper border. Back to the starting line, only still a few steps behind all of the other kids his age and we're going to have to play catch up. Not Nicholas' fault, and not mine either, but I do have to wonder if this will be the story of our lives.

There's a knock on the door, and the doctor enters and takes a seat on the rolling stool across the room. I wasn't expecting him to be my age, but he can't be older than around twenty-seven. For a second it is disconcerting to think that my peers are finishing medical school. I don't know why I'm so surprised. Of course they are. Why shouldn't they be? Not everyone made the same decision I did to hit the career pause button. He introduces himself and says he has two children who are the same ages as mine.

I'm not sure if I should offer congratulations or commiseration, so I tell him that and he laughs. I like him. We keep talking about the kids and all of my questions. I have a lot of those.

"We can certainly spread out the revaccination schedule if you'd like. It will give us time to see if we can get that paperwork issue sorted. Was there anything else you wanted to ask?" Like when the last time was that anyone other than my husband made eye contact with me? Did Ellen actually look at me when we were having our conversation a few minutes ago? I can't remember. I don't think I looked at her. I was focused on keeping the kids away from her desk. Come to think of it, though, I do have another actual doctor question.

"Abby, the baby, she won't sleep anywhere besides her swing. There's a warning printed right on it that says not to let her do that. Is she going to suffocate? Or am I stunting her spine or something? Because Nicholas never sleeps either. I mean literally never, and honestly, I don't know what else to do. I'm exhausted, like, all the time. Nicholas, don't touch that." I turn my attention to my son, who is pulling at the stethoscope around the doctor's neck. The doctor just smiles and hands Nicholas the hammer they use to check reflexes, assuring me it's fine.

I don't know if I should tell him what I'm about to say. "I know this sounds insane, but I actually begged my husband not to go to work today. Legitimately begged. As in with real tears and groveling and clothes grabbing. It was quite pathetic."

He wheels himself a few inches toward me and leans

forward, elbows on his knees, not breaking eye contact. He can see me, which is good, because I've been walking around in this shell of myself and, to be honest, I wasn't entirely sure I was still here. It's also terrifying. If I would have known this was the conversation we were going to have, I would have put on some make up, or at least not been wearing sweatpants that are fraying at the hem and dotted with cracked and peeling formula stains. I look like I feel, which is to say like a scattered mess.

"I should probably tell you that you should follow the manufacturer's recommendations," he says solemnly before a slow smile spreads across his face. "But what I'm going to tell you is that it's exponentially safer for children to be in the care of a mother who is well-rested and feeling as good as possible, and that you should do whatever you need to do to get yourself to that place." He's implying that I'm not currently in a very good place, and it makes me swallow hard because I know he sees it. Is it that obvious, or rather, would it be if anyone was ever looking? His brown eyes are staring up at me, piercing into me in a way that makes me feel too exposed, so I cough and turn my head away.

"So, she can sleep in the swing then?"

"I've honestly never heard of a spinal injury caused by a nap in a swing, if that's what you're asking. But, again, I'm supposed to tell you to follow the recommendations." He shrugs and then goes right back to where we were a minute ago. "Let's talk for a minute about how you have been feeling, though. Have you been following up with your OBGYN on your own self-care?" I don't know how he peeled away all the protective layers of children I piled on top of myself, but somehow we're back to me again. "It's not unusual for young mothers to feel sad or even have unwanted thoughts. You should know if you are going through anything like that, doctors are here and it's our job to help you with those things."

The lump of emotion I tried to swallow earlier is stuck behind my sternum now, making it harder to breathe. "Uh, thanks. I don't really know if I'd say I'm sad, exactly. More like stressed. Really, really stressed. But I feel like my anxiety levels are relatively normal for anyone who would be going through the transition period and dealing with the behaviors we are. I don't think it's my hormones." And I sort of resent the implication. "I think maybe it's just an adoption adjustment thing." I forgot to add that I meant an adoption adjustment for Nicholas. Except I'm not really sure if that is exactly what I mean.

"Well, I've heard that quite a few adoptive parents feel the same symptoms biological parents feel. It's not officially recognized, but you might want to look into Post Adoption Depression Syndrome and see if anything sounds familiar." I'm not alone in this? Other people go through this too? "But back to Nicholas, he's my patient today. What behaviors, specifically?" he asks. I tell him about the journal I've been keeping and everything I wrote in it this week, then I launch into a few things I could have written last week if I had been keeping the journal then, like when the Sunday school teacher tried to put him in time out for hitting a little girl in his class. Nicholas refused to sit in the time out chair and instead took off all his clothes and rolled around naked under the table until the teachers came and pulled Eddie and me out of the worship service to deal with him ourselves. The doctor takes out a pad of paper and a pen and writes two words before tearing the top sheet off and handing it to me.

"When you check out today, make sure Ellen gives you the number to Early Intervention before you leave. After what you've told me, I think Nicholas could really benefit from an evaluation. It's free, you've got nothing to lose, and if they do decide that he is eligible for resources then you would have help in coping with some of the behaviors you've described." He's referring us for a special education evaluation? Why didn't I think of that?

# Chapter 9

The examiner is sitting on our living room sofa, with her perfect posture and her buttoned sweater set over ironed khakis, and she still hasn't touched the glass of water she asked me for. It's sitting in front of her on the coffee table that I probably should have dusted better. There are fingerprints all over that table because Abby has been using it to learn how to pull herself up. There's a puddle of water gathering under her glass now that the ice has melted. She asked me for a coaster forty-five minutes ago, but I pretended not to hear her because I don't think we actually own any of those. Maybe I should get a paper towel or a tissue or something. Not that we have real tissues, but the thought of them does make me notice that Abby's nose is running. I carry the baby into the bathroom so the examiner can't see me wipe her face with toilet paper.

When we walk back into the living room our guest shifts from her perch on the edge of the couch cushion so she can face me. I wonder if I should offer her a lint roller for the dog hair that is probably going to be clinging to her sweater when she leaves.

"Have you noticed that when you ask Nicholas a question he doesn't actually answer you?" she asks. I don't know what she's talking about. Nicholas speaks all the time. He is a constant stream of noise all day, every day. If there is one thing I'm not concerned about, it's his verbal skills. I just took him to the doctor, and even the pediatrician said his word count was right on target.

"I'm not sure I'm following you. Nicholas is very chatty." What she is telling me doesn't even make sense. How could he be so social if he didn't understand what people were saying to him? He will pull strangers in the grocery store into full-blown conversations. Old ladies are happy to indulge him about whatever is on his mind. How can he have a language processing problem?

"Yes, but language is quite nuanced," she offers. "Right now, I'm talking about the things he takes in, not the things he puts out. He seems to be struggling with receptive language."

What in the actual hell is she going on about? This child is still only two years old. He won't be three for another month.

She can see I'm not buying it, so she clarifies, "For example, if you say, 'What would you like for dinner?' have you noticed that his response has nothing to do with food?" Well, that's true. He would probably tell me that he likes airplanes and keep playing with the toy in his hand. Even so.

"Is that not normal for a toddler?"

"A young toddler, perhaps. But we are entering the preschool age now. At this point, it's actually considered a significant delay. He had trouble answering the majority of my questions today. Also, as you saw, he struggled to grip the crayon to draw the circle and the straight line."

She's not even mentioning the other fine motor tasks she tried to get him to do, tried being the operative word. I don't mean to smirk at the thought of him refusing to cooperate, but watching her squirm was a little amusing, and at least it's becoming pretty obvious that I am not the only one who can't seem to get him to comply.

"I'm going to recommend weekly sessions with an occupational therapist and a language coach," she says. "I will be in touch to set up another meeting. Because of the delays we saw here today, Nicholas qualifies for an Individualized Education Program. You might also hear it called an IEP. It's a form that guarantees him access to these services free of charge as part of his education."

"Thank you. I'm familiar. I was a public school teacher," I interrupt before she starts to further explain the paperwork I am already trained to write. In Florida, giftedness was mandated under special education. All of my students had similar plans, although that was slightly different because as a gifted teacher I was serving an advanced ability rather than a disability. All of my experience is on the opposite end of the spectrum.

"I appreciate that, and of course we will get him whatever he needs, but our concerns were primarily about behavior," I remind her. It will be great if he can hold a crayon correctly, I suppose, but what is any of this going to do to get him to stop trying to bite other kids at the library or punch holes in his bedroom wall?

She purses her lips at me and gives me a canned response about how with the correct interventions we should hopefully begin to see an improvement in other areas as well. Learning how to communicate effectively should help ease some of his frustration. Then she notes that a structured environment and scheduled routine are of paramount importance. Yes, I imagine they would be for people who button every single button on their perfectly pressed cardigans. On the other hand, I'm just trying to make it through the day over here. Her eyes scan the room and graze the discarded toys piled in the corners. For a second, I imagine her living room. It's probably immaculate. I bet she has some sort of white wicker basket with a monogrammed liner, and she has trained her children to put their toys away the second they stop playing. "Children truly do benefit from a calm, structured environment," she tells me one more time, to stress her point.

"I'll keep that in mind," I smile sweetly at her before I show her out.

By the time Eddie comes home, I'm too exhausted to handle another thing. Abby's molars are coming in and she hasn't stopped crying for the past three hours, and Nicholas managed to find a bottle of hand sanitizer in his room at naptime. He must have scaled his dresser. I kept it up there for after diaper changes. It's my fault for assuming he was still asleep. I should have known not to trust the quiet. He emptied the entire bottle on the floor and used it like finger paint. So today, in addition to receiving our special education recommendation, we learned that hand sanitizer removes the finish from hardwood floors.

"Hi, Honey. How did your day go?" He tries to engage me and I dump all of it onto him at once as I hand him the baby. The examiner and her sweater set, and Nicholas and his finger paint, and the floor we are going to have to have refinished. He thinks for a second before responding.

"That's disappointing. I looked at that hand sanitizer the other day and thought we should move it. We really can't keep stuff like that in his room. We're lucky it was just the floor this time. He could have put it in his mouth instead. We can replace the floor. We can't replace him." The measured tone of his reaction is infuriating. I feel chastised, which in itself is humiliating and puts me into defensive mode.

"So, this is my fault?" I step back from him, incredulous.

"Um, no. Also, what?" He stretches each word out slowly.

My answer spills out fast. "If you didn't think the hand sanitizer should be in there, you had months to move it. You're saying you wanted to move it, actively thought about moving it, but you didn't because why? The only explanation is because I put it there. You have no responsibility here because you were just going along with your wife. So, you think this is my fault."

"Do you hear yourself?" he asks, cocking his head. He's irritated, but also honestly seems confused.

I do hear myself, and I realize how convoluted it sounds, but that doesn't change the fact that he didn't move the stupid hand sanitizer when he evidently knew better than I did and foresaw it as a potential danger to our son, yet left it in the room. He's correct that it could have been much worse. If he knew that and did nothing, then that is horrendous and irresponsible. Now I'm not just overwhelmed, I'm angry. At him. At myself for not seeing that same danger, because if I had I definitely would have moved the bottle. The anger piles on top of all the other layers of chaos I've had to deal with today and the tears are out before I can stop them. It's not that I care that much about fighting over a bottle of hand sanitizer, it's more that my husband just put the final touches on this emotional lasagna that's been cooking all day.

"Why are you crying?" I wish I weren't, and I also wish he didn't have to ask.

"I can't talk to you about this right now," I sniff. "I need to make dinner."

Maybe if I can focus on something else for a few minutes, something I can actually accomplish, it will make me feel better. I take two cans of tomato soup from the pantry and walk over to the dishwasher to retrieve clean dishes to set the table, but when I open it I discover the load inside is dirty. The sink is piled full of more dishes that need to be washed. There is not a single clean bowl or spoon in this entire house, and it's the final straw. I slide down onto the kitchen floor, hug my legs as tightly as I can, and sob uncontrollably into my knees.

"Hey," Eddie pulls me to my feet. "You need to go lie down. I've got this."

I wander into our bedroom and I do try to rest for a few

minutes, but the giggling that's coming from the kitchen now is making me too curious to ignore it. I want to see how he turned the mood around that fast. I have to sneak back down the hallway to peek at my family.

The dishwasher is running. Eddie is standing at the sink washing the rest of the dishes. Nicholas is at the table, eating. He sees me and smiles. Eddie motions with his head for me to join them again.

"Nicholas and I have decided that tonight is Silly Spoon Night." He emphasizes the words with great importance, beginning to explain what they are doing. I look down at the table. Nicholas is dipping tiny pieces of a grilled cheese sandwich into one of my grandmother's antique German teacups. She truly would have loved that. She would do anything to bring a smile into a child's heart. I've only ever seen them used at Thanksgiving, once, in the 80's. I have not used this one since she entered hospice care and we split her china set amongst the family. But her cup is sitting on my table now, filled with canned tomato soup and generational memories. There's also a melon baller sitting on the table in front of him, dripping with orange-red liquid.

"You're going to have to make a very important decision," Eddie continues, looking at me expectantly. "Would you like to drink your dinner from this priceless over-sized Eeyore mug from Disney World, or eat it with an ice cream scoop? Of course, if you are feeling extra fancy, you could attempt to do both." He mimes dipping the ice cream scoop into the mug.

Nicholas laughs. Abby doesn't understand, but from her

high chair across the room she laughs as well because she sees her brother doing it. I point to the mug and take a seat. Eddie slides a grilled cheese onto a paper plate and puts it in front of me. He also sets the mug down, filled with soup. I look up at him and try to apologize for earlier with my eyes. He nods at me and walks over to the stove to get his own sandwich.

"Hey," he tells me. "I got you something today."

He takes a leather-bound Moleskine notebook from the kitchen counter and places it in front of me. "I think you should start writing again. You used to write all the time. And you love those mom blogs. You could start your own."

I do love reading the blogs that have started popping up everywhere. Other moms share the smallest details of their lives, recipes, and home decorating. Their websites have been a lifeline as I struggle to make connections in our new city.

"Thanks, but what would I even write about? Today I microwaved some chicken nuggets."

"I'm sure you'll think of something."

Later, after the kids are for once asleep at the same time and we are alone with space to breathe and think, he lies next to me in our bed. I can feel his hand start to stroke my arm. Has it been a week since the last time? Maybe. I can't remember. I promised myself long before we got married that I would never let it go longer than a week, and I don't think I ever have, other than those few weeks post-partum when the break came at the doctor's orders. But I'm so tired of having so many people take so much from me all day, every day. All of the touching, it just never stops. He's stroking the same arm that carried our daughter all day and signed the paper for the Early Intervention examiner. Now he wants me to take the same hand that not even an hour ago was wiping tiny butts and noses and put it where, exactly? I miss the days when my body was mine and only mine and no one needed anything else from it.

He deserves to have me at least make an effort, though, I know he does. I reach over and begin to reach down, pausing just under the elastic of his boxers. It's not that I don't want to, I'm just kind of indifferent to sex at all right now, really. If we never did it again, sure, I would miss it sometimes, but I think I would also be equally relieved to at least have that one thing crossed off my to-do list forever. Plus, let's be honest. It's hard to feel sexy when you are at your highest weight of your entire life, and your skin is riddled with stretch marks.

"Can I ask what you're thinking about over there?" he whispers. He must be able to feel the indifference in my hand.

"I'm sorry. It's just a little overwhelming to be constantly taking care of everybody's needs." Although, I guess he must feel that way too. He's supporting an entire family. That would be why every piece of advice I've received over my entire life in church and in women's magazines and through conversations with trusted friends is culminating in this moment to tell me that I'm still supposed to be moving my hand. Except he just moved it away.

"Can we try something?" he asks. "Take your clothes off."

"Only if you turn the light out," I negotiate. "And the

blanket stays."

He sighs, "I wish you would believe me when I tell you I think you're beautiful. Because you really are." I do believe he thinks that. I also believe he has to think that no matter what I really look like, because it's the only way he's getting laid again for the rest of his life.

"Yeah, yeah. We've been through this. You have a recently acquired cellulite fetish." I roll my eyes.

"Stop. Don't try to make it weird. Fine, your body looks a little bit different now than it did two years ago. I know you don't like that, but I actually think it's pretty hot. Your body changed because you made an entire human being. And who put her in there? I did." He props himself up on his elbow. He's really getting into this speech. It's kind of cute. "So, looking at you right now actually makes me feel pretty powerful, okay? More than I did when you had smaller boobs or washboard abs." I don't know if I love how much he assumes my confidence is wrapped up in what he thinks. I am, in fact, fully capable of having my own opinion about my own body that is not the same as his. But his heart is in the right place. He just wants me to feel good about myself.

He continues, "I think this new body is a hell of a lot sexier than the old one because now we both know what it is really capable of. I've seen you put your body through a tremendous amount of pain this year, and now I would really appreciate it if you would let me explore the other side of that coin."

"What?" I don't know what he is talking about, and for the record, I am always going to miss my former abs. Zumba and yoga at the YMCA don't seem to be doing a heck of a lot in the way of getting them back. But I really don't know what he's talking about or why any of this is relevant to our bedroom situation. What is the opposite of intense pain like childbirth?

"Oh," I realize. That.

"Exactly. Now don't fight it. Let me be the one who takes care of you first.

My father's side of the family would call it a kitzel, the German word for tickle, the way Eddie later caresses my back with just his fingertips while I rest my head on his chest. I want to stay here, in this temporary nest, where he is the only one who understands why the anxiety is building up all around me and also how to take the weight and lift it off, at least temporarily.

"How was your day?" It occurs to me that I never asked him. I run my finger through a few scattered chest hairs and twist my neck to look up at him.

"Better now that we got to this part of it." He smiles and kisses my forehead.

"What about work?"

He shakes his head as if he doesn't want to talk about it.

"Did something happen?"

"There's a lot of writing on the wall. I have a feeling they are closing the P.A. office." That's not necessarily the worst news for us. He's still working remotely for the Florida office. He could probably keep working from home for a while if they closed the Pennsylvania location. But it does mean a lot of his friends are about to lose their jobs, and maybe he should start looking for something else too, just in case. That won't be easy, though, jobs are hard to come by at the moment.

"That sucks. Anything else?"

"Nothing bad. The other thing is probably good for my career, really. They asked me to help manage part of a project."

I sit up and tilt my head. This seems promising. "That's great, right?"

"I guess. It's a great resume builder. Our company is inspecting the guide rail at some national parks. So, it means a lot of traveling around the country to visit them. It would be a lot of overtime, plus a per diem, which would really help us out financially."

"So, what is the problem?"

He hesitates. "You seem pretty stressed out around here right now, and I know the timing's not great with the kids being so young, but I sort of have to do this if I want to keep my job." I'm not sure why he was nervous to tell me that. It's not like any of those things are shocking to me.

"Okay. And?"

"And if I do it, I'm going to be gone for three months."

# Chapter 10

In September Eddie starts to travel. Every three weeks or so he will be able to stop back at home for a day or two, as long as the park he is surveying is within driving distance. In the meantime, other than my solo parenting, not much else has changed at home. We have been doing two sessions every week in our home with the special educators: one with a teacher tutoring Nicholas in language, and one with an occupational therapist. They also recommend that he starts sessions with a speech therapist soon. He prefers occupational therapy over the language classes; all he has to do is play. Lisa, his OT, engages him with toys and games while she observes to see where his challenges lie. She has also been the first person to offer tangible support.

The sensory brush she recommended reminds me of a vegetable scrubber. When he is overwhelmed, I use it to brush his arms or legs. When I tried it on myself I thought it hurt, but Nicholas laughs and says it tickles. The brush has done wonders to calm his tantrums, but people look at you strangely when you use it in public. Earlier this week Nicholas started tantruming in Target while we were picking up a pack of diapers. There were more than a few funny looks when I pulled out the white plastic rectangle and started to brush him, but it is better than the "that child needs a spanking" comments or too-loud-on-purpose whispers about mothers who can't control their children in public that we used to get.

Last week Lisa let us borrow a weighted vest that felt like a small bag of cement and made Nicholas look like a miniature policeman. He wears it for short periods every day and it does help to calm him down, but we need to return it so she can use it for other clients. Lisa tells me there are companies that make weighted blankets filled with plastic beads or sand and, although they can be quite expensive, they have been effective for helping kids like Nicholas sleep through the night. We can't afford to spend two hundred dollars on a blanket, but I did buy an imitation down comforter on clearance and a few bean bags, so I can try to sew them inside and make one of my own.

She says heavy work like pushing or pulling something is helpful to calm his brain. Have him push the laundry basket down the hall for you when you are washing clothes or push in the chairs after dinner. Even carrying a bucket of water or sand around the yard could help to focus his energy, she suggests. Try to make it fun, it shouldn't feel like a punishment, just a strategy in the form of a game. Also try the indoor trampoline park, he will like to bounce. As soon as I told my mother this, we received a surprise backyard trampoline of our own via a giant Amazon box delivered to the front porch. So far, all of Lisa's suggestions have been making a positive impact. They are baby steps, but we are seeing some improvement, and at least I know what to do when the meltdowns begin. Water and sand are especially helpful. I've started filling a shallow storage tub with water to keep him occupied in the kitchen long enough to give me time to cook.

Today the weather is crisp and clear, and he is outside swinging from the tire that hangs by a fraying rope attached to our oak tree. He spins himself in endless circles. Lisa stands next to me, a tote bag filled with kinetic sand and chewable jewelry on her shoulder. She is watching him from twenty feet away.

"Does he do that often?" She directs her curiosity at me.

"Swing?" I ask, balancing Abby on my hip.

"The spinning."

"Actually," I say "now that you mention it, yeah. All the time. We have a Sit 'N Spin in the basement playroom and he will spin around on that thing for hours. I know that sounds like an exaggeration but it's not. It's like he never gets dizzy." He spins in circles while he's playing with matchbox cars or airplanes, too. I thought he was just using his imagination.

"That's interesting. Have you noticed if he is sensitive to certain things like fabrics or smells?"

"Uh, the tags on clothes really bother him. And last summer he cried for two hours when we spent a day at the beach because he didn't like the way the sand was sticking to his sunscreen." There's also a twenty-minute battle each time we have to put socks on his feet, and I've stopped using the Crock-pot because the smell of dinner cooking all day melts him into tears. He's just a very particular child. He knows what he likes, and he's bothered a little bit extra by the things he doesn't. Okay, maybe more than a little bit.

"What about eye contact? Does he look at you when you speak to him?"

I laugh, "Good luck getting him to sit still enough for five seconds to actually look at your face, but I think so. He's very friendly. He does look at people when they talk to him, as long as the conversation is about airplanes or something else he likes. If not, you'll lose him pretty quick. But he does try."

She nods and smiles, keeping her eyes focused on the tire swing. "You said he avoids clothes because of the way they feel, but does he ever try to make himself feel things in ways that seem a bit strange to you? Like, does he ever hit himself or bang his head into something on purpose?"

"Well, now that I think about it, yes. He also runs into walls. I don't mean he bumps into things. I mean he will run full-speed at a wall and jump straight into it, fall down, laugh, and do it again. I know it has to hurt because he gets bumps and bruises from it. I figured boys, and Nicholas in particular, just had a lot of extra energy."

"That can be true, but most kids won't actively try to feel pain. Even when a child is very high-energy, once they figure out something hurts they usually won't do it again. What you're describing is called sensory-seeking behavior. That's just a fancy way to say he likes to try to get as much physical sensation as he can, even though sometimes it might not be safe."

My mind drifts to the pool party our Mom N Me group had over the summer. I turned around for less than a minute to get a diaper for the baby and some sunscreen out of my bag, and in that time Nicholas found his way onto the diving board. He was two at the time and didn't know how to swim, but that didn't stop him from climbing the ladder and jumping right into eight feet of water without his swim vest. Thankfully, there were already other women in the water and everything was fine. I still shudder at the memory.

Has he ever been evaluated for autism?" Lisa's voice pulls me back.

"The disease Jenny McCarthy writes about? No. I mean, he's only three."

"It's not a disease," She corrects me. "It's just a slight neurological difference some people are born with. It's not something I can diagnose, but with your permission I would like to recommend an evaluation. I think it could be beneficial."

Our conversation stops when Nicholas jumps off the tire swing with a thud. He runs to me and pulls something from his pocket.

"Mommy, I found this outside for you because you're my one true love." He shakes his entire body with pride and shuts his big blue eyes behind thick lashes. Lisa told me in our last session that when he shakes that way it's called stimming. As in stimulation, or over-stimulation, as the case may be. The OT smiles as Nicholas crushes a wilted dandelion into my hand, then asks for a snack. I thank him and put the flower behind my ear as we all walk to the kitchen so he can work with his therapist on how to properly hold a spoon as he eats his yogurt.

I agree it can't hurt anything to do the autism testing, which begins with an oversized white envelope appearing in the mail. There's a questionnaire for me to fill out, over fifty times it asks me to rate things like how often he engages with peers or if he is sensitive to lights. A similar form was sent to the school. I circle my answers and stick it in the mail, then wait for the phone call to schedule our appointment with a psychologist.

In the meantime, I spend every free moment on the internet scouring blogs and Facebook pages. It's an addiction, like any other, but I tell myself it's healthier than smoking or downing a bottle of wine, and I have to do something to cope with the stress. I can type with one hand faster than most people can with two because there is always a baby in my other arm.

My favorite blog is called *My Life and Kids*. It's written by a woman named Anna and every Friday she and her friend Kelley, who writes a different blog, work together to host an online party they call "Finding the Funny." Anna has three kids, around the same ages as mine, but her life seems so much brighter. She excels at making motherhood seem fun and she is genuinely nice to everyone who comments. I have a blogroll, which is just a list of websites I check religiously, multiple times every day. I've never met these women, but I know them. Through comment boxes we are checking in and keeping each other sane. *Those new curtains are adorable. How did the appointment go yesterday? Did your family like that chicken recipe?*

My own blog is new. I named it *Binkies and Briefcases* as a reference to the elusive work/life balance women don't seemed to be entitled to find. "Binkies" is what we call pacifiers in our family. It's a reference to the fact that you can bury yourself with children or corporate life, or try to do both, but it feels like you can't do both well at the same time, and either way it will be the kids or the job that define you, never mind who *you* actually are. My blog is mostly pictures of my kids, recipes, and do-it-yourself craft projects. There are a lot of tutorials to help teach other women how to make things for their own families on a budget. The goal, after all, is to get people to read the work. Or perhaps the goal is just to confirm for myself that somewhere between the binkies and the briefcases, I am here.

There are quite a few women blogging in central PA, and sometimes we go out to dinner at local restaurants or meet up in public. Yvonne, an older home decor blogger, says we are the everyday historians, documenting the little parts of our lives that make them worth living. Yvonne compares us to Laura Ingalls Wilder in that we don't know why anyone would be interested in our simple, ordinary lives, but they are, so we will be here on the internet documenting this phase of humanity with our words. Years from now our children and their children will have our pictures and our recipes, and so will anyone else who wants to feel a sense of family.

Anna's blog is growing more popular every day, and for good reason. She is hilarious as she recalls the story of her first tattoo and has a warm, friendly banter with her mother.

One day she posts an embarrassing story about the time in college that she had too much to drink and released her bowels all over a group of her boyfriend's fraternity brothers as they carried her down the steps. Her telling makes it laugh-out-loud funny. It also reminds me of a story of my own, but I am not as brave as Anna is, and there is no way I could put stories that personal on the internet. Still, I want to share it with her; if nothing else, because she said in her post that she was feeling really awkward and nervous about that story, and maybe our shared embarrassment will make her feel less alone.

Although I see her as a friend, in reality I have never met Anna and she has no idea who I am. That doesn't stop me from typing a long email introducing myself and recounting the story of my twenty-first birthday, when I got food poisoning and ending up pooping in the backseat of my car while my dad and my boyfriend sat horrified in the front. Then when we finally made it to my sister's bathroom so I could clean up, I accidentally flooded her toilet, and subsequently the entire bathroom, by trying to flush a very dirty tampon. My mother saved the day by walking in when I was half-naked, covered in my own filth and screaming, just to calmly and silently reach her bare hand into the toilet and unclog it. As I tried to issue a tearful apology to my mom, all she said was, "Stephanie, I have three children. I would not have gotten this far in life if I were afraid to touch a little bit of poop. That was not the first time, and it won't be the last. Just remember this in another thirty years when it's your turn to be the one changing my diapers."

I'm still too embarrassed to find any humor in my story,

but I hit send hoping it will make Anna feel better for sharing hers. Like her, I also married that boyfriend soon thereafter. Immediately, I'm flooded with regret. Can you unsend an email? I cannot believe I just sent a stranger an 800-word essay, unprompted, about the time I shat myself in front of my boyfriend and my father. What is wrong with me? This is why I can't make friends.

To my amazement, Anna emails me back the following day. *This story is amazing! Please, please, please let me share it on my blog. And you HAVE to link up to Finding the Funny this week. I'm so glad you sent this. I haven't stopped laughing. Your mom is the greatest. I checked out your blog and I love those puppets you made from recycled sweaters. Haha, sweater puppets. Did you use that title on purpose? Also, your kids are adorable. I know you said you don't want to share it on your own blog, but plllleeeaaaaseee let me publish this.*

She liked it. A lot. And my email didn't scare her, but the idea of publishing something so personal on a platform as large as hers is terrifying. Oh, screw it. If Anna and I both have such similar stories, there have to be other women out there who have them too. I compose another email.

*That sounds insanely scary, but if you can be brave enough to share your story, I guess I can too.*

*Awesome,* she writes back. *I'll put it on my schedule for Thursday and then I hope to see you link up to the Finding the Funny party on Friday.*

My heart is racing Thursday morning and my palms are sweating. It feels surreal to see my words published on her website. Reading through the comments, every one of them is positive. A few women are sharing embarrassing stories of their own. There is a big uptick in traffic to my own website as people click though Anna's link. It actually feels...good. Anna's blog provides a space that we can visit friends without the need to coordinate schedules, arrange childcare, or even shower. It offers a way to connect with other women in specific, personal ways on our own time and be able to laugh at even the more unpleasant parts of life.

I link up to her party with the story of a time I accidentally showed up to a wedding wearing the exact same dress as the bridesmaids. There's nothing quite like walking into a bathroom and being confronted by six women all wearing the same outfit you are, demanding to know who you are and what is going on. The next week I link up the story of the time at the hospital, after I delivered Abby, when I assumed the knock at the door was from a nurse, and accidentally invited in a priest, who saw me standing there naked.

For several weeks in a row my stories are featured as the most popular ones from the Finding the Funny party, meaning they are getting the most clicks. More people are reading my posts than any of the other bloggers who linked up. I might actually be sort of good at this. It's not long before I get another email from Anna.

*Hey, I am loving your stories! I was thinking about starting a private group for writers to support each other. Nothing fancy or formal. All online. Just a few people I like. I want to keep it small. You in?*

Is she kidding? *Um, duh. Of course. Thank you for thinking of me!*

*Great,* she replies, *here's the invite.*

It soon becomes obvious that Anna did not use any criteria for curating this group beyond her own taste. She did not care what professional connections anyone brought with them, she simply invited friendly writers she liked. My website is tiny. I barely have three hundred readers on a good day. I have nothing of value to offer these women, but they welcome me with open arms. There are women here who have social media followings in the hundreds of thousands, and a few others with small sites like mine, but there is no judgment and no comparison. It's just a small club for women who also happen to be moms who like to write. Anna caps the admittance around forty members because she wants to curate a safe, friendly atmosphere and build the intimacy of our group. It's a place to promote your work and help find writing jobs, but more importantly, to make personal connections and say things you might not be able to share anywhere else. We do use our platforms to share each other's work, but we also begin to support each other in real life through pregnancies, births, moves, divorces, deaths, and surgeries, and in the process become an inseparable sisterhood. We are spread throughout the country, but those of us who live in close proximity meet in person, first at blog conferences, then for coffee dates or an occasional ladies' night out.

I am animated at dinner, discussing my writing group with Eddie.

"You have three hundred people coming to your website every day? That's great." He encourages.

"It's actually kind of terrible in terms of how those

metrics are measured," I say through a bite of spaghetti, turning to cut up a meatball for Nicholas.

"Sure, your website isn't Amazon or anything, yet," he continues. "But imagine speaking in front of three hundred actual people every day. There are schools that have smaller attendance than that, but you wouldn't discount them, right? If you had a storefront and three hundred customers came through every day to buy things, that would be amazing. It isn't any less amazing just because it's online."

I roll my eyes at his eternal optimism in my regard, but I can't help smiling.

"All right, fine. I really like it," I admit. "But it's taking so much time, it feels like a job I'm not getting paid for. Granted, a job I really like. I just wish I knew how to become a real writer and actually contribute."

"Pretty sure you are a real writer as long as you, you know, write stuff. Also pretty sure raising our kids counts as contributing."

"Fair enough, but how do I make it a job that sends paychecks?"

"No idea. Oh geez, let's get these kids in the bath." On spaghetti nights I have Nicholas eat without a shirt and put Abby in the high chair wearing just a diaper, because the kitchen looks like a crime scene when we are finished. Eddie picks Nicholas up by the armpits and flies him to the bathroom making airplane noises, while I follow behind picking noodles out of Abby's hair.

A seed has been planted and I can't let go of the idea of becoming a professional writer, although I don't even know where to start. What would a confident person do? I decide the best answer to that question is to email the editor of our local paper and introduce myself as a freelancer. I don't have a writing resume beyond my own blog, so I hope a strong email will suffice.

*Hello, my name is Stephanie Giese and I am a former elementary school teacher making a career transition into writing full-time.* I include a few sentences about my work being award-winning; he doesn't need to know I'm referring to an eighth-grade essay contest. I would love to send him a few pieces on relevant education topics or cover family-friendly events.

I do not expect to hear back, but a week later there is a gentle rejection in my inbox.

*Hello, Ms. Giese. Unfortunately, we do not currently have a budget for freelance work and do not hire full or part-time employees without a journalism background here at the paper, but I have passed your information along to the editor of our sister publication, a local parenting magazine. Best of luck to you in your new career.*

It never occurred to me that the small, local parenting magazines I've seen at the grocery store and the library would hire writers.

A month goes by before I find a new email from a name that I don't recognize with the subject line "Seeking Author for Potato Article." I almost delete it as spam, but when I do open it, I find:

*Ms. Giese, I received your contact information from the editor of the York Daily Record. You come recommended as a freelance writer for education and parenting topics. Do you have availability to complete a reported piece this week on the topic of which local restaurant has the best mashed potatoes? We were thinking of using categories such as kid-friendly, gourmet, etc. Please let me know your availability as soon as possible.*

I'm not sure what she means by reported piece on an opinion topic, but I email back asking for more information. Is she looking for a specific word count and what are their compensation rates? How many restaurants would she be looking for me to compare?

Another email from her and I have my answers, and just like that I'm officially a professional writer.

All of that is great, but the truth is that writing one paid article every few months is not a career, and we are drowning in student loans and other bills. Not to mention that I'm learning that I am not cut out to be home all day with babies. I'm jealous of the women who excel and enjoy being home. I think it's maddening, feeling like I abandoned my education and my career to become a failed housekeeper and reliant on a man for everything from our roof, to our food, to which doctors we can see through his insurance. It makes me resent my family, particularly my husband, and I need another focus if this marriage is going to work. Something bigger than bottles and diapers that uses my professional skillset but lets me keep the kids with me because as much as I don't like being a housewife, I actually do love being a full-time mom. I hate how the chores multiply so much faster when we are home all day because more people eating more meals in your house every day or playing in mud or paint leads to exponentially more dishes and laundry, and then all those extra chores fall on me just for being the only adult who is around at the moment. But I like being there for every new word, first step, and knowing all of their friends and food preferences. I love being able to go to the park whenever we want, being able to meet my grandmother for lunch on a whim, or being able to take Nicholas and Abby to the free kids' movies our local theater shows at 10 a.m. on Wednesdays. I really enjoy the Mom N Me classes we've been doing at church and the library. If only I could make a career out of something like that. Maybe I can.

"Babe?" I ask Eddie tentatively. "What would you say about me starting a business?"

"What kind of business? Like tutoring or something?"

"No, like an actual business. I was thinking it would be cool if York had a community toy library. You know, like a regular library, but instead of books families could borrow toys." Toys are expensive and kids outgrow them so quickly. Plus, I could teach classes and the kids could go to work with me.

"That's a cool idea, but we don't have the capital to start a business. I'll support you, as long as we don't go into any more debt over it. And I think it's going to be really hard to take on a project that big while the kids are little."

It is hard, but I love it. It takes some creativity to figure out the finances, but I decide to cash out a life insurance policy and use the money to rent a space in a strip mall. My mother also invests in my idea and gives me the cash to buy our toys and some furniture. I call it Tiny Toes. I hope eventually it will become a non-profit organization, but ironically I can't afford to file for non-profit status because it's cheaper to start a business that makes money than one that doesn't. I form a single-member Limited Liability Corporation to protect our family from risk, just in case the business fails or I get sued. As such, I am officially a small business owner and Tiny Toes becomes the first privately owned for-profit toy library in America, or at least that's what the insurance agents tell me because they can't find a precedent, and that makes it challenging to find liability coverage.

Renting used toys to infants is considered extremely high-risk because of recalls, choking hazards, and not being able to account for how the toys are handled when they are out of my sight. The lack of precedent and my own lack of equity also make it impossible to get a small business loan, but that doesn't matter since we are trying to avoid collecting more debt. After meeting with more than twenty different insurance agencies and creating a detailed plan for how we will inspect and sanitize every item in our inventory every day, I finally get the coverage we need.

Most other toy libraries were created by established charities or churches during hard times like the Great Depression. The recession is making it a great time to start another one, because families need the services we are offering. As the owner I can set limited hours for the business, so I spend about five hours there every weekday and Saturday morning, usually toting Nicholas and Abby along. We close for the afternoon, when we noticed a lull in interest anyway, so that I can take my children home to nap and get them dinner and into bed, then Eddie stays home with the kids and I go back to reopen for evening hours and bedtime stories to give working parents a chance to use our services. The paperwork and press releases I do from home while my kids are asleep.

Eventually, I find an artist who donates her time to paint circus animal murals on our walls, get local news crews and papers to cover our story, join a small business coalition, and hire our teenage babysitter to work part-time on-site to cover the hours I cannot be in two places at once. Eddie coded my entire website himself and created my logo and graphic designs for the membership cards and staff uniform. I handle all of my own payroll, inventory, advertising, and bookkeeping. We don't have a large client base, but we do sell memberships and offer story times and enrichment classes as well a fun, safe indoor meeting place for playgroups.

To my surprise, the toys become a secondary part of our business model. Parents come to play with their children for the day and socialize with friends, but they rarely choose to take a toy home, so in order to stay afloat I start to focus on developing our classes and renting our space to private groups. Tiny Toes is able to offer a variety of classes every month by bringing in teachers with other skill sets. In addition to the bedtime stories, science, and beginner French classes I teach myself, we offer Spanish, art, and theater classes. Other teachers can use our space and set their own schedules. I watch their children while they teach, and I advertise for them, but they have to pass a background check and have clearances and we split the profit 50/50. The applicants are almost always women with young children who are looking for a way to increase their income on a flexible schedule without adding childcare costs. I'm not making a lot of money, and in fact I don't think we will turn a profit for a while, but for a first-year business we are on track to do well and I've discovered a passion for creating family-friendly business opportunities for women.

# Chapter 11

I drive across town, with Nicholas and Abby in tow, to the psychologist's office when the day of our appointment finally arrives. The man who greets us is tall and bespectacled. I forget his name immediately after he tells me what it is. He will be taking Nicholas into a room to talk and play with blocks and puzzles. I can watch through the two-way glass, if I'd like, but I won't be able to hear. He will use this interview with Nicholas as well as my responses on the questionnaire and the responses from Nicholas' preschool teacher to make a diagnosis. After an hour, he invites me to come back in a week without the children to discuss the results of the screening.

"Do you want to come with me to hear the results next week?" I ask Eddie when the kids and I are back at home.

"I mean, it's just going to be a yes or a no, right? Either way, he is still the same kid, it doesn't really change anything. I'll stay with the kids so we don't need to hire a sitter."

So, a week later I go back to hear the results alone.

"Nice to see you again, Mrs. Giese." The psychologist shakes my hand.

"Stephanie, please." I try to make this meeting feel less formal. It doesn't work because he pulls out a file folder and sits crossed-legged, balancing our son's paperwork on his lap.

"So, let's talk about Nicholas," he begins. I only raise my eyebrows in response, so he continues, gesturing to another chair and inviting me to take a seat as well. "He's very young for an evaluation, so let's start there. If you decide to have him reevaluated in the future, you might find different results. But for now, here we are."

"And where is that?" I ask, folding my arms across my stomach and leaning toward him as I sit down.

"Well, I reviewed your responses as well as his teacher's. The way they are scored puts the behaviors you are seeing at home or at school on a scale from mild to severe. You and his teacher both reported answers that scored in the severe category for autistic markers."

"So, he does have autism?" I question.

"Well, I didn't say that." He adjusts his glasses, then removes them to wipe a smudge away on his shirt. "The third component we look at is his in-person interview. He did struggle to answer our questions, but I see here he already has a diagnosed receptive language delay, so that has been accounted for. Nicholas is quite advanced in social skills, isn't he? I might even call him a social butterfly. He was very friendly during our chat, and he looked me in the eye several times."

"Okay?"

"Those are not behaviors consistent with autism. As such, I'm not comfortable making the diagnosis, especially considering his age."

"I'm sorry, are you saying two out of three markers came back severe, and he also had difficulty answering your questions, but you won't diagnose him just because he looked at your face?" It sounds as dumb when I say it out loud as it feels in my head.

"It's a bit more complicated than that," he scoffs, but he doesn't explain how so.

I don't know whether to be relieved or agitated, so I settle for simply confused. My son does not have autism. That's...good, I guess? Although, how is it possible that just looking at one person's face can negate the severity of his mother's and teacher's experiences and his own interview responses? If it isn't autism, what is it?

On cue, the psychologist says, "I see here there is a history of adoption? A traumatic background could account for the same behaviors you are seeing at home. His behaviors really are quite similar. Trauma changes the brain and severe anxiety, especially as a result of previous trauma, can present in the ways you are seeing. Unfortunately, since there is no documentation about his birth mother's pregnancy or her time with him, we just don't know what happened there." Is he saying Nicholas can't have autism just because he's adopted?

"He was only a year old when he came to us," I offer. He has had a stable home life since.

"Be that as it may, the first year of brain development is

99

the most crucial. The violent outbursts, the sensitivities, the anxiety, the sensory-seeking behaviors." He moves his hands in a circular motion as he goes down the list. "Those can all be explained by trauma, even in limited exposure. Could they be autism? Maybe, but considering his history I can't definitively say, and it would be unethical for me to make a diagnosis that was purely speculative." How is it purely speculative when there is a full file folder sitting on your lap giving you data to support the diagnosis? My face must be asking the question for me because he continues, "It's the classic nature versus nurture dilemma, and unfortunately we may never know for sure. I'm not in the business of making uninformed guesses. But do I understand those behaviors are difficult to parent. If I were you, I would look into the same services people who are on the autism spectrum receive. A classroom aide or perhaps ABA therapy would be highly beneficial for Nicholas."

Except we can't access services for autism without an autism diagnosis, that's the entire reason why we are here, and he knows it. The diagnosis is the ticket into every school and community-based service and every healthcare option that would serve him. There is no such thing as trauma-based services for children in school, or in our community, or in our state's Medicaid program, and there's no official diagnosis for trauma-induced-autism-like-behaviors. If he had given us a yes, then Nicholas would magically be able to access different classrooms, home-based programs, therapists, and Medicaid.

"There is such a thing as Sensory Processing Disorder, which is when a person is extra sensitive to sensory input but does not necessarily have the social difficulties an autistic person would," he says. "If pressed, I would probably place Nicholas more along those lines." But he didn't write that down on any of those papers in his lap, and even if he had it wouldn't be considered a disability in the same way autism is.

As it is, we are leaving with nothing but a recommendation to try to find non-existent equivalent services in the private sector ourselves and pay for them out-of-pocket, while our taxes continue to pay for the same services for other people's children who exhibit the same symptoms. But only children without traumatic backgrounds, apparently. I clench my teeth and breathe as deeply as I can so my voice won't shake.

"If Nicholas were my biological child, and you had the same information, would I be leaving this room with a different diagnosis?" I look into his eyes and ask.

He closes the folder and strokes his chin, considering the question before offering, "Again, I can't speculate on things beyond our reality. I have an obligation to diagnose Nicholas as he came to me. His history does not allow for me to make a diagnosis with the information I have. If you disagree, when he starts kindergarten you can ask to have him retested by the school district." He stands and gestures toward the door before leading me out.

Nicholas is only in preschool, so I suppose it doesn't really matter at this point whether or not he has a diagnosis, but I find the idea that a trauma history can be the only thing standing in the way of getting one to be maddening. Are we to assume then that there are no autistic children in foster care, or that it will be harder if not impossible for them to receive services if there are? How can you tell the difference between severe trauma and severe autism? Is he saying eye contact is the only difference? And the kids who can make eye contact and have a traumatic background then get none of the other services? That seems insane and detrimental. I can't wrap my brain around it. This examiner has to be wrong. I'll have Nicholas tested again.

At home, I park the van and let the screen door slam too hard behind me when I walk into the house.

"Well, how did it go?" Eddie asks.

"He said no," is all I offer.

"Huh. I'm kind of surprised. I was looking at a checklist online while you were there and he has like ninety-five percent of the symptoms. Did he have any other suggestions?"

"Nothing particularly helpful," I sigh, kicking my shoes into the coat closet. "He thinks it's all because of trauma. If that's right, then I guess the next step should be to find him a therapist?" Silently I also commit to change Nicholas' diet. Maybe if we stop eating gluten or red dye it could help.

"Hm, well, I leave that to you then. You know so much more about this stuff. I'm so glad you were a teacher."

"I really don't." There were not any Here's What You Do If Your Kid May or May Not Have Autism classes when I was in college. "I'd actually really appreciate it if you would do, well, anything when it comes to this stuff." I unload my frustration onto my husband.

Eddie's demeanor shifts. "I guess I thought paying the bills, and making sure we have health insurance, and being an active father counted as doing something," he snips. "I'm not one of those guys who refuses to do laundry or dishes. I fed the kids and got them in bed tonight, didn't I? Just tell me what you need me to do, I'll try to do it."

"Just, never mind. Yes, congratulations on being an adult and washing your own underwear and going to work every day, exactly the same way you would if we didn't exist. All right. Thanks." I drench my words in sarcasm and end the discussion. He's never going to understand that what I need is for him to occasionally be the one to figure out what needs to be done in the first place, then do it without waiting around for me to take charge and delegate, but it's not really worth a fight. He's trying, and I guess if we were to put it on paper our distribution of labor is pretty even. It's not like I'm mowing the lawn, or changing the air filters, or remembering to update the registration for our cars. There are plenty of things he does do. It's just that it's so exhausting to be running my own business in addition to being the one making such huge decisions about Nicholas every day, and I wish this felt like more of an equal partnership when it comes to the kids. He has made zero sacrifices of his body or his career. As it stands, I guess I'll be the one to find a therapist, just like I was the one who filled out the paperwork, and went to the meetings with the psychologist, and just like I go to every doctor, occupational therapy, speech, and most school meetings alone.

# Chapter 12

I tried to Google therapists in our area who treat children, but the only result outside of being admitted to a hospital was the same practice that did our autism evaluation. We're not in a big city like Tampa or Baltimore anymore. This is rural, central Pennsylvania. I drive past three different cow pastures on the five-mile trip to the pediatrician. Most smaller businesses and private practices in our area don't even have websites. There has to be another way to figure this out, and I'm too stubborn to give up now. The Yellow Pages was delivered a few days ago and has been sitting on the kitchen counter ever since just because I'm not sure if its glossy cover can go in the recycling bin. Now it seems as good a place as any to find a therapist, so I lug out the heavy book and start turning pages. I haven't used the Yellow Pages since, well now that I think about it, I may never have used the Yellow Pages as an adult and I'm not sure where to start. Should I look under C for *Child Psychologist*? What's the difference between psychotherapy and psychology? Is there a difference? Will mental health services be listed under M? Do I try P for *pediatric*? I finally find a page that looks promising and start making my way down the list.

I expected to have to make a few calls before I found someone willing to see a preschooler, but after thirty-four phone calls I'm feeling more than a little bit discouraged. Over and over, they all say the same thing, "Your son is three? Sorry, ma'am. Our practice doesn't serve children that young. You could ask your pediatrician for a referral to, oh, you already saw them? I see. No, then I'm not aware of anyone else in York County. No, I'm sorry, I'm not familiar with any trauma specialists in our area. Best of luck."

A few do recommend books about parenting children with attachment concerns. It's common in families with adopted children, they tell me the very obvious thing I already know. Still, I buy all of the books. One office recommends calling an adoption agency, but when I do the only post-adoption support they have in place is a group of other parents with similar concerns who meet in a different county. They get together once a month to vent their own frustrations about the lack of other resources available. I understand that a lot of people find support groups helpful, but I cannot get behind the idea of paying a babysitter and driving for an hour and a half just to sit in a circle where everyone has the same problem and listening to them complain, cry, and one-up each other's battle scars. I am already at full capacity and I do not have the bandwidth. It's just a depressing reminder of how few actual supports exist for families like ours.

Four weeks and many failed attempts later, there is only one therapist's name left on the list and I don't feel especially good about it. The Center for Creative Arts and Play Therapy sounds like they are listed in the wrong section. Their name conjures images of finger paint and Mommy N Me Music classes. Nicholas is already spending every day with me at the toy library, and this doesn't sound any different. I, of all people, understand the value of play, but we need a licensed therapist. There are no credentials listed in their advertisement, just a phone number and a fanciful quote about the power of art.

"Hello?" a woman's voice answers.

"Yeah, hi," I sigh before launching into the same thing I've repeated dozens of times in previous calls, which now includes a disclaimer that I've already contacted every other therapist in the Yellow Pages. Picturing Nicholas having to lie still on a sofa and tell her about his day is laughable. I tell her that he has a language processing delay and warn her that he's only three, and a very active three at that. I don't know how much he will even be able to understand in therapy. He's already receiving quite a few services, although they are mostly educational and not really helping his behaviors at all. A lot of the behaviors are very normal for children transitioning out of foster care. They might go away if we just keep providing a safe, stable environment. I know that, but something bigger is wrong. I can't explain it, I just feel it.

I know I sound crazy. Who goes through this much trouble just to get someone to agree something is the matter with their preschooler? Crazy people, that's who. And also mothers who know in their gut that something actually is wrong.

"I would love to meet him," after waiting patiently for me to finish she surprises and relieves me with her reply. "My name is Betsy. I'm a Licensed Clinical Social Worker." She is the first therapist to answer her own phone and the first to tell me to call her by her first name. "I specialize in play therapy. I also have a colleague I can recommend who specializes in art and music therapy, if that's a direction you'd like to go, but for Nicholas at this age it sounds like play therapy might be a good fit."

I don't know what that is, which must be something she hears a lot because before I can respond she continues, "If you decide I'm a good match, then Nicholas would come and play in my office for thirty or forty minutes, and afterward you and I will sit down and talk about what I observed. I look for patterns in the way he plays. We can learn a lot about a child from the way they interact with toys. Then after a few sessions, we will come up with a treatment plan." I should be advised that it costs eighty dollars for a forty-five-minute session, do I want to schedule? If so, we will also need to schedule a separate intake meeting first for her to collect some information about him.

If all he has to do is play with toys for half an hour, we can definitely handle that. Although it seems like an odd thing to pay for because he can do that for free at home or at Tiny Toes. Doing something has to be better than doing nothing, though, so I take the next available appointment.

The kids need a bath, so I put Nicholas and Abby in the

tub together. I can't risk having him alone and unsupervised for the amount of time it would take to bathe his sister by herself. They are happy and giggling in the suds until Nicholas, unprovoked, slaps Abby in the face. She starts to cry immediately, and her cheek turns pink.

"Nicholas," I scold. "That was mean. Tell your sister you are sorry. We do not hit."

"I didn't hit her, Mommy," he lies to my face.

"I just saw you do it, young man, and now you're in extra trouble because you aren't telling the truth."

"Mommy, I promise," he looks into my eyes with such sincerity that I begin to doubt what I just witnessed. If it weren't for the preschool-sized handprint on her cheek, I might actually believe him.

"It wasn't me. I'm nice to Abby. That was the other Nicholas. He is mean."

Well, that's a new one. Maybe I should blame Batman for this alter ego business. My mother bought him the DVD set of the old television show with Adam West.

"Just tell your sister you are sorry." I demand, pulling Abby out of the tub and wrapping her in a towel.

"I'm sorry the other Nicholas hurt you, Abby."

I roll my eyes and tell him that there is a three-minute time out waiting for him after this bath, for hitting and now also for lying.

"Mommy, no. I didn't do it." He wails.

"Uh, huh. Well, maybe you'll get lucky, and the other Nicholas will show up to take your time out." I purse my lips and widen my eyes at him. He faces away from me and splashes his fists down into the soapy water.

Turning to lay Abby down on the floor and wriggle her damp body into pajamas, I hear him mumbling to himself.

"Mommy doesn't believe me. He did it. There is another Nicholas. I hate that guy."


Betsy's office is a small rented room in the back of a yoga studio. I was here a few days ago to meet her and drop off some forms, but I didn't realize the yoga classes were held at the same time as her therapy hours. That would have been nice to know before I barged my family into a silent room full of spandex-clad women bending themselves into pretzels.

"I can see their butts." Nicholas says too loudly, before I can shush him.

"Can I help you today?" The instructor is pleasant but confused by our presence.

"Oh, um, I have an appointment?" I offer, but it isn't enough.

"Are you sure you have the right place, Hun?" This isn't exactly a child-friendly class.

"I think so. We are here for therapy." I try to whisper, half out of respect for their yoga and half because of my own embarrassment. I really did not expect that I was going to need to announce it to twenty complete strangers today.

"Right. Of course. Just take a seat. She'll be right with you, I'm sure."

The only place to sit is a line of cafeteria-style chairs under the window. Otherwise, this is one large, mirrored room with the kind of bouncy wooden floor you would expect of any dance or yoga studio. There are two closed doors along the wall opposite our chairs. One has a sign designating it as the bathroom, and the other is Betsy's office. I try to will her door open with my mind, but it stubbornly stays shut.

I balance Abby on my lap and Nicholas stands next to us, bending and reaching, imitating the yoga stretches. A few women smile in his direction, others glare at me, not happy about the interruption to their class. I try to ignore them and stare straight ahead, with all of the advice we've received from well-meaning friends or online strangers playing in my head.

*Make sure he is not eating sugar.*

*Rub essential oils on his feet before bed.*

*Have you had him tested for Lyme Disease?*

*I'm sure he will grow out of it.*

*You know what they say about those vaccines, and he had them all twice.*

*Boys will be boys, it doesn't mean they need therapy.*

Finally, the door opens and a slender, blonde woman wearing geometric prints and chunky bracelets makes her way over to us, smiling without showing any teeth. This is Betsy.

She reintroduces herself to me, then bends her knees to lower herself enough to look Nicholas in the eye.

"Are you Nicholas? My name is Betsy. It's nice to meet you," her voice is soft, and she extends her hand to shake his. "I met your mom the other day and I'm so glad she brought you here to see me today. Would you like to play in my sand table?"

"You have a sandbox inside?" Nicholas bounces, taking

her hand and pulling her toward the back room without so much as a glance in my direction.

Her office is lined with shelves filled with toys, mostly small figurines grouped into categories: animals, people, outer space, super heroes, underwater adventures. There are also dolls, pretend kitchen items, costumes, and a dollhouse. A child-sized table filled with sand sits prominently in the center of the room. It's actually very similar to the toy library, only where my office is filled with bright colors and noisy plastic toys that talk, Betsy's is more subdued and none of these toys requires batteries.

Betsy leads Nicholas into the room, asking him what kind of toys he likes to play with at home. When he tells her airplanes, she points to her shelf of vehicles, and he shrieks. Trucks, Hot Wheels, miniature construction equipment, and all sizes of planes and helicopters sit at the ready.

"You have an A-10 and an F-15?" He doesn't ask for permission before grabbing both off the shelf and holding them above his head as he zooms around the space.

"He says he wants to be an Air Force pilot one day," I tell her.

"Wow, you know a lot about planes. I didn't know that was what kind they were," she says to Nicholas. Then Betsy turns to me, "You're welcome to stay for the first session, but if you are comfortable, I might be able to get to know Nicholas a bit better if our following sessions are just the two of us. Or you can step out today and continue to wait out on the chairs, or even go grab yourself a coffee." She seems to be encouraging the second option.

I don't drink coffee, but we passed a Starbucks on the

way in. It never occurred to me that I wouldn't be staying for the session. I am always there for his other therapies.

"Are you sure you don't need me?" I ask tentatively.

"Bye, Mom." Nicholas runs over my foot, still holding the planes above his head.

"We'll have fun," Betsy assures me. "You mentioned some possible attachment concerns at our intake. This will give me a chance to see how Nicholas reacts when he's separated from you for a few minutes. I just ask that you return in half an hour so we have time to debrief and collect your payment."

I slip out with Abby as Nicholas crashes the A-10 into the sand. With Abby buckled into her car seat, I drive aimlessly for a few minutes exploring the unfamiliar neighborhood. She drifts off to sleep quickly and I don't want to risk waking her to go into a store, although I have discovered a new children's consignment shop a few blocks from Betsy's office. Maybe that will be an option on future trips. For now, I pull into the Starbucks lot and park, just waiting for the clock to tell me it's time to go back and pick up Nicholas.

Silence is an unfamiliar, empty space and the tears that come to fill it catch me off-guard. I don't know if I'm crying because of guilt, or shame, or just because I didn't expect everything to be this hard. I thought raising a preschooler would be mostly finger painting, preparing snacks, a few long nights, and fighting to get him to eat vegetables. There are thirty other women in the Mom N Me group from church, ten more from our library play group, and still dozens more from pre-school. None of them are taking their children to psychotherapy. Or if they are, they definitely are not talking about it. I know because I asked everyone for recommendations when I was trying to figure out who would see us. I was met with mostly wide eyes and head shakes, a few I'm sorries, and even fewer promises to ask around to see if anyone they knew could help. I must be doing something wrong, but I don't know what it is. If our family were the norm, then it wouldn't have been so hard to find a therapist. Simple supply and demand tell me there must not be that many people looking, or there would be more therapists serving three-year-olds, right? I would give anything to just be normal. I would happily trade any mom my seat crying in this parking lot for a few temper tantrums over broccoli if she wanted to take my place.

We are up to weekly speech therapy, occupational therapy, academic tutoring, and now play therapy. There are four appointments at a minimum every week, which total about eight to ten hours including travel time, and that doesn't count the regular doctor's appointments. It also doesn't include the hours I have to spend researching, making phone calls, filling out paperwork, and talking with the insurance company, or the fact that the pediatrician wants me to take Nicholas to a gastroenterologist because he was in the emergency room twice last month for refusing to poop.

The GI is an hour away because that was the only person in our area the insurance would accept. Nicholas' stool became so impacted that he started having colon and prostate spasms and was in so much pain we thought he had appendicitis. Now they think he may need to have a procedure done on his prostate if we can't get this under control. Taking care of Nicholas' medical and educational needs has become a full-time job. Why is my kid the only one I know refusing to potty train to the point that he may literally poison himself with poop? And what is giving all of my attention to her brother doing to the baby? If the first year of development is as important as everyone says, am I creating a cycle by diverting so much attention to Nicholas while Abby is an infant? Is she going to have the same problems? I don't think I can do all of this all over again.

Abby stirs in her seat, and I wipe my face and shift into drive, back to the office/studio. The yoga class is gone. Betsy invites me into her office, where Nicholas continues to dig in the sand.

"He did well today," she says. "He was engaged and talkative. I really enjoyed my time with Nicholas."

"What did you do? Can I ask that? Is it confidential?"

She smiles, "Nicholas? Can we tell Mommy what we did today? Is that all right with you?"

"Airplanes. Boom. Crash." Nicholas seems to give his consent, so Betsy fills me in.

"Today was just free play for Nicholas so I can get to know him, discover how he likes to play, and start to take note of any patterns I see. You can see he really favors the cars and airplanes. He enjoys spinning their wheels."

"Ha. Yeah. I figured."

"One thing I noticed was that Nicholas likes to fill things. He spent a lot of time filling cars with sand, burying things, or putting the toys inside of each other rather than developing stories. Do you notice that at home? I found it interesting."

"Um, yeah. He does do that." My mind drifts to the matchbox cars I found in his room filled with half-chewed gummy vitamins and tiny pieces of torn computer paper.

"Okay, those are the kinds of things we will be looking to observe. The way children play can tell us a lot about them. For example, based on that I would guess Nicholas might tend to eat quite a bit of food. To the point that it would be hard for him to know when to stop."

"Oh my god, yeah he does. He will eat four or five helpings if I don't stop him. The last time my sister visited for a barbeque I was distracted. He ate, like, four adult-sized sloppy joes and a hamburger, then hid in the coat closet and threw up." It's a problem. All that food needs to come out, and when he is so stuffed it hurts him to get it out, he won't go. Hence the bathroom issues. It never occurred to me therapy could help with that too.

She nods, not surprised. "That is the same 'fill it up' tendency I saw today in his play at the sand table." A few months ago, that would have sounded like a bunch of hippy nonsense, but now she's the only one who seems to understand why Nicholas is acting the way he does. "I find play therapy is great for kids who might be too young or not have the language skills for traditional talk therapy methods. It's hard to get a three-year-old to sit still and talk about feelings," she laughs. "So, if you decide to continue, we will work together to figure out what Nicholas is telling us while he plays."

Because of his history and what the previous psychologist said, Betsy also offers to bring an attachment specialist into her office for a session with us. She says the specialist would video our interactions with Nicholas and send the tape to a team in Chicago to be analyzed. Then we will know for sure if a diagnosis like Reactive Attachment Disorder would be appropriate, but she didn't see anything today that gave her that impression.

Six months later we are still seeing Betsy once a week. Because we have high-deductible insurance, we have to pay in full for every appointment until we meet the arbitrary amount assigned by the insurance company, which is so high that we've never been able to hit it. Between therapy, the attachment specialist, and doctor's appointments, there is always more month than money and the groceries, diapers, and gas for the cars are all being charged to our credit card. Several bills from the pediatrician are already a few months late and might be sent to collections.

Betsy has relocated to the top floor of an old Victorian-style mansion that sits just off the highway, in a section that has been rezoned for commercial use. She was true to her word and set up an appointment for us with the attachment specialist. We spent hours taking turns in front of the camera, Nicholas interacting with me or with Eddie, then with both of us, then just Nicholas playing alone. We watched the tape with Betsy and the specialist as they pointed out things like how often Nicholas looked at our faces or at me while my back was turned. It should be a relief that the specialist and his team didn't see any signs of RAD, and for what it's worth he also doesn't think Nicholas has autism, but instead it just feels frustrating that we still aren't any closer to finding an answer. We are paying hundreds of dollars every month for treatments, but no one even knows what we are treating. I had to call my father sobbing because there is a stack of hospital bills sitting on the table, and there is no way we can afford to continue therapy and doctor's appointments for Nicholas and also pay our mortgage.

"Stephanie, don't be ridiculous," I could almost hear him roll his eyes through the phone. "It's not like I'm going to kick my grandchildren out of their house. Every young family has a hard time starting out. Our parents helped your mother and me, and Helen and I will be here to help you. I'm sure your mother and Ed's parents feel the same. Just pay what you can when you can." The guilt is overwhelming, especially when I think of all the families who don't have a daddy-owned mortgage, or health insurance (as unhelpful as ours may be financially, at least it grants us access to our doctors and therapists), or two healthy partners to share the parenting. Eddie and I both feel like complete failures.

Diagnosis or not, our kid is still the only one pulling down his pants at the preschool reading rug and scooting around to smear his poop on the floor like a dog that has worms. We are still the only family I know calling a friend who is a nurse to come over and help us give a three-year-old enemas twice a week because he was hospitalized again and is still refusing to poop, but the GI specialist said there was nothing physically wrong. Nicholas is literally being anal retentive. He's refusing to poop because he just doesn't want to. He holds it so long that it hurts, and then because it hurts to go he avoids going, and then it just gets worse. We repeat that cycle ad nauseum.

A full adult dose of medicine in his milk twice a day does nothing. We've had to resort to bi-weekly enemas and have still needed a few trips to the doctor so the pediatrician could disimpact his stool manually, which means at least two or three times a week I'm pinning a screaming child down so that an adult can put something into his rectum just to get him to poop. When none of that works, we still end up in the emergency room again and again. It's for his own good, I know that, but Nicholas doesn't, and if trauma really is the root of all of this, then the additional trauma this must be causing surely isn't going to help.

"In my opinion, this is behavioral," the GI doctor says when all of the tests confirm his suspicion that Nicholas is perfectly healthy. "A control issue. It's common for kids who have experienced trauma to have toileting issues." Here we go blaming the t-word again. "Frankly, I'm impressed by the strength it must take for him to be doing this, but it's not healthy. Your son needs a therapist, there's not really much else I can do for him. I'm afraid if we try too many medical interventions, we might end up making the problem worse."

Thankfully, we already have a therapist, so Betsy starts to bring it up in their sessions and lets us borrow a book called *It Hurts When I Poop*. I find it comforting that this book exists. If someone saw a need to write it, that must mean there are other people going through the same thing. I read it to Nicholas a few times each day while he sits on the potty. I have also started curating a small library of books I saw in online adoption forums that are supposed to help with attachment concerns. *Llama Llama Misses Mama*, *I'll*

*Always Come Back, The Kissing Hand*, and *The Fathers Are Coming Home* are now our regular rotation at bedtime. Although, no matter how many books I read or songs I sing, Nicholas still won't sleep for more than three hours each night, which means neither do we.

It has only been a few months since his doctor gave us that first referral, but now between the play therapy, speech therapy, occupational therapy, doctors' appointments, specialists, and hospital visits, my schedule is completely full. At least once a day I need to close the toy library during regular business hours to take Nicholas to an appointment because none of his therapists or doctors have evening or weekend hours. I can't afford to hire anyone else to run my business for me and my one part-time employee is pregnant and will be leaving soon. This schedule is not sustainable and I'm not willing to sacrifice helping my child. So, after less than a year in operation, I have to shut down the toy library for good. For the second time in less than two years, my decision has been made for me. I know I should try to stay focused on how lucky we are that we have a two-parent household, insurance, and Eddie's job, and the support of our families, but it's still hard not to resent the fact that my career has been stripped from me twice without my consent and the lack of diagnosis for Nicholas means no one can even tell me why.

I might not be able to work full-time, but I can't sit by and watch us fall into bankruptcy either. My writing assignments are sporadic and only pay an average of two hundred dollars per month, so I find an ad on Craigslist. A local non-profit is hiring part-time teachers for their parenting classes. Having a degree and experience in education and parenting my own children makes me qualified, and the hours are ideal. A few evenings each month I teach a scripted child development course to new parents, and two or three Saturdays per year I teach a co-parenting class to former couples who are court-ordered to attend, mostly after nasty custody disputes.

They are the same types of classes Eddie and I took to become licensed for our adoption: basic child development and age-appropriate, touch-free discipline techniques, using I-statements to help you communicate, and the difference between natural and logical consequences. Sometimes I help run a family program in the evenings at public schools. The classes are free to the community and childcare is included, so I can bring my own children to work. I enjoy teaching again, and although the paychecks are small, the light schedule is family-friendly. It feels ridiculous to me in light of how things are going with Nicholas, but because of my position I receive a badge that labels me a Parenting Specialist.

# Chapter 13

*May 2011*

I gave the kids canned soup for dinner and put them to bed early. Eddie picked up Taco Bell for us on his way home from work and now we are sitting on the couch watching *Fringe* and eating nachos. Our beige sectional is already ripping at the seams and covered in apple juice stains and crayon, so a few more drops of liquid cheese won't hurt it. The traveling has finally stopped and he is home each night. There's an adorable baby boy in this commercial, crawling around wearing nothing but a diaper, his tiny little rolls of fat spilling over onto each other. I want to reach through the TV to hold him and blow raspberries on his chubby belly. I turn to lock my eyes on Eddie. "We should have another baby."

He doesn't even look at me before he answers, "Hard pass."

"Oh, come on, remember how great they smell?"

"You mean for the five seconds a day when they aren't

covered in puke or poop?"

"Remember when they learn how to say your name?"

"Remember how we already have two kids we can't afford?"

"Aw, remember when they learn to give kisses and it's like they are eating your whole face?"

"Remember how you had to lie on an operating table and be awake while they cut you open and removed your organs?"

I smile, "Yeah, I do. Let's do it again."

"Nope."

"Please? Eddie," I'm serious now. "I want another baby."

"Steph, look at me," He finally turns to face me, and his eyes are hard. "I need you to hear what I am telling you and understand it. I do not want any more kids. For real. Now watch your boy from Dawson's Creek fight these monsters."

"Or..."

"No."

I crawl across the sofa and put my hand on his thigh. He ignores it and dips another chip into the now cold yellow liquid. He doesn't respond when I start to kiss his neck, but when I move my hand higher he speaks, his mouth still full. "Just watch the show."

"But I want you," I protest, batting my eyelashes against his ear.

"No, you don't. You want a baby, and it's not happening."

A switch flips in my head, and now I'm furious. Still leaning on his thigh, I pull back enough to glare at him.

All I Never Knowed

"You know, it's really great how you get to unilaterally make these decisions. That's exactly what I was always hoping for in a partner."

"Oh my God, you are so ridiculous."

"Am I? Am I ridiculous to think that maybe when you know your wife wants a baby you should talk to her about it instead of just shutting it down and acting like you are the king of this family?"

"Oh, fuck you." He takes my hand and flings it off his jeans.

I fold my arms across my chest and sink back into the cushions undeterred. "That would be lovely, actually. That is how babies get made, after all. But you still won't, will you?"

"Do what? Fuck you? Tonight? Yeah, right."

"Then fuck you, too."

The commercial break is over and we sit and stew in silence for the remainder of the show. There is no way that Peter would do this to Olivia if she decided she wanted to have his inter-dimensional love child.



That is the memory playing on a loop in my head as I stare at the two pink lines. It's too late now. This is happening.

It's after eight o'clock by the time he gets home. The kids are asleep. I'm sitting on the sofa in the living room, in the same spot we were watching *Fringe* last month, and Eddie can tell I've been crying. One look at my face and he knows there is something awful I don't want to say.

123

"Steph, what is the matter? Did you wreck your car or something?"

"No." I start sobbing all over again. I hate that I can't control it.

"Did somebody die? Are the kids okay? Jesus. What is it?"

"I'm... pregnant."

"Oh." It takes a minute for the news to hit him. "That's great. Why are you sad?"

He's beaming. Is he serious? Now I want to hit him.

"I. thought. you. would. be. mad. at. me." Heavy breaths I can't rein in are shaking my shoulders.

"Wow. What kind of an asshole do you think I am?" The kind that lets your wife anticipate the opposite of this reaction, for starters.

"I don't know." I wipe my face on my sleeve. "You're happy?"

"Of course I'm happy, but are *you* happy? Geez. Come here." He moves the baby gate that is separating the living room from the foyer and walks over to sit next to me on the sofa. I fall into him, covering the front of his polo shirt with warm tears and snot in the process. "Thanks for that," he laughs, leaning me back for a second so that he can take off his shirt. "These hormones are going to be fun."

"Shut up. You are the worst."

"Obviously. Hey, guess what?" He tilts my chin up so I'm looking at his face and touches my nose with the tip of his index finger.

"What?"

"We're going to have another baby."

"So I noticed."

"Guess what else?"

"What?"

"I'm quitting my job." We've been talking about it for a while. In addition to all the park trips, working for Florida means he has been making occasional visits back to Florida. I'm constantly alone with the kids. He has been traveling too much, and recently his company has been doing more steady layoffs. They've already closed the office building where he worked, so Eddie has been working from our basement on the desk we moved out of the toy library. It's really time for him to move on while he can still do it on his terms. He will be ready to take the P.E. exam soon, and he's more likely to get hired now when he's not worth quite as much as he will be in a few months if he passes the test and gains the ability to sign and seal plans. He won't actually leave his current job until he finds another one; this just means he is going to start looking. Hopefully he'll find something that doesn't take him away as much. The timing is not great. The economy is awful. I lie down and put my head in his lap.

"We're so screwed."

"Yeah, good thing I married you for your money," he smirks.

"You're not funny."

"Eh, I think I'm pretty funny."

I don't know how long we sit like that. He runs his fingers through my hair until I fall asleep.

# Chapter 14

*December 2011*

He had to take a significant pay cut to do it, but Eddie found another job. This one doesn't require any overnight travel and there will be steady work in the local engineering field for a while because Pennsylvania is fracking for natural gas. I still don't know how I feel about fracking, but for now it's feeding our family.

Tonight we are going up to the church for a date night at the Christmas play. Eddie takes our coats and weaves his way through the crowd to hang them up, while I stand holding Nicholas' hand in my right hand and Abby's in my left. My belly is so big that it is hard to breathe. Before long, Eddie returns and picks Abby off the ground as we greet dozens of familiar faces.

We've been attending more regularly, and Eddie has joined their recreational volleyball league. I've been volunteering for the moms' ministry and the clothing closet. Sometimes they have board game nights with free childcare. We've made some connections with other young married couples, including the nurse who is helping us with Nick's enemas and his wife. Eddie has also been invited to play guitar for the worship team. The tickets to the play were free, and our new friends will be there. The nursery is open, and we won't need to hire a babysitter. We might as well get in one more date night alone before the baby comes.

My c-section is scheduled for the 30th and I have already been in the hospital once this month for early labor. They gave me a prescription to take that will stop the contractions, but at this point we are just supposed to head straight to the hospital so that they can deliver the baby if the contractions start again. The curtain opens after bedtime, so we put Nicholas and Abby in their matching reindeer footie pajamas and hope they might fall asleep in the nursery. Not that they ever do.

When we arrive, the hallway is so packed that it is hard to move. Our church typically draws over 1,000 people on a Sunday, and their free holiday events for the community are very popular. As we are standing in line Mrs. Carter, the children's choir director, comes up to us carrying a basket of handmade lollipops from her family's local candy store. I wonder if the holiday vest she is wearing was also handmade. Mrs. Carter is one of the few people I stand a full head taller than. Her silver white hair makes her easily recognizable among the crowd.

"Oh, I'm so glad you made it. I can take Nicholas with me from here if you'd like," she offers, although I don't know why she would.

"Grandma," Nicholas exclaims and runs to wrap his arms around her legs. She is obviously not his grandma, but Mrs. Carter smiles. He has taken to calling her that, and she enjoys it.

Eddie and I exchange a puzzled glance so she continues, "The children are singing in the play." Choir doesn't start until age four. This is the first year one of our kids has been old enough to sing. We had no idea.

"They are?" I look around and for the first time I notice that all of the other children in Nicholas' age group and older are dressed in suits and ties or black and red Christmas dresses with tulle. My child is wearing fleece pajamas with reindeer feet. "Um, he's not really dressed for that."

She waves a hand at me dismissively. "He looks adorable. And I can always hide anyone who is uncomfortable in the back." There are at least fifty kids in the choir. It's a big church. Maybe no one will notice.

"Okay, I guess." We allow Mrs. Carter to take Nicholas and we sign Abby into the nursery, then we follow the line of people filing into the large gymnasium. Round tables have been set on the floor and topped with white linens and our tickets send us to our assigned seats, facing the lighted stage. It isn't long before the children's choir begins to walk on. Nicholas is not in the back like Mrs. Carter suggested he would be. Instead he is standing, fully decked out in his pajamas, directly in the center of the first row. He locks eyes on me and starts to wave excitedly with both hands and shout, "Hi, Mom." There is a flurry of giggling from the crowd. When he realizes the laughter is directed at him, he is only encouraged. The children around him start to sing, but our son does not sing along. Nicholas steps out in front of all the other children and stands center stage blowing large, exaggerated kisses to me and various other women he knows and talking to them as if we all came to see his one-man show.

"Oh, Miss Liz is here. Yay. Hi, Miss Korie. Miss Jen, Miss Jen, it's me Nicholas. I'm on the stage. Do you like our song? Did you see my mom? She's right there. I love you, Mom."

There is not a single adult in the room who can stop laughing at my preschooler, but they are all trying to muffle their response out of respect for the other children, who are still trying to sing the songs they've been rehearsing all year, the way they are supposed to be doing. My face must be red enough to match those reindeer pajamas. The choir sings three songs, and the audience claps politely between each. Nicholas takes the opportunity to bow deeply every time, as if the applause is directed solely at him. He comes up from his bows to blow more kisses with huge arched motions.

I am hiding my face behind my hands, but I don't think I have ever seen my son look happier or more alive. Eddie is beaming from his seat next to me. He thinks it is hilarious and doesn't seem to understand why I would be embarrassed. Nicholas was born to connect with an audience. They have fallen in love with him. For the rest of the evening every person who walks past our table on their way to the restroom or the water fountain stops to whisper to us about our son. The men pat my husband on the shoulder and nod approvingly. The women look at me with sympathy.

"Was that your boy up there?"

"He is quite a character."

"You must have your hands full with him at home, but I don't think I have laughed that hard in years."

# Chapter 15

*February 2012*

It's almost six o'clock and Eddie should be home by now. Nick and Abby are in the living room watching Toy Story, and I am stretched out on the couch, with the sleeping baby balanced on my still-round, although now deflated belly. Penelope Christine was born five days after Christmas. We call her Penny. A tiny little thing with a full head of hair, she only weighed five pounds when we brought her home. I reach over and grab the phone off the coffee table, careful not to wake her. The familiar tone of the beeps echoes back at me as I press in Eddie's number. There's a rotisserie chicken in the refrigerator I can pull out when he gets here.

"Hey, what time do you think you'll be home?"

"I got stuck in some construction traffic. I'm thinking probably twenty more minutes. See you soon." Click.

*If I did it now, the kids wouldn't be alone for long.*

One thought, just one thought, but I don't know where it came from. It was in my head, but I don't think it was mine. That isn't what I want. Is it? No. It definitely isn't. It's like someone else has taken control of the teleprompter inside my brain.

*They are fine watching the movie. Just do it in the bathroom. Put the baby in the crib. Lock the door. He'll be home soon. They won't see you.*

Oh, no. No, no. No. This is bad. I stare at the phone in my hand, and my thoughts drift back to the manila envelope in our file cabinet. I can't call the doctor. That's how it starts. That's how it started for her. There are consequences when you tell. A siren in the distance reminds me exactly what those consequences are.

I can't sit here with three children and these thoughts inside my head, but I don't want to call a doctor or a therapist or a pastor right now. I could call a hotline, I guess, but I don't know how that works. I'm too skeptical of the anonymity. They could always trace it back to me. I run through a checklist in my head of the people who would probably not be mandated to report me and decide to call my mother. She's in a graduate school program working on her PhD in counseling. She might know what to do. I put Penny in the portable crib we keep in the living room for naps and diaper changes and move into the kitchen, where it is easier to pace the floor and be out of earshot from the kids.

"Steph?" she picks up on the third ring. I didn't realize I had been holding my breath.

"Mom," my voice cracks. "I don't know what's happening."

I tell her about the unwelcome thought and the way it

came out of nowhere for no reason. No, it never happened before. No, I don't actually want to kill myself. No, I did not think about a method, Jesus Christ. To my relief, she doesn't think I'm going crazy.

"You just had a baby. This is not unheard of. What you are describing sounds like an intrusive thought." It has a name? "Now, first of all, have you started any new medications recently?"

Actually, yes. "Just a new kind of birth control." They made me switch to the progesterone pills because I'm breast feeding. Apparently, my normal pills had a different hormone in them that wasn't great for the baby.

"Is that Pumpkin on the phone? Hi, Pumpkin," Nicholas calls from the other room. My children call their grandmother Pumpkin, which she hates, but everyone else thinks is adorable. Originally, my mom asked to be called Grammy, but every time she saw Nicholas she called him Pumpkin. She said that word so much that he thought it was her name, so the kids have been calling her Pumpkin ever since.

"Well, I'm not a medical doctor. So, I say call your doctor. But it could just be a reaction to that." Her voice is steady through the receiver.

Does birth control give people these kinds of thoughts? That sounds insane. I've been taking birth control pills since I was nineteen years old, just not this particular hormone. But if there is one thing I am definitely not doing right now, it is calling a doctor to find out. I head to my computer and start looking up side effects of various kinds of birth control. Not surprisingly, the internet is full of conflicting information.

"Just please stay on the phone with me until Eddie gets home," I beg my mother.

"Okay, but why won't you call your doctor?"

"Mom," I whisper, "they Baker Acted her for this."

I don't know much at all about Nicholas' birth mom or the circumstances that led up to his adoption, but I do know that in his paperwork there is a record that states that this is the exact reason my son ended up in state custody in the first place. The Baker Act is a controversial law in Florida that allows for people to be involuntarily institutionalized if there is evidence that they have a mental illness and pose a threat to themselves or others. I have no idea if a similar law exists in Pennsylvania. All I know is that if they can do it to her, they can do it to me. I will not risk my children.

"Stephanie," my mother tries to reason with me. "Your circumstances are very different. You have a husband and a very strong support network. Nicholas' birth mother was homeless and alone. Even if you did need some sort of in-patient treatment, which I don't think you do, because I've known you for twenty-eight years and this is the first time there has ever been an incident like this, then your kids would just stay home with Eddie. Do not let that fear stop you from getting help."

It hardly seems fair. We have so much in common, but his birth mom always had to draw the short straw. Even with this. My own mother doesn't see how much I have in common with my son's first mom. She looks at me and only sees her daughter. She sees a highly educated woman who probably has the baby blues and should just switch her medication or talk to a professional. But I see the parallels. All of them. I know that I'm technically unemployed, and we can't pay our mortgage, and I'm sitting here grasping with my own version of the very thing that cost my son's birth mother custody of her child. It's not my fault that I was born on a higher rung of the social ladder and I have all of these people around me holding me up, but now I'm here and I have the privilege of raising the son we share, the little boy who went into custody when he was the exact same age Penelope is right now. I'll be damned if I'm going to do anything that even has an inkling of potential to make Nicholas or any other children lose another mother.

Mom sighs. "Besides, didn't you swear to raise him just like you would a biological child? Would you call the doctor for yourself if Nicholas weren't adopted?" Some questions are just too complicated to answer in the hypothetical. Would I be living this moment if I didn't have children? Do I want to know that answer? I don't have the time or the patience to play games with what ifs. I can only deal with what is. It's my turn to sigh at her.

The front door opens, and the older kids run to Eddie screaming and announcing that Daddy is home. The stress must be written all over my face because the first thing he does is ask me what the matter is. I hang up with my mother.

"Oh, I had sort of a bad reaction to my birth control," I tell him. "Maybe I'm allergic to it or something?"

He loosens his tie and undoes the top button on his shirt as he sinks into a kitchen chair. "I'm definitely getting a vasectomy."

Later, my mother calls to check in again. I assure her I'm

fine, truly, I do feel better now. It was just a strange, scary one-time thing, but there is also something else I wanted to discuss. My father wants to retire, which means he is liquidating some assets. He needs to get the cash out of some of his investments, one of which is our house. The time has come for us to either refinance or move, but we can't afford to do either. I don't expect her to have a solution, I just need to be able to talk it through.

# Chapter 16

*Fall 2012*

I stopped taking the pills immediately, and I haven't had the thoughts again since. Eddie scheduled himself for a vasectomy. Now we just need to figure out where we are going to live.

"Mommy, Mommy. Come look," Nicholas calls from the other room. The sun is not up yet, but he is. He's gotten out of bed and is standing in the open door leading to the girls' bedroom, where they are both still asleep.

"Something is wrong with Penny's tummy, it is going up and down like this," he sticks his own stomach out in an exaggerated way. "I think there is something in there, like a frog. We gotta get it out."

"Shh," I hush him. "Don't wake the girls. That's just air. Her tummy is going up and down because she is breathing. Your tummy does that too while you sleep."

"Penny can breathe all by herself?" He yells, astonished. "Wow, just like me. Great job, Penny. Yay," Nicholas claps and jumps up and down, causing the baby to stir and then wail. Abby rubs her eyes and sits up in the twin bed across the room.

"Well, now you're all awake, I guess."

I get all of them dressed and put them on the sofa with a few bowls of dry cereal and sippy cups filled with milk, then sit down to think about my mom's proposal. She thinks we should pool our resources, buy land together, and build a house for my family. She could give me my inheritance now as opposed to after she dies and update her will so that her remaining assets will only be split between my brother and my sister. Then in a few years when she has finished her doctorate degree, she could relocate up from Maryland and we could add an in-law suite or a second house on the property for her. Eddie doesn't like taking money from my parents, doing that was how we got ourselves into our current situation after all, but it makes a lot of sense. We could have a better house in a better school district than we can afford on our own, she could be there to help with the kids while they are young, and in the future once the kids are grown and she is older we will be there to take care of her. Tons of other cultures recognize the benefits of multi-generational living; I have no idea why it is looked down upon in our own.

Eddie emerges from the bathroom, where he was getting ready for work. He perches on the arm of the sofa, straightens the collar of his shirt, and leans down to kiss the top of my head.

"All right, I'm leaving. Do you want me to pick up a pizza or something on the way home?" Since the baby was born, five-dollar ready-made Little Caesars pizzas have become a staple of convenience.

"I think we should sell the house." I keep my eyes forward and look out the window instead of at him.

He sighs. "Yeah, I've actually been leaning in that direction, too. But it's going to take a long time to build another one, and Nicholas is starting kindergarten. Where would we go in the meantime?"

In Pennsylvania kids don't legally have to go to school until the age of eight. We could decide not to send him to kindergarten, but I don't love that option because he is already so far behind. After two years of preschool, library classes, Mom N Me groups, weekly tutoring, therapies, and a mother with an education background home full-time, Nicholas still can't identify a single color or write most letters. He is four-and-a-half-years-old and not potty trained. Not starting school for three more years won't help. There's a strong push for homeschooling in our area, but you have to apply for permission to do it if your child has special needs and there is no guarantee we'd get that permission. Plus, Nicholas could lose his resources if we decided to homeschool. Right now, the occupational therapy, and the speech therapy, and the tutoring are free, covered by our taxes. If we homeschool, he won't need those services any less, but we will have to pay for them ourselves.

I called a few private schools thinking the small class sizes and structure would be good for Nicholas and it wouldn't matter if we moved to another district at some point during the year, he could still attend the same school.

Moving, possibly twice if we sell early and need to get a temporary apartment, and starting a new school with longer days for the first time is a lot for any kindergartener. Having a steady environment would help ease some of the transitions. Unfortunately, all of the private schools I called requested that I send a copy of his school paperwork, and once they saw his file every one of them told me that his needs were beyond their capabilities. They wished they could be more help, the refrain would go, but they just did not have the resources to serve him properly. The lack of toilet training alone makes him a poor candidate. Not that we could afford the tuition anyway.

We could always do another year of preschool, but the teachers there strongly recommended we send him to kindergarten. They warned we should be prepared that he might need to repeat a grade or two, but there are so many more resources available to him in a public school building than they can offer in the small church-run preschool. They try so hard, but everyone can see he just needs more than they can offer in a two-hour church program.

I turn to look up at Eddie. "Maybe we could look into cyber schools?" I offer. Online charter schools are still public schools. He would have the same access to services. "If this house sells, I'm sure your parents would let us move into their basement for a few months until our new one is built. If school is online, it should be easy to do it from anywhere, right?"

So, we sign up to start kindergarten online in the fall, at the same time we put the house on the market. While the school does continue to send an occupational therapist and a language therapist each week to work with Nicholas in our home, they do not make any exceptions to the curriculum for him. He is expected to meet the same rigorous standards as every other student. He must be present for live instruction for several hours each day, at the prescribed time, sitting still in front of a computer to follow their schedule. He misses huge chunks to attend therapy or go to doctors, and the work is harder than we anticipated.

The first day he is expected to memorize and identify every continent on the planet and write something about each of them. There is just no way that is happening. We are still working on recognizing letters and spelling his last name. According to this curriculum, I'm supposed to teach him about Picasso and Monet and have him recreate pieces in their styles. He struggles to hold a pencil and doesn't understand when his class uses color codes or learns patterns because he still can't recognize colors by their names. The academics are a disaster. I receive frequent phone calls from the teacher assigned to him to remind me that he needs more support in the home if he is going to have a successful year. I roll my eyes and flip her off through the receiver, but I patiently wait as she chastises me on the latest call. Finally, she finishes, and I can hang up.

"Mommy, in all my years I have never seen this much work. I don't like school." Nicholas sinks into his booster seat at the kitchen table.

"In all five of your years, huh?" I sit in the adjacent chair and put my elbow on the table, turned sideways to face him. "We'll figure it out, we just have to do some extra practice."

"I don't think that will help. It's too hard. I was borned

with a bad brain," he pouts.

"No, you were born with a special brain, and we just need to find the best way for it to learn."

Halfway through the semester I still haven't figured it out. School is the worst part of our day, and both Nicholas and I usually end up in tears yelling at each other. The girls aren't getting nearly enough attention and I've started to rely on the television as a babysitter. Abby does do a three-hour preschool program twice a week, but otherwise they spend most of the day parked in front of PBS cartoons.

Having the house on the market with three young kids and a dog means constant interruptions, along with never-ending vacuuming and bathroom cleaning added to our schedule. I keep a laundry basket at the bottom of the stairs to fill with scattered toys and shoes whenever we need to rush out the door and leave the house clean and empty for a last-minute showing. The kids and I spend the majority of those showings parked across the street, just waiting in our van with Lucy because by October it is too cold to go to the park with an infant and too expensive to go anywhere else.

Eddie has done a lot of updates to the house. He remodeled the downstairs bathroom, replaced moldings, refinished floors, and we completely replaced the outdated kitchen with used cabinets and countertops we found on Craigslist. It looks much better now than when we bought it, but the market is still slow and, despite all of the work, we have no equity in this house. Once again, it's going to cost us thousands of dollars to move, but since my father is the one who asked us to do it, he is willing to absorb the cost.

It sells on Halloween night to the couple who came to

see it while we were out trick or treating. This year I made the kids' costumes myself out of things we already had around the house. Abby is Mary Poppins in a hand-me-down coat from a cousin, carrying an umbrella. Nicholas' cheeks are smudged with my mascara as Bert the chimney sweep, and Penny is a penguin in an outfit I made out of a plain white onesie and two pairs of black tights.

By Thanksgiving we have moved our entire family into my in-laws' house in Baltimore. Eddie's parents, Ed and Cindy, have relinquished their office as a make-shift nursery for Penny, and Eddie and I sleep in the finished basement with Nicholas and Abigail. Eddie leaves at five a.m. and commutes two hours each way every day to Lancaster for work. He doesn't get home until bedtime, around eight o'clock. At first, I tried to continue teaching part-time, but the load is too much with the extra travel and childcare. It's a two-and-a-half-hour round-trip commute, which is too much to ask of three kids under the age of six, not to mention that my paychecks aren't worth it. At fifteen dollars an hour, I only make thirty dollars for a two-hour class, and most of that is poured straight into the gas tank to cover the cost of the commute. It doesn't make any sense to force the kids to spend hours in the car each week for a profit of barely ten dollars per class, so I need to quit. I'm doing almost all of the parenting alone, although at least now Cindy, or Nana as the kids call her, is here to help and we can divide things like cooking and grocery shopping between the two of us. I can leave the girls with her if I need to take Nicholas to an appointment, but due to some health concerns of her own she can't watch them for longer than an hour. Still, having another woman around is amazing. I'm looking forward to my mother being with us full-time.

Ed and Cindy's house is on a beautiful water-front lot along a secluded gravel road. There is plenty of space in the front yard to play, but it's winter so it's freezing and none of the children can swim. I'm afraid to have them too close to the creek. Nicholas loses his first tooth catching a football outside with a neighbor.

It's time to call and tell his school that I need to change our address. We purposefully chose a charter school that advertises themselves as an option in all fifty states, so I'm shocked when the man on the phone tells me moving across state lines means they can no longer serve Nicholas. I have to mail back all of the materials within thirty days, and his therapies will stop until we enroll him in a new school. They will be happy to forward a copy of his IEP paperwork at that time.

He still can't hold a pencil, button his pants, zip his coat, or use a fork. Nicholas needs occupational therapy. I have also learned that in the state of Maryland, kindergarten is mandatory starting at age five. I would prefer to just keep him home with me for half a school year until our house is built, but it would be illegal not to send Nicholas to school now that we live here, and we do need the therapies.

Do we really live here, in the legal sense? We've purchased two and a half acres of former farm land in Pennsylvania and have started the process to get our building permits and have utilities installed. Well, my mother purchased the land and attached our names to hers on the deed. There is running water and a shed that is technically large enough to live in, although it is probably not stable enough to survive the winter if we get a heavy snowfall. We could stretch the truth enough to make the case for that being our permanent residence, if pressed. It is only going to be a few months, a year at most that we need to stay in Baltimore. But when you are five, a year is twenty percent of your life. We can't afford for Nicholas to fall twenty percent further backward, and besides, the more that I think about it the more I think it would be nice to have a team of professionals to handle Nicholas five days a week and finally have more time to devote to my girls. So, we enroll him in a Baltimore County public school.

What I did not think about was that registering for public school requires proof of residence, including a lease or property deed and a utility bill in your own name. We do not have either of those things living in someone else's basement; therefore, in order to get my son into school I need to go to the Department of Education building to be interviewed and file paperwork in person declaring our family homeless.

Pulling into the parking lot, my stomach lurches. *His birth mother was homeless and just did not have the resources to take care of him.* I can hear Christy's voice describing the toddler she wants to entrust to me.

It's not the same. It's not the same. It's not the same, I mutter to myself. Holding my coat closed with my arms clutched around my midsection, I can see my breath as I walk into the building. I called ahead of time to make an appointment and they are expecting me. It only takes a few minutes and a short interview about our living arrangements. I take the pen and watch myself sign the declaration of homelessness. I know this is only a technicality, but that doesn't make it any less humiliating.

"He can start in January when we come back from winter break," the clerk assures me. Then she asks me for the fourth time whether I feel like our living arrangement is safe. Again, I tell her it is. No, I suppose I don't have an employer, but that doesn't really have anything to do with this. She nods at me, but it doesn't seem like she believes a word coming out of my mouth.

"Just the same, here is some information about free and reduced lunches, and here is a paper that tells you where you can find some help in the community." She hands me a paper that lists area soup kitchens and halfway houses, and she gives me another with directions on how to contact the unemployment office.

# Chapter 17

*March 2013*

The phone rings, and before I pick it up the caller i.d. warns me that it's the school. Nicholas is never sick, unless you count endless bathroom issues, and there is only one other reason they could be calling.

"Hello?"

"Yes, hello. I'm looking for the parent or guardian of Nicholas Giese."

"Speaking. I'm his mother."

"Hi, Mrs. Giese. This is Mrs. Jordan, the principal at Middletown. I'm calling because there has been a bit of an incident here at school today." Of course there was. She pauses for me to ask what happened, but I stay silent and wait for her to go on. She starts by stating the facts. "During math instruction, Nicholas stood up in the classroom, removed his pants and undergarments, and shouted the phrase 'feast your eyes' while motioning to his genitals. The teacher was able to get him to put his clothing back on and return him to his seat, but it seems he got quite a reaction and that encouraged him to repeat the behavior."

"What?" I choke on a laugh.

"This is a very serious matter, Mrs. Giese."

"Yes, of course." I have to clear my throat and regain my composure. He pulled down his pants in front of the entire kindergarten class and shouted, "Feast your eyes." Twice. Well, I guess he's never watching *Brave* again. Damn that tiny animated Scottish man who lifts up his kilt and shouts those very words. Thanks, Disney.

"I'm going to need you to come into the office so we can discuss further disciplinary action."

"Um, if you're sure that's necessary. I can be there in twenty minutes."

"Then I will see you soon."

In her office she stays seated behind the sprawling oak desk overwhelming the cramped space and motions for me to take one of the smaller grey chairs facing her. I oblige and sit, self-conscious now about the tattered sweatshirt and leggings I'm wearing because I left the house immediately upon receiving her call. The last time I was called to a principal's office it was to go over a stellar performance evaluation. The look on her face indicates that Mrs. Jordan does not share my previous employer's perception of me. She exhales a slow steam of air through her nostrils. Her computer is telling her we are homeless, and her experience is telling her our son is out of control. Now I'm sitting here with a day-old ketchup stain on the hem of my shirt and judging by the sore tightness in my chest, I'm almost positive I am about to start leaking breast milk in her office.

It's not a stretch to see that she thinks I'm trash.

"That's a lovely handbag," she deadpans, eyeing the Dooney & Bourke bag Eddie bought me from the Orlando outlets as a birthday gift the first year we were married.

"Uh, thanks." I reach into it and pull out my phone to switch off the ringer for this meeting. It's the same pay-as-you go cellphone I needed to use to answer her call twenty minutes ago. We bought it at a gas station after we cancelled my cell phone plan to save fifty dollars a month. My friends tease me constantly for being the only person they know who still uses a flip phone.

"Hmmm," she pushes the sound through her pursed lips. I can tell I've just confirmed something unpleasant for her, but I can't tell what she wants from me.

"Well, Mrs. Giese, what are we going to do about Nicholas?"

"I was under the impression he spent the majority of today in the office," I offer.

"Yes. That makes his second in-school suspension in two weeks," she says. Her glasses slide down to the tip of her nose. She tilts her head down so she can look at me over them.

I continue to stare into her face but say nothing. Now is not the time. I have to bite the sides of my cheeks to keep from starting in on how inappropriate the last punishment he received was. Two five-year-old boys chasing each other around on the sidewalk before school, imagining they were policemen and pretending their fingers were guns. They both got suspended. Nicholas also had to miss the Valentine's Day party last month because he was so excited for the party that he couldn't stay in his seat. He was being too rambunctious for his teacher to control. He spent that day in the office as well.

"We need to be a team here," she continues. "So, I would like to know what you intend to do at home."

I tell her I am going to take away his favorite toy, the train that Santa brought him, until he can earn it back. She pulls her lips in tighter.

"It's very unusual for such young children to act out sexually. Do you have any idea where he may have learned such behavior, Mrs. Giese?"

"Yes. I know exactly where he saw that. It's a scene in a Disney movie." She can get those other ideas out of her head right now.

"Well, then you may find it helpful to limit his screen time going forward." She puts her elbows on the desk and leans toward me. "Have you ever considered the possibility of having Nicholas tested for ADHD? Many parents find medication extremely helpful."

That's it. The gloves are off now. She has no idea how many times this child has been tested, which is just further confirmation that she has not read the accommodations she should be offering.

"Have you considered smaller class sizes or classroom management seminars? May I ask exactly how it is that my son was placed in an environment that allowed him to be able to engage in this behavior twice? Why are there over thirty kindergarteners in one classroom? Actually, while I am here I would love to schedule another IEP review." The classes are over-crowded as it is, and a lack of substitutes means teachers need to split classes and take on extra students whenever one of their colleagues is absent, which is basically every day.

They added a classroom aide to Nicholas' most recent IEP, which was a big check in the pro column for our experience with Maryland schools. Every state has different rules. Here, he did not need Medicaid to qualify for an aide. He is entitled to have an adult in the room dedicated to helping him manage his behaviors, but she quit just a few weeks into working with him, and they never bothered to replace her. They also never bothered to notify me when she quit. Nicholas told me that himself, and when I followed up with the teacher it was confirmed that there had not been an aide in the room to help my son for weeks.

The principal uses her index finger to push her glasses back into place. "We certainly agree that it would be ideal to have smaller class sizes. However, Nicholas is the only one of those thirty-eight kindergarteners who exposed his genitalia to his peers today. That may be something you wish to think about." Like I don't think about it every day and wonder what the hell I'm doing wrong.

For weeks at Ed and Cindy's house, Nick tries so hard to behave. Each time he gets into trouble at school he makes me a card to apologize with the words "Sorry, Mommy" scribbled onto folded construction paper surrounded by crayon outlines of a flower. His teacher has run out of patience for his shenanigans, and he is in trouble at school every day. Most days it doesn't sound to me like he really deserved it. He spends more time in the school office than he does in his classroom, and I'm out of ideas. He is still chronically constipated, and he has started having spells every once in a while when he says he feels like there are bugs crawling on him. At first, I thought he just couldn't deal with the sensation of pins and needles when his legs or feet fall asleep, but this seems different. He will scream and cry for over an hour and beg me to take them off.

"Get them off me, Mommy. Please, help me. The bugs are everywhere. Take my feet away. Take them off me," He yells and claws at his legs like he is in a horror movie, but none of us can see anything wrong. I guess maybe this is just part of the Sensory Processing Disorder the therapists told me about, but it seems intense.

We visit our land in Pennsylvania frequently. The permits have come through and we've started to break ground for the house. We still drive up to attend our church in York each Sunday because it's important to us that the kids keep their relationships with their friends, and we maintain our own friendships, too.

"Have you considered having the church elders lay hands on him?" an acquaintance from our former Mom N Me group asks when we run into each other. She asked how we were doing, and I was honest, Nick's not well.

"Like an exorcism?" I raise my eyebrows, it's hard to contain my skepticism.

"What? No. Exorcisms aren't real, this is different." She protests. "They just sit around him in a circle, put their hands on him, and pray for a few hours." My own Catholic background begs to differ, it sounds exactly like an exorcism, but I bite my tongue and let her continue. "What you are dealing with sounds a lot like spiritual warfare."

Sorry, what now?

"You think Satan is possessing my kindergartener and the church elders could pull him out?" I question her. What kind of sixteenth century bullshit is this?

"I wouldn't put it that way. But you say you've tried everything else, and I'm just saying it couldn't hurt. If you don't want to go to the elders, then the next time it happens you should try to command the evil spirit away in the name of Jesus. That's what they do in the Bible."

I mean, she's not wrong in the sense that it is what they do in the Bible, but that was thousands of years before we understood the way the brain works. Not that we really understand it completely now.

It seems crazy, but no one has any better ideas and what do I know? I do believe in the power of prayer and Eddie and I pray for our kids all the time, but I'm just not going to approach a group of full-grown men and tell them my friends and I think it's possible that the devil has possessed my six-year-old. I'm also pretty sure this is probably just another part of his Sensory Processing Disorder. We have been dealing with Nicholas' sensory issues for years. Although, I suppose my friend is right that it wouldn't hurt to try something. So, the next time Nicholas feels the invisible bugs I stick my hand straight into the air and yell, "In the name of Jesus Christ the Son of God, I demand you leave this child alone. Leave my son. Go." Nicholas immediately stops scratching his legs and looks at me, his head cocked sideways. After a long, silent minute he gets up and goes to sit in his beanbag chair in the corner. Did that actually work?

Of course, it couldn't be that easy, though. The bugs are back the next day. I keep trying, but the makeshift exorcism never works again.

# Chapter 18

"You want to do what?" I turn to my husband, thinking I must have misheard him.

"I want to go on the mission trip to Africa," Eddie tells me in the car on the way home from church on a Sunday afternoon in April. Penny groans her displeasure with the car seat from behind me, and I contort myself to hand her a stuffed pig. Eddie continues, "We've been really caught up in our own family drama for a long time. I just want to be a part of something that's bigger than me for a little while and I think the team could use my engineering skills. They need someone to design the water tank they are building with a village in Burkina Faso."

"I mean, can't you just design the tank from your computer right here and then let other people go build it?" The other men who have signed up for this trip so far are all older than him by about twenty years, and they are in a completely different stage of their lives. We have a kindergartener, a preschooler, and a toddler. I don't love the idea of him leaving for half the summer to fly around the world playing White Savior for a month and leaving me to deal with all the stuff at home he is trying to escape, but I also don't want to be a jerk about it, and it feels like it would be a pretty big jerk move to say those things out loud. He's trying to do something meaningful with his life, and he did go along with my all plans to foster, adopt, leave Tampa, and support my toy library. Plus, when our house is finished he will be living with my mom indefinitely. I've survived at home with the kids by myself for longer than this.

"You know what? Never mind. Of course, you should do it." I resolve to be supportive.

His parents make no such resolution and are worried out of their minds. Things at their house become tense because Eddie is insistent that he has to do this, and they think it's irresponsible for him to go while he has a young family at home. They print articles on the dangers of rebellions and African regimes and leave them on the kitchen counter, and they book themselves on a cruise so they won't have to spend the time he is away worried about their son.

Nicholas doesn't seem to be concerned with the idea of Eddie going to Africa, he just wants to know what kind of airplane his dad will be using to get there. In June they all leave, Eddie on a flight to France and then Burkina, and Ed and Cindy headed to the port of Baltimore for their Caribbean cruise. I find myself alone in a house that is not mine with all three of our kids. At least school is over for the summer, so the pressure to get Nicholas to perform is gone. Mostly, the kids watch videos or play at my feet in the basement while I write. For the first two weeks my husband is gone, I publish a piece of our love story on my blog every day, starting with when we shared our first kiss during a game of Truth or Dare when we were fourteen.

My friends in Anna's online writing group send encouraging messages. I read them on my laptop, bouncing Penny on my shoulder, trying to get her to sleep. Abby and Nicholas are a few feet away playing the Just Dance video game on the basement TV.

*That love story is so sweet, I can't wait to see what happens tomorrow.*

*Thanks*, I reply. *I had to do something to remind myself why I still like this guy. Haha.*

Eventually the conversation migrates to the business side of blogging and a conference a few of us attended in the spring.

Kathy: *Honestly, I'm so tired of paying so much money to sit in a room and hear things I already know. I swear, I learn more here in this group from you guys than I have ever gotten out of a conference.*

I think about the time I wanted to know how to get published on a national scale and these women showed me how to write for *The Huffington Post*. From there, other editors saw my work and I got more jobs, and conference organizers started reaching out and asking me to speak.

Erin: *For real, by the time you add airfare, the hotel, food, and all of that on top of the price of the ticket it's ridiculous, and you don't even get to talk to the speakers. You pay all of this money, and they always regurgitate the same stuff you can find out for free by Googling it. The parties are fun, and I like seeing other bloggers in person, but it's just not worth it.*

Their words plant the seed of an idea in my brain. *You guys,* I type. *We should totally start our own conference.*

Everyone: *Haha. Yeah, that would be cool.*

*I'm 100% serious,* I tell them. There are three New York Times best-selling authors in this group and the *I Just Want to Pee Alone* parenting anthology book Jen just put together, which included essays from almost all of us, also hit the NYT list. That book was number one in the Humor category on both Amazon and iTunes. We briefly knocked Tina Fey out of the top spot, which anyone has to admit is impressive for a self-published collection of silly stories from a bunch of moms. We have a combined social media following in the millions, our websites are profitable small businesses, and we have earned the right to be taken seriously. Yet, there is a distinct lack of both tech and writing conference options for women in the Baltimore/D.C. area, which is exactly where I happen to be at the moment.

*I think I have an idea. You know how the Erma Bombeck writing conference is held on a college campus? We could do that for bloggers. If we host it at a college and include dorm rooms and cafeteria food in the ticket price, it would be so much cheaper for attendees and we could bill it as an all-inclusive kind of retro slumber party experience. It would also be so cool to have our speakers interact more intimately with attendees than other conferences do,* I tell them.

At the last conference I attended, I bought the ticket because I have been a fan of the keynote speaker for years. I wanted to meet her, but there was no time built into the schedule for a meet and greet, so I ended up on Twitter tweeting at her in the middle of the night. She responded and we met in the hallway of the hotel first thing in the morning so she could sign my book and say hi. When other attendees saw us talking there, a line formed behind me and she graciously did an impromptu book signing standing in the third-floor hall, but even that speaker said she was disappointed this was the only way she had been able to interact with the people who came to see her. Otherwise, she had been mostly hanging out in her hotel room, alone in an unfamiliar city. There has to be a better way.

My alma mater is in Baltimore City. It's a tiny women's college built in the 1800's with gorgeous architecture, and I know they host conference groups in the dorms over the summer. We can host it there and put together a conference that actually focuses on education. In fact, that could be the entire theme. We'll call it The Blog University, or BlogU, we will call our speakers "faculty" and even have office hours with them where attendees can talk to the writers and speakers they admire one-on-one, get books signed, or just hang out. We also aren't afraid to embrace the "mommy blogger" label and work with sponsors in the parenting space and cater to women with families. Yes, absolutely, your breast-feeding infants are welcome, and we aren't going to make it weird. Bring them to class with you and we will help you find a private place to pump, and store your breast milk in the shared dorm fridge. No one is promoting a balanced version motherhood and professionalism like that yet.

*You honestly think other women would pay us to fly out there and hang out with each other in person?*

Yes, I do. And what's more, I think it would be beneficial to them because we can give them a better, cheaper option where they learn more than they do at other conferences marketed to women and feel more comfortable in their own skin at the same time. Ours will be unique not just because we welcome parenthood as a worthy topic of exploration, but because it will focus on balancing writing on the internet, self-publishing, and traditional book publishing. We will keep it small and sell a limited amount of tickets, which will increase demand but also make sure that we can focus on giving our attendees the experience they deserve. Between the thirty-seven of us in this writing group, we have plenty of established relationships with sponsors. It will be a lot of work, for sure, but this is certainly doable.

*That sounds awesome, Steph*, my friends tell me. *If you can secure a location and figure out the logistics, we'd definitely be down to help.*

By the time Eddie comes home from Africa, I'm a small business owner once again. The Blog University, LLC becomes the second corporation I founded as a sole proprietor. Our first national conference is scheduled for June of 2014. When tickets go on sale, as I expected, we sell enough to cover all of our costs and also turn a small profit in the first year. I am not surprised that people liked the idea, but I am surprised at how far they are willing to come to see us. I thought we would draw crowds from New York, Philadelphia, D.C., and Baltimore. In reality, in addition to the locals, women are also flying in from Canada and Europe for this conference. People of any gender identity are welcome, of course, but only one man purchases a ticket.

Just like with the toy library, my clients are primarily women with young children seeking family-friendly business opportunities, and it's a vastly underserved market.

A few months into planning, a small box comes in the mail. The note inside reads:

*To our fearless leader,*
*We love you and you are doing a great job, but we can't allow you to run a conference teaching other people about social media and technology from a burner phone you bought at a gas station.*
*Love,*
*The BlogU Planning Team.*

They all chipped in their own money and bought me an iPhone.

# Chapter 19

*Fall 2013*

Our new house is finished by October. It's a craftsman style ranch at the top of a steep hill. The basement, which will eventually be my mom's apartment (affectionately called "The Pumpkin Patch"), and bonus room above the garage won't be finished for another year, but the rest of our home is finally livable. We have two covered porches, black shutters, and yellow siding that Eddie insists is actually cream-colored. We are finally here. It's only two houses down the street from Nicholas' elementary school, and Eddie's commute has been cut down to fifteen minutes. The kids are watching Harry Potter in the living room while I unpack more boxes.

"Is that a g, Mommy?" Nicholas asks from the sofa in our new living room, pointing to the television screen. I follow his finger and scan the walls of Hogwarts, thinking maybe there is a Gryffindor banner somewhere in this scene. Was Hermione writing something?

"Where, Honey? I don't see any letters in the movie right now."

Nicholas laughs and shakes his head. "No. You're silly, Mommy. You have to listen for the letters." He starts to hum along with the background music that is so faint I have never noticed it, despite seeing this movie at least a dozen times. He raises his voice to emphasize one particular note each time it comes back. "Is that a g?" he asks again, swinging his bare feet against the base of the couch.

I shrug. "I'm sorry, Bubba. I don't know." He wants me to identify the individual music notes in the instrumental overlay by ear. I didn't know this was going to be on the test.

Nicholas starts to hum again, then he pauses to tell me, "That one is an a." I have no idea if he is right, but I take his word for it. I wouldn't be surprised. Although the shift would be indistinguishable to most people, I can see him starting to get frustrated. Building. I know the signs. His breathing is heavier now than it was just a second ago and his hands are balling into tight little fists, pounding on the cushions. "But I don't know if the other one is a g. I need to know. I really need to know. Can you call Daddy?" he asks through gritted teeth.

I wish I could just lie to him and say the stupid thing is a g, but if I do that it won't take long for him to figure me out. It won't be hard for him to find someone who knows more about this than I do to correct me. Once he realizes I would lie about something as insignificant as a music note, he won't trust me with the bigger, more important things. How many more problems could that cause in the future when the stakes are higher? Is it better to avoid the meltdown now or let it happen and make sure he knows that I am trying my best and I am at least always striving to be honest with him? We can't have both.

"No, sweetie. Not right now. Daddy is working."

He pounds the cushions harder, then starts on his own legs. A rhythmic thud in time with the music but hard enough that it must hurt. "But Daddy plays guitar. Daddy knows. You don't know about music. You don't know anything." He has no idea what he just said is disrespectful. He just knows that in this moment he feels that it is true. It wouldn't occur to him to think about my feelings. We are still working on empathy.

"Watch it." I narrow my eyes and point my finger at him. He's right, though. I really don't know anything about music. "I might not play any instruments, but I can still help you. I can try to look it up on the computer." I walk into the next room, grab my laptop and bring it back to the sofa so I can sit next to him and search. We do try, but after several attempts there is still nothing turning up. I don't know what else to type in. There are no results that provide us with the sheet music for this one particular scene in Harry Potter. I'm not sure how to find the entire score for the series, and even if I could, I don't know how to pick out this one note and match it to this scene.

Think. I am an adult, I should be able to model problem solving for him. Maybe there's an app I can put on my phone that can identify music notes. We also have an electric guitar tuner around here somewhere. If I hold it up to the TV, would that work?

No, it doesn't.

His fists are still pounding, and his face is red. I can see him tensing as he starts rocking back and forth. He's escalating, and I'm getting desperate. I don't have any more time to be searching and downloading apps. I know I only have another minute or two before my son is going to erupt. "Let's play a g on the keyboard and see if it sounds the same," I offer and reach out to try to rub his back. He shakes me off and runs toward his room, but he bumps into his sister, knocking Penny down in the process. He says nothing to her but slams his bedroom door and beings pounding what I assume are his fists onto the wall.

It's hard to ignore the banging, but I'm trying. The girls are now both crying, and I'm doing my best to try to convince them everything is normal. I force my voice to stay level, despite the tension I feel rising in my own chest.

"He wasn't trying to hurt anybody, and he doesn't mean what he said, he's just angry. He loves us." Every part of me winces as I hear myself say it. It's exactly the kind of language I don't want them to internalize. It will destroy me if I hear these words repeated back to me one day about another man who is just treating them the same way their brother always did. There's another crash coming from his bedroom and the sound of breaking glass keeps me from spending too much time reflecting on the lessons I'm teaching my other children.

I open the door to find him standing to the left side of his desk. "Nick. Stop. Remember what Ms. Betsy says. Stop, think, and plan. Or you could use your senses. What do you see right now? What do you smell? Let's practice feeling grounded."

"I don't care what anybody says, I hate you!" he screams.

"I'm sorry you feel that way, because we love you." The response is so automatic now I don't even have to think about it. Instead, I am scanning the room for the newest damage.

"Would you like to talk about what happened here?" First, I point to the hole in the wall behind the door. Then my eyes fall to the picture frame that is shattered on the floor. A glossy two-dimensional memory of the three of us, smiling in a booth at McDonald's, covered now in jagged shards of broken glass.

"I'm not talking to you. Get away from me."

"Did you hurt yourself?"

"You don't even care." His rage has given way to tears.

"I care a lot. Let me see it."

"No. Don't touch me. I'm leaving. I hate this family. I'm going away." It's heartbreaking, but it's also hard not to smile. Such a normal thing for a little boy to threaten after a fight with his mommy, and for a moment I forget that we are different. A bitter pill that I know one day I might hear him say these words and have to let him leave for real.

"Where are you going to go?"

"Away from you." He stomps his way out the front door and down the driveway. There is a bus stop on the street and he stands there waiting. It's forty-five degrees and he's wearing short sleeves, sweat pants, and flip-flops. He has nothing with him. No money. No food. No coat. I wonder how long it will be before he gives up and comes back inside.

The girls look out the window and scream for him to come back, yelling that they love him and they miss him, and they are sorry. I tell them not to be sorry because they didn't do anything wrong, he's just having a temper tantrum. They are not responsible for their brother's behavior. He'll come home soon.

"But Mommy, what if the bus comes?" I'm more concerned with well-meaning passersby. As usual. What I do not need is for a stranger to see a child by himself on the street and stop and try to talk to him right now. Lord only knows what he would say. Or do. I grab his jacket and start walking.

"It's pretty cold out here, huh?" I stand next to him, keeping my eyes on the street, as if we are just two people waiting on the next bus. He says nothing, but I notice his head move towards me. He pulls it away again quickly when I start to turn.

"I think you left something back there." I motion toward the house and hand him his jacket. He snatches it fast but doesn't put it on. "Also, I was wondering what you would like me to do with all your LEGO, since you won't need them if you run away."

"What?" So he is talking to me.

"Your LEGO. They would be too heavy to take with you. Not important. We could talk about it later. I hope you remember our phone number. You'll have to call me since I don't know where you're going." I think it's starting to work on him. "Hmm, I'm kind of hungry. I wonder what kind of food they have where you are going. Anyway, it looks like this bus is running pretty late. I think I'm going to go inside and make some Bagel Bites. Then I'm going to put them on the kitchen table, just in case anybody who likes Bagel Bites would like to eat some. See you later. I hope you come back one day to visit."

I turn around and walk back up our driveway. It takes thirty-seven steps before I hear him start to follow me. I don't dare turn around, just walk straight into the house and take the pizza bagels from the freezer. The door alarm pings, and he walks in, silently. No one says a thing. He sits down at the dining room table with his sisters and they wait for their snack to be ready.

A few minutes later I have all of my children home, sitting around the table that was handed down to me from my father, eating their afterschool snack and laughing, making the memory I can only hope will erase what just happened. While they are busy, I slip into his bedroom and start picking up the glass. That's my job. Someone has to be there to pick up the pieces.

# Chapter 20

*October 2013*

Dr. Walker, Nicholas' new principal, did call last week, after I was home from my first meeting with Pastor Bob. We scheduled a review of Nicholas' paperwork, which is how I've found myself sitting in the conference room just outside the nurse's office. It has been three years since his last school district evaluation, which means he needed to be tested again. We are here to review the results.

He is repeating kindergarten, but it's not going well by any estimation. He has not received a score above thirty-seven percent on any graded assignment. He is failing every subject, and his behavior in the classroom is hard to manage. His classroom teacher spends most of her day trying to subdue or contain Nicholas, which is not fair to her, or to him, or any of the other students in the class. That teacher is not in this meeting.

Mrs. Haugh is the resource teacher who pulls Nicholas out of class for small group instruction. I recognize her because she is the teacher with an edgy buzzed haircut who walks Nicholas to our mailbox after school. We live just a few houses down the street, but she doesn't want to let him cross the busy parking lot by himself. She is alone with me in the conference room, explaining the latest re-evaluation report. Because we moved from out-of-state, they were able to request a new evaluation and update his paperwork. Nicholas received an IQ score of seventy-one. The requirement to be diagnosed with an intellectual disability is a score below seventy, two standard deviations below the mean. He missed the cut-off to qualify for services by two measly points.

"If the IQ score was just a bit lower, then he would qualify as what we now call intellectually disabled. It used to be referred to as mental retardation." Ms. Haugh explains.

But they aren't, and he doesn't. She continues, "He has made significant progress in receptive language, which is wonderful. Unfortunately, that improvement means he no longer qualifies under his original diagnosis. Can you produce a different diagnosis from a qualified professional?"

"No," I sigh and look at the ceiling. I wish they would just expand the damned autism parameters already. It feels like they change them every three seconds to broaden the scope of the spectrum, but under the current definition they still can't recognize a kid like mine, with significant trauma in his background. The reevaluation report on her desk includes yet another autism screening from a school district psychologist, but once again it was useless. Like the first appointment Nicholas had in preschool and every one since, this examiner declined to give a diagnosis on the basis that, although he demonstrated many spectrum behaviors, in the school psychologist's opinion, Nicholas was too social to have autism. He's only six, he has almost every marker, but no one has been willing to give him the diagnosis. I don't think I will ever understand why trauma-induced autistic behavior is not a diagnosis that exists. Or at least they could make trauma a category on its own.

We're at an impasse. She can't give him any of the diagnoses that could come from within the school, such as a learning disability. Every state interprets the federal laws differently, and occasionally there are variations in local interpretations as well. In our region of Pennsylvania, they use the discrepancy model for testing, which means there has to be a gap between a student's performance and their ability in order to diagnose disability. If Nicholas were only struggling in math or reading, this would be a different conversation. Maybe then they would say he had a Specific Learning Disability, but he is not only struggling in one subject. When ability matches performance, meaning the test scores and evaluation report match what a teacher is seeing in the classroom, especially if the performance is the same across all subject areas, then a child is considered to be meeting their potential, even if that potential is extremely low, and there is nothing more the school can do.

The score of seventy-one proves his ability is very low. His performance in the classroom is also well below average. There are only thirteen disability categories that qualify for an IEP eligibility, which means not every child who does not do well in school is able to receive services. A student has to have a documented disability in an approved category in order to qualify. The categories are: Specific Learning Disability (which also covers things like dyslexia), Other Health Impairment, Autism Spectrum Disorder, Emotional Disturbance, Speech or Language Impairment (which is how Nicholas originally qualified, but because he has improved so much in that area, he is not eligible any longer), Visual Impairment, Deafness, Hearing Impairment, Deaf-Blindness, Orthopedic Impairment, Intellectual Disability, Traumatic Brain Injury, and Multiple Disabilities.

Nicholas does not meet the qualifications for any of them. Our hands are tied.

The law is telling us that on paper he's just a dumb kid, let it be. He doesn't have the ability to do any better and he's not quite impaired enough to be considered intellectually disabled, so don't bother wasting the resources trying to get more out of him. Nicholas has been tested by four psychologists in as many years and still has no diagnosis. It's expensive to offer services, and he is not worth the money. Neither Ms. Haugh nor I agree with that philosophy, but no one consulted us when they wrote the laws.

Besides the Intellectual Impairment option, with his symptoms an autism diagnosis would be the easiest path to give us the paperwork we would need to move forward, but Nicholas can't seem to get that diagnosis either. Every professional we've seen is blaming his issues on trauma. Trauma is not a category serviced under the Individuals with Disabilities Education Act. He is out of luck.

We could try for the Emotional Disturbance category,

but so far it is proving next to impossible to get an official mental health diagnosis at this age. His teacher and I both think he might have been hallucinating a few times both at home and at school, but other than those few episodes with the invisible bugs that could have just been sensory-related, he hasn't shown that kind of behavior to Betsy or anyone else in our family. Without more perspective, it is difficult to tell the difference between hallucination and imagination in a six-year-old. Without a diagnosis, there are no services. He's not going to be able to function in society if no one can figure out how to teach him to read and do simple math, but the way the laws are written is preventing the school from being able to offer any help.

"That outside testing may be something you'd like to pursue in the meantime. For now, I'm afraid our hands are tied here in school. His performance is low, and the new tests show his ability is also low." Although not quite low enough to qualify for any kind of aide. "When ability matches performance, the state guidelines tell us there is nothing more we can do." She is as frustrated by this as I am but trying to maintain her professional composure. There is no documentation to support anything else. No one ever wrote down a Sensory Processing Disorder diagnosis when they suggested he might have it, and it didn't occur to me to insist on getting it in writing at the time, so we can't use that either.

"We are looking into private testing. Again. But right now, can he qualify under the Other Health Impaired category? He was diagnosed with Failure to Thrive as an infant. Schools have used that diagnosis for him before. I have the old plans," I offer. It's a stretch, but in the past some schools have used that catch-all category to squeeze him under the radar. This is ridiculous. I can do this paperwork in my sleep. I'll do it for them if they want me to. It doesn't seem possible we are actually having a conversation about taking resources away from a former foster child who has been receiving special education services for years and is currently failing every subject in his grade, a grade he is repeating because he also failed it the first time around.

"I'm afraid that just won't be possible this year without something more concrete. That might have been appropriate when he was younger, but I can't justify using a failure to thrive diagnosis from infancy in elementary school, especially when Nicholas does not have any known physical limitations and has proven he does have the ability to make progress."

Right. The progress that he is being punished for making at the moment.

"I notice it says here that Nicholas was adopted. Do you know anything about Fetal Alcohol Syndrome and whether that may have been a possibility?" she asks.

"The only thing I know is that his birth mother tested clean at the hospital." Everyone always wants to blame the birth mom, but this isn't her fault. Four years of testing, and I have no proof of anything else to give the school. He is about to lose his access. I dig my fingernails into my chair and inhale deeply through my nose.

She sighs, "Then unfortunately there is nothing we can do. Sign here. The IEP will be revoked and replaced with a

504 plan so that Nicholas can continue to be served in the general classroom." A 504 plan does protect children's rights in the general classroom setting, but it doesn't recognize his disability. It does not promise him any services the way his IEP did, it does not allow the school to use a different curriculum for him, and then there is the biggest problem: Nicholas can't actually function in a general classroom.

It's not fair to him, or the other students who are distracted by his behavior and losing their teacher's attention, or the teacher who has to spend the majority of her day dealing with just one child. And now that he won't have an IEP, it will also affect his teacher's evaluation when she can't get him to perform as well as his peers. Teachers' job performance is judged according to how well their students do on standardized tests. The law is telling me that it is impossible for Nicholas to pass his grade level. They say he doesn't have the innate ability to do it, but when he fails that will not stop our state from scoring his teacher poorly if she can't get him to perform. Only now she needs to pull that performance out of him with fewer resources and less support because they are taking his right to services away.

It also means that any access he might have been able to receive to community-based services will disappear. It might not be a huge problem now, in kindergarten. I know the teachers here still have his best interest at heart, they will do what they can. But eventually he is going to grow up and be an adult with special needs. I'm not going to live forever. With a diagnosis, he would be eligible for programs that can help take care of him. Community-based services confirm children's diagnoses through the school district via the IEP paperwork he no longer has. Without one, he will not qualify for any help outside of school either and is much more likely to end up a statistic.

Every child in America is guaranteed the right to a free, appropriate, public education. That is the language used in the law. I refuse to believe any of this meets the guidelines for what should be considered appropriate.

"The general classroom cannot possibly be the most appropriate environment. Test him again." I know it's not her fault, and I don't mean for my words to sound as cold as they do.

"It seems he has been tested several times recently. We've reached the limits of what we can do here at school. We know it's frustrating. We agree that Nicholas needs to be serviced, so we are going to continue offering the small group instruction and speech classes he has been receiving." It's a nice gesture; now that he has lost his diagnosis, they don't have to do it. I appreciate the offer, but without the IEP there won't be anything in writing to verify this verbal commitment. I sigh and nod only once, without speaking.

"I understand this is a difficult day, but I will make this right for him. I promise," Ms. Haugh vows. Her eyes are glazed with the tears she is holding back and I can hear her voice stretched thin. We are both angry, but not with each other. "It might take some time, but we will figure this out," she tells me. I wish I could believe her.

There is a delicate knock on the door, and another woman invites herself to our table. She introduces herself as Mrs. Crowley, the guidance counselor. She apologizes for being late, she was driving from another meeting in a building across town. She attempts to smooth her curls into place and sighs heavily, lowering herself into one of the blue plastic chairs with protruding metal legs. The bump is still small, but she is visibly pregnant and uncomfortable.

"I'll sure be glad when the fall weather kicks in," Mrs. Crowley fans herself with one hand. Weather is always a safe introduction. I've been too distracted to notice, but now that she mentions it, the room is filled with stale air and is much too warm. There is no air conditioning in the school. She opens a folder and looks down at some handwritten notes as Mrs. Haugh clears her throat and recaps the meeting to this point. Mrs. Crowley nods and smiles, sensing there is some tension that needs to be diffused.

"Continuing his services sounds like a great start," she says. "I also wanted to let Mrs. Giese know about a few ideas I had to help Nicholas be more comfortable in his classroom. He seems to need a lot of breaks throughout the day." She looks at me for confirmation, so I nod again. Then she continues, "I thought maybe we could give his teacher a stack of envelopes for her desk. I will put index cards in them that say, 'Read this, then smile at me and send me back to class.' That way we can discreetly ask him to deliver a message to me or any other staff member throughout the day. The short walks through the hallway might help a bit."

"That sounds like a good idea," I agree.

"Also, have you noticed that Nicholas seems to be, I don't want to say paranoid, but I'm having trouble finding another word. He is certainly very anxious here at school. Do you see the same thing at home?"

"Can you be more specific?"

"For example, if he sees two teachers talking in the hallway, he assumes they must be talking about him, and whatever they are saying must be bad. Then he seems to fixate on his imagined version of their conversation and get more and more concerned throughout the day, to the point that it starts to negatively impact his ability to stay on task in the classroom."

"No, I haven't noticed that at home." But I also haven't been looking for it, and he's not surrounded by strangers in our house the way he is at school.

"Hmm. Well, I was wondering if I could have your permission to pull Nicholas out of class occasionally. I meet with a few small groups, although the students in those groups are usually older. I could also eat lunch with him once a week. I'm happy to do what I can, but of course I'm not a substitute for a therapist." She tilts her head subtly, but I see it. She's too professional to ask outright.

"He does have a therapist. He's been going to play therapy on and off for a few years now. We've started going more regularly lately. I'll bring up your concerns at his next appointment, but I haven't seen them myself. You're welcome to talk to her if you want."

"Thank you. I'm glad to hear he is getting that service. I would love to be part of her team. I'll get some paperwork for you to sign before you leave that will give me permission to talk to his therapist."

"Sure," I sigh. I don't have to say anything further for us all to know that, while they are being very kind, none of this is going to solve the problem we are here to discuss. The diagnosis has become a necessity.

"If you wish, you can request a full battery evaluation," Mrs. Haugh interjects as though she can read my mind. "It's a series of about fifteen tests performed over the course of one day by a psychologist. It's meant to give us a full picture of Nicholas and how he learns. Be aware, though, it could be up to a year before the test occurs. Is that something you feel you wish to do?"

"We haven't really been left with much of a choice, have we?"

"I will take that as a yes. I'm also going to get you an application for Medicaid. The testing is very expensive for the school district and they will be able to reimburse us for it, but it can take quite a while to process an application."

"That won't be necessary. He doesn't qualify." We've been through this every year since he was two. He doesn't have an eligible diagnosis, and our family's earnings are over the Pennsylvania income bracket. Nicholas has to have one or the other to get a yes. If he had qualified for a state-sponsored adoption this would never have become an issue. Children adopted out of foster care are supposed to have access to Medicaid until at least the age of eighteen, and children with medical needs also qualify in Pennsylvania. It seems like Nicholas should be eligible on both counts, but nope.

"It's worth a try," she says calmly. "I'll be right back."

"We have tried."

"Well, that's unfortunate."

I'm getting really tired of hearing that.

# Chapter 21

*March 2014*

I kick the door open as quietly as I can because Penny is drooling on my shoulder and Abby is still asleep in the car. The farm where we spent the afternoon wore both of them out. The house phone rings, but I ignore it as I put the baby down in her crib and walk back out to get my other daughter. Once Abby is inside, tucked under a blanket on the couch, I glance at the caller ID and see that it was the school. Actually, they called several times. My heart starts to sink when I realize that I turned my cell phone off during the preschool field trip. When I switch it on there are eight missed calls from the same number. I don't know how long Nicholas' school has been trying to get in touch with me, but if they've called this many times, it must be important. I try to take deep breaths and stop my hand from shaking as I dial the number to call back, but something in me already knows this is bad.

"Hello? This is Stephanie Giese."

"Mrs. Giese. Hi. My name is Mrs. Crowley and I'm the guidance counselor here at Nicholas' school." I know who she is, we were in a meeting together a few months ago. "We've been trying to get in touch with you for quite a while." She is worried.

"Yes, I'm sorry about that. I was chaperoning a field trip for my daughter." Didn't they try to call Eddie? Surely, he could take one phone call. Why does this stuff always fall on me? "What's going on?"

"I don't mean to alarm you, but there has been what I would consider a very serious situation here at school today." She explains that in his kindergarten classroom Nicholas got into a bit of trouble for being off-task and was very upset with himself for getting reprimanded. He wasn't paying attention, kept talking to his neighbors, and lost a behavior token. Nothing that was especially note-worthy, it was all very normal behavior for an almost- seven-year-old. That is until he was so shaken by getting into trouble that he took a pair of scissors and threatened to remove his own arm, and then the situation continued to escalate from there. He became paranoid and delusional. Something about a blonde girl? They removed him from the other children, but he continued to scream that she was there and coming to get him. No one in the room was blonde, and even after they sent out all of the women and left him with male staff, he still said he could see her, so she seems to be a hallucination. He has been in the office all day with four adults, and they still can't calm him down, but he has deescalated since the first few times they tried to call and is no longer trying to hurt himself.

"Although," she notes, trying to find a tiny silver lining, "he has been very sweet and he's using excellent manners toward everyone else, even in his current state." I allow myself a small piece of relief, briefly thinking of Mrs. Crowley's now largely pregnant belly and Nicholas holding scissors. "But he's become a danger to himself." A gasp of air that might pass for a laugh in other circumstances escapes on its own. The whole conversation just seems so surreal. His guidance counselor isn't finished.

"I was actually calling to see if we had your permission to call in a mobile crisis unit or transport him to the hospital. He seems to be suffering a psychotic break. It's very important that we work as a team to get him immediate care." I don't know what a mobile crisis unit is, but when used in combination with the words *psychotic break* in reference to your kid, it's definitely not a good thing.

I feel my legs give out under me. The tears want to come, but I can't let them. Not now. I have no choice but to be strong if I am going to convince her to release my son to me.

"I'll get him. I'll take him to someone." My voice is stretched thin while I speak to her from my place on the carpeted floor. I have no idea what I mean by that, but I know I need to get him home.

As if she can read my mind, Mrs. Crowley says, "You had previously shared that you were taking Nicholas to therapy?"

"Yes." That's true. I could call there first. "He has been going to play therapy. I will call and see if she can see him today or tomorrow."

"While that couldn't hurt, I'm afraid we may have

moved beyond the realm of play therapy. Nicholas also needs to see a child psychiatrist. Immediately. Do you have a pen? I'm going to give you a list of names. I will send them home in Nicholas' folder as well. Call and ask who takes your insurance. Get him an appointment as soon as possible."

Her voice is kind, but it has a more commanding edge than it did in our last encounter. "In the meantime, do not leave Nicholas alone tonight. If he has another episode like this, you will need to take him to the emergency room at York Hospital. York, okay? That is important," she pauses for emphasis. "The other hospitals in our area do not have the resources to treat mental health emergencies. If that happens, tell them it is not the first time and that he needs treatment. Mrs. Giese, I know this is a lot of information. Do you understand?"

"Yes," I whisper into the receiver. Yes, I do understand that a professional just told me that there is a very real possibility that I might need to make the decision to have my kindergartener committed tonight.

I put the girls back into the van and ignore their protests so we can retrieve their brother from school. My head is spinning with all of the things I should do. There are so many phone calls to make and no rule book to follow. By the time I get to him, Nicholas seems fine. He is calm and responsive and acting like himself. If I hadn't spoken with Mrs. Crowley, I wouldn't have guessed anything was wrong. Should I keep him separated from my other children? How would I even do that? Should I send the girls to their grandparents? For how long? I just wish someone would tell me what I am supposed to do.

I will do anything, but I am terrified that whatever decision I make now could be the wrong one. What if I end up making it worse? I'm looking into a sweet little freckled face standing in front of me with missing teeth. He still believes in Santa Claus and the Tooth Fairy. He's not even going to be seven years old until later this month.

Am I turning my son into some kind of monster? Am I making it worse than it is by forcing him into all those doctors and psychologists and therapies? Has it become a self-fulfilling prophecy? Does he think he has to act crazy because my actions showed him he was? Or would it have been so much worse if I hadn't? Is this as bad as it is going to get? This is already a nightmare; the entire school administration has locked down the office and spent their afternoon in a fight to keep him and everyone else safe. How could it possibly get worse than this?

The fear is paralyzing, and the questions without answers will not stop bombarding my brain, but I have to do something. Once we are home, I park the kids in front of the television with some pretzel sticks before I pick up the phone and keep making the calls.

First, the number on the back of my insurance card to see which of the names Mrs. Crowley gave me are covered by our plan. I circle a few from the list school sent home in Nicholas' folder, then start calling the ones that will accept us. Most send me straight to voicemail, after a warning to call 911 if this is an emergency. Is it? No, I don't think so. They couldn't send anyone to help me get a psychiatry appointment, could they? I continue to move down the list.

There are only four names that both matched the guidance counselor's recommendation and take our insurance.

My hands are going through the motions, but my mind is too preoccupied to form coherent thoughts. I don't have it in me to form an entire prayer, so I just keep repeating the two things I need most until someone answers the phone.

Strength and clarity. Please. Just strength and clarity. Give me the strength.

*Press one if you are a new patient. Beep.*

It's finally ringing.

"Hello?"

"I need to make an appointment for my son. Today, please." I tell the woman who is handling the scheduling for the psychiatrist's office exactly what the guidance counselor said, that he was in danger of harming himself at school and that he should be seen right away. It all pours out in one breath.

With less urgency than I think is warranted, she asks about his current state, and I have to admit that he seems to have calmed down significantly. I haven't personally witnessed any of the behaviors his guidance counselor described. She asks me if he actually attempted to harm himself or only made the threat. I believe there was actual intent. He had the scissors, but again, I didn't see it. All I can do is repeat what his guidance counselor told me.

"She did say she thought treatment was necessary immediately," I stress.

"Our next available appointment is in June." She is unsympathetic. She has an office full of patients with more immediate needs.

"That is three months from now." Does she intend for our family to live in limbo while we wait? He will have to get through the rest of the school year before June comes around. How do we do that without any help?

She puts us down for the appointment and repeats the same thing that the guidance counselor told me about taking him to the hospital if he has another episode in the meantime.

I stare at the phone for a minute while the bile threatens to rise up from my stomach. The kids seem fine in the other room nibbling on their pretzels and watching cartoons. Now I have to tell Eddie. I dial his number, and when he answers I go through the whole story, as calmly as I can.

He is silent for so long that I think we might have been disconnected. Then he simply asks, "What do you need me to do? Should I come home?"

I peek into the living room at the kids perched on the sofa with their snack in brightly colored plastic bowls. It's a good question. What would I expect him to do once he got here? At the moment, it doesn't even feel like I'm really doing anything out of the ordinary. There's only one more hour to go before five o'clock, the regular time he'd be leaving for the day.

"Um, I guess not." Is what I say out loud, even though I'd rather scream, "Yes, idiot, are you serious? Come home and hold onto us, and do not let go." I have no idea how to answer anyone honestly about anything anymore.

"Three months, huh? That doesn't seem good." His voice pulls me back to reality.

"Yeah, three months. That's what they said."

"Maybe you could try to call the church. They might know something we don't about some kind of resources in the meantime. Or you could at least talk to them about what to do now while we're waiting," he suggests as if a theology degree can solve this. I'm not sure why I am the one who has to make the call. Although, I suppose it's as good of an idea as any.

"Okay. I guess I'll try that then," I tell him as we hang up.

I was hoping talking to Eddie would bring more comfort than it did, and I start to realize that it isn't his fault, but there really isn't any comfort to be had right now. He can't make this better and maybe that means no one can. My hand is shaking so hard as I dial the number for the church that I have to hang up and press the buttons a second time. As the phone starts to ring once more a deep sense of dread overwhelms me because I realize that someone I actually know is about to answer, and I have no idea what to tell the receptionist, whom I'm going to have to face again on Sunday.

"Hello?"

"Hi." My voice sounds so hoarse and distant that I barely recognize myself. I can hardly force the words out. The ones I am saying don't really make sense. "This is Stephanie. I just need to. Please. Can you get? I think it might be an emergency. Well, they told me it was. It doesn't seem like it now, though. I, I think we really need a pastor?"

"Ok, sweetie. I'll find someone. Hold on." In the silence the stress of the last two hours catches up to me, and I can't hold the tears back any more. By the time the children's pastor answers the phone I'm sobbing so hard that it is impossible to breathe, but I try to focus on telling him my story the same way I just told it to Eddie.

"They said he needs help right away, and I don't know what to do." When I finally finish explaining what happened at school, my entire body is convulsing.

"Wow. Well, I can certainly see why you felt the need to call. You are doing the right thing reaching out for help," he assures me. "Unfortunately, something like this is really beyond our capabilities for counseling here at the church. In this sort of situation, we'd recommend Nicholas sees a child psychiatrist as soon as he can, someone who might even be able to prescribe medication if he needs it." I tell him we do have an appointment, but she can't see us for a while.

"That's very good. I'm glad you were able to get an appointment. It sounds like you are doing all of the right things. Would you like us to add him to the prayer list in the meantime while you're waiting for that appointment?"

"I, I don't know." He means well, I know, but it feels so hollow, and it never occurred to me until this moment that it could hurt to have a name added to a prayer list, but if we add his name then people will start asking why he is on it. They will want to know why they should be praying. Then what am I going to tell them? Will they pray for him out loud at the same time that they silently pull their own children away from the little boy who now might be a danger to them or their children? How many more friends will that cost him? If the kids at school think he's weird after this, his friends at church are the only ones left to offer any peer connections.

"I think we'd rather keep this information private for now if you don't mind," I answer after a minute.

"I understand. But I will certainly be praying for him myself while we're waiting. Perhaps they'll have a cancellation and you can get in sooner than you think?" He tries to offer some semblance of hope. I wish I could feel it.

"Yeah. Maybe. Thank you."

"Any time." I hope to God there will never be another time like this one, but I can already feel that there will be.

It's too much. Maybe I shouldn't, but I have to tell someone who actually gets it before I break too, so I sit down at the computer and type it all out. I send a long S.O.S. out to the group that Anna put together. I need help. Actual help. I need someone to step up and do something real, right fucking now, not three months from now, and not just prayers and kind thoughts without actions behind them. I don't know how to get through this one.

Almost immediately they are there. Jessica's adult daughter has autism, and she reaches out with love and practical support and advice. She offers to connect me with other parents who have needed to make the decision to hospitalize their children if I want to talk to someone who has been there and come out on the other side. Nicole is a therapist in her professional life. She sends me a private message. As I start to read it, the door opens. Eddie decided to come home early after all. He sits on the sofa between Nick and Abby and silently rubs Nicholas' hair while he helps himself to a pretzel from Abby's bowl. I nod at him, then turn my attention back to the computer and the message waiting for me on the screen.

*Hey. I can't treat Nicholas, since I've never met him, so this is not professional advice. I'm glad to hear that you're seeking treatment for him. I hope you also consider it for yourself. But I am reaching out to you as a friend. I see you are in crisis right now, and this is what we are going to do to get you through that until you can get to those appointments. It sounds like you are asking for a focus while you are waiting.*

She is careful with her phrasing, the same way my mother always is because she doesn't want to lose her license for just trying to help a friend. She adds disclaimers and clauses like "some people have found it helpful to" or "some of the research says" and never directly tells me what to do. I do everything she implies could be of any sort of benefit.

We repurpose his beanbag chair and buy a fairly indestructible photo album, the waterproof plastic kind meant for infants to chew. Then we transform a small corner of Nicholas' room into a "cocoon" with soft blankets and cuddly things where he can sit in the beanbag and look at the pictures of family and friends when he gets upset. Now there is a designated place to go: a safe, soft place to hold him when he doesn't know where to put the feelings. The photo album is supposed to pull him back to reality and to be a physical reminder of all the people in his life who love him and are happy he is here. These people would be sad if anything ever happened to him. I talk to his teacher and his guidance counselor and we create an identical cocoon for his classroom. All of the children are welcome to use it, but we all know that it's mostly for Nicholas.

As we wait for his appointment, I'm concerned how his

behavior is going to affect his relationships with his peers. At school Mrs. Crowley offers to do a few empathy trainings for the other children in his classroom. They can also give him more time on the swings, which seem to do wonders to calm him down, or they can have the custodian pull him out of class for one-on-one mentoring and so that he can do heavy work, like push the bucket of mop water. The custodian is a retired grandmother who took on a part-time job cleaning the school, she would love to work with him. It might help him focus.

His teacher is concerned because he can't concentrate and his grades are suffering, not that they were stellar in the first place. Frankly, I don't care about his report card. We are trying to save his life. The alphabet will still be there next year, but I'm getting more and more worried that my son might not.

Tucking him into bed on Thursday night, his eyes are closed and he whispers, "Mommy, why do people have nipples?" Kids are curious about the strangest things.

"Oh. Those are for mommies to feed babies."

"Do boys need them?"

"I guess not really."

"Then can I cut mine off?"

The words freeze me in terror, but I try to respond calmly.

"No, honey. That would hurt very bad. Why do you ask?"

"I don't know. I just think I want to. You know that blonde girl on the commercials? She talks to me sometimes. She told me I should try that. Good night."

Was that enough to take him to the hospital? I don't know what constitutes intent. Where is the line between a six-year-old asking his mother an innocent question and the time mine decides to pick up a knife?

That night Eddie and I sit up discussing options. How do we stop him if he tries something violent at home?

"I mean, I don't know, there has to be some kind of training, right? They teach hospital workers how to restrain people, what are we supposed to do?"

"Martial arts, maybe? But I feel like it would take a long time to learn, and I don't want to hurt him."

I took a year of karate lessons when I was younger. In that year we learned how to block and throw punches, a few specific kicks, and broke some boards. There was no instruction about how to safely restrain a violent child without hurting your attacker. There is also no extra time or money to devote hours each week to classes at this stage of our lives.

"Handcuffs? Is that awful? I'd hate to use them, but it's better than the alternative."

"I feel like those would hurt him, though."

"We could buy the fuzzy kind," Eddie shrugs.

"From the sex shop? Can you imagine? That's exactly what we need, for him to go to school and explain to a teacher how we made him wear pink furry handcuffs when he was being naughty."

"Could we call an adoption agency or a school and see if they have any trainings?"

"I tried that. They do, but they only offer those trainings to their staff. They won't let us come." It would be too much of a liability to teach parents how to physically restrain their own children. It's understandable, no one wants to tell an adult to use force on a child. But it leaves us in the precarious position of needing to protect him and everyone else in the house with absolutely no idea how.

"I don't know, man. I'm out of ideas. Maybe we can find something on the internet?"

A few poorly lit YouTube videos become the only crisis management training we receive. Wrap your arms around him from behind, locking your hands, they say. Keep your own head tilted to avoid breaking your nose when he starts to flail. Widen your stance to keep yourself stable. Eddie makes me practice on him, but it's easy for him to escape my grasp. My arms are barely long enough to lock the way they need to in order to keep him in, and he's stronger than I am. One day Nicholas will be that big, too. Hopefully it will never come to this.

"Don't worry," Eddie tells me. "Nicholas is still little, and he can't control all his motor skills. You can hold him. You'll be fine." Sure, probably. But for how long? And what are Abby and Penny supposed to do when their brother is too big for them to hold this way?

# Chapter 22

I hear the front door shut behind him as he tosses his blue vinyl backpack onto the dining room table. There's never any question that Nicholas is home.

"Can I have a snack?" He is standing right in front of me, but his voice is carrying through the entire house.

I nod at him and remind him to put his shoes away before he starts his homework.

"Here, let me see your agenda." I motion toward his backpack, but he slides it slightly further down the table while he kicks his shoes across the room toward the foyer closet, where they land with a thud against the wall.

"Nah. That's not a good idea." He reaches into the bowl of popcorn I've just set down. I tell him I'll decide that for myself, thanks, and he needs to hand the book over. He groans. "I don't want to. You're going to go turbo when you see what she wrote." I have to suppress a laugh by pretending to clear my throat before I suggest that this might go better for him if he tells me what happened first.

I'm confident I can handle any note from a first-grade teacher. Whatever he did this time can't be that bad, it didn't even warrant a phone call or an email. Agenda notes are like the lowest rung on the Stuff-Mom-Needs-To-Worry-About ladder.

"Well, it was like this," he starts. "You know how there was a field trip today?"

"Yes." I vaguely remember signing a form last week. I think they were going to see a play at the children's theater or something.

"So, I was sitting next to Melody, and it was dark, and I thought I wanted to kiss her so I did."

This time the cough that comes up out of my throat is real. There goes that theory about agenda notes. "And how did she feel about that?"

"I don't know, but her mom was not happy."

"Oh?" I guess Melody's mother was chaperoning this trip.

"Yeah, her mom said 'I'm watching you' all mean and got real close to my face, like this." Nicholas gets up and walks around the table to demonstrate by wagging his finger so close that it brushes my nose. "Plus, my teacher said it's not okay to kiss each other in school, but we weren't even in school and I still got in trouble. Did you know field trips count as school even though you leave?"

I confirm yes, I did know that, and he's shocked that I'm not learning anything new. "Then how come you didn't tell me? This is your fault, Mom."

This is going nowhere. I'm going to need to change the course of this conversation.

"Nick? I think I need to agree with Melody's mom and your teacher." They are too young to be kissing in theaters. "You don't need to be kissing your friends in school or on field trips or anywhere else right now. Let's save that for when you are older. And the next time you want to kiss a girl, do me a favor and try to understand how she might feel about it first."

"But you kiss me and daddy."

"Yes, that's because we are a family and I love you. Do you love Melody?"

"Ew, gross, no." His face twists at the preposterous notion.

"Do you like her?"

"Mom, stop, you are so weird."

I fold my hands on top of the table and look straight at him. "If you can't talk about liking a girl, then you are not ready to think about kissing her. You have to care about her first. Please try to remember that."

He rolls his eyes and shovels another handful of popcorn into his mouth. I should have made him wash his hands first. How do his fingernails get so dirty? I hand him the pencil that is waiting on the table so he can get started on those spelling words.

"Mom?"

I sigh. What could it possibly be now? "Yes, Nick?"

"You love me and I love you?"

"Yes, Nick."

"And that's what makes us a family?"

I smile and tousle his hair, then get up to throw in a load of laundry and remind the kids we need to leave in a few minutes for our first appointment with Dr. Black. We finally made our way through the waitlist. I have no idea what to expect from a psychiatry appointment, but I assume it must be similar to every other appointment and evaluation we have done over the years. The huge stack of new patient forms I filled out this week is balancing on top of my purse so I don't forget to take them with us.

Traffic was terrible, and we are running five minutes late, so I call the office from my car and the woman on the phone snaps at me that it is against their policy to wait for longer than ten minutes past an appointment time, and we should be considerate of the doctor's time. I'm sweating and anxious when we park and exit the car. I hold Abby's hand and carry Penny's car seat draped over my other arm, weaving through the parking lot. Nicholas' shoes light up as he bounces in puddles next to me. We manage to sign in with two minutes to spare, but as I hand my driver's license and insurance card over to her to be copied, the woman behind the desk tells me we have cut it very close and should try harder to arrive earlier for our next appointment. I bite my tongue and swallow what I'd like to say to her about my ability to control school dismissal times and construction traffic.

"I'll keep that in mind," I smile my canned response at her. We wait another hour in the lobby before Dr. Black emerges and calls our name.

She is a short, round woman and her white lab coat hangs nearly down to her ankles. She escorts us down the hall to a small room that is overrun by a highly-varnished cherry wood desk. I was here last week to drop off Nicholas' intake packet, but I didn't make it past the lobby, so this is my first glimpse of her office. Two adult-sized chairs sit against the wall, and a bookshelf holds some well-used toys. Other than the contents of the shelves, it looks like any generic office: sparse walls, dark wooden furniture, faux plant gathering dust, obligatory framed family photo on the desk. An accountant or human resource officer could work here. There is nothing that indicates this space is focused on mental health.

Before she can say a word, Nicholas removes a basket of plastic blocks from the shelves and dumps it onto the floor. Abby is silent, but she asks with her eyes if she is allowed to join her brother. I hold my index finger in the air, a quiet signal to her to wait for the doctor to tell us what we are supposed to do.

"Oh, that's fine," Dr. Black says. "The only rule with the toys is that you need to put back whatever you take out."

Abby smiles and joins Nicholas on the floor. Penny has fallen asleep in her car seat, her legs hanging off the edge, which I'm sure I will pay for in lost sleep later tonight, but for now is a blessing because I can focus on this conversation.

I lower myself onto one of the chairs and sit facing her desk. With the car seat set next to me on the floor, I'm rocking the baby with my foot. The doctor types quickly on her computer, I assume to access our file. Her lips purse into a tiny triangle, and her forehead wrinkles as her eyes scan the screen. It doesn't take long. There is no small-talk. She saw what she needed to see in the inch-thick stack of paperwork I brought in last week.

"Nicholas seems to have a fairly extensive history for a child his age, so I feel comfortable making a general mood disorder diagnosis. That should allow him to get some more services at school. In the future we might consider another diagnosis, but this will suffice for now, as he is still very young." Just like that, I think we have what we need to get the school to reinstate his IEP. It's a huge victory, but bittersweet because she has just confirmed that there is something wrong with my son's mental health, and now something new is nagging me.

"What other diagnosis?" I wonder out loud. As soon as she answers, I wish I had not asked.

"Well, just be aware that as he is getting older, we might want to start to consider something along the lines of bipolar disorder, schizoaffective disorder, or schizophrenia. But he is too young at this point, I personally would not be comfortable assigning any of those labels until at least adolescence. The mood disorder will be enough to get him what he needs for now."

Did she just say schizophrenia? Like, actual schizophrenia? I don't know whether to feel justified because I've been fighting for years to get people to recognize something is wrong or to be terrified because that possibility sounds much worse than anything I imagined.

The only memory I have of anyone with schizophrenia is an older woman who would occasionally walk into our church when I was young. She was always dressed in layers of winter clothing, no matter the weather, and everyone assumed she was homeless. She would burst open the doors in the middle of service and shout nonsensically until an usher would calmly escort her away. Looking back, she wasn't dangerous, but as children her behavior seemed scary. My friends and I only referred to her as "the crazy homeless lady." We did not intend for it to be mean, only descriptive. The adults told us she couldn't help it, she had a condition called schizophrenia that made her brain sick. It never occurred to me until this moment that she must have a name and a family. Oprah also did a show about a schizophrenic child once. That little girl was nothing like Nicholas.

"Okay, as far as an action plan, based on what you've shared and his history, I think I would like our first step to be trying a medication called Risperdal." Dr. Black pulls me back to the present.

"What does that do?" I try to pretend I'm still focused on what she's saying and not replaying the word *schizophrenia* in my mind on loop. Calm down. He might not even have it.

"It's an anti-psychotic medication that will help him regulate and control impulsive behavior. Our hope is that it will help keep him safe. We will need to monitor his blood every few months. This medication can cause weight gain and it may affect his triglycerides."

"Anti-psychotic?" A new word swarms in my brain alongside the first one.

"Yes, it's just a classification for the drug. It's one of a few that are safe for a child his age. We prescribe it for mood disorders, and it is also used for patients with autism. Has he been evaluated? That may be something to consider."

I thank her and confirm he has been evaluated in the

past and is on the waitlist to be evaluated yet again by the school district. But I can't stop thinking about that fact that she wouldn't need to prescribe an anti-psychotic medication unless she considered my son's behavior to be psychotic in the first place.

Dr. Black clicks a few more buttons on the computer and prints a prescription for the medication. She tells me to be sure to schedule our next appointment before we leave. She would like to see him once a month, for now, so there will be yet another standing appointment on the calendar. After three months of waiting, the entire meeting took less than fifteen minutes.

Standing to leave, the room spins. I must have gotten up too quickly. I squeeze my eyes shut and try to correct my vision. My head is pounding, but what else is new? Show me a mother of young children who does not live with a perpetual headache. It's been a stressful afternoon. I gather the girls and tell Nicholas to follow me. We stop back at the front desk to schedule next month's appointment before we all climb back into the van. After getting everyone buckled, I dig through the glovebox until I find a small bottle of Advil and open the lid of Abby's sippy cup to take the pill with a gulp of her water.

At home I feed the kids a quick dinner of rolled lunch meat, grapes, and crackers. The tax bill stares up at me from the kitchen counter. Our property was reassessed and increased in value when we built the house. We knew it would happen, but we didn't realize the bill would be this high. We owe ten thousand dollars this year, which is more than any other house in our borough, which are all older and smaller than ours, and I have no idea how we are going to pay it. In another week or so there will be a brand new bill from Dr. Black. Who knows how much her office visits or the new prescription cost? Eddie has his P.E. license now and his salary is higher, but there is only so much overtime he can work, and we do not have ten thousand dollars sitting in the bank. I need to find a way to make more money.

My website has been doing well, it's making a few hundred dollars from advertisements each month now, and I am writing more. I have had essays published on bigger online outlets and in a few books. BlogU is thriving, the conference was more popular than I expected, and there is a demand to do it again over the summer or maybe create a few online courses. Brands want to sponsor me. I am making enough to hire a high school student to watch the kids a few times a week as a mother's helper so that I can get some work done, and I have five women working for me as independent contractors in charge of various aspects of the conference like securing sponsorships and managing our social media accounts. Despite all of that, the reality is that writers make even less money than teachers do. By the time I account for self-employment tax, healthcare, and retirement benefits, I would need to pull in six figures as a freelance writer to make my take-home pay equivalent to what I could earn by teaching full-time again.

Until I can break into bigger outlets more consistently, I have to be realistic about what I can earn without a journalism background and with the time it takes to parent Nicholas. Our local parenting magazines give me steady work, but at the rate they pay, I would need to write a minimum of twenty articles every week, and each one takes me at least four hours from start to finish. I can't research, interview, transcribe, write, and edit in less time than that. Eighty hours a week is the equivalent of two full time jobs, working year-round without vacation, and since Eddie's job is more consistent and carries our insurance, I would still have to be the primary parent. It's not realistic or sustainable for me to rely on writing. However, if I took a job with benefits, my health insurance coverage might be better for our family than Eddie's high-deductible plan, and we could divide the parenting responsibilities more equally. He might even be able to cut back his hours.

I think I need to go back to work. The kids are older now, Nicholas is in school all day and in the fall Abby will be also. Lindsay, our babysitter, is graduating this year and taking a gap year to decide if she wants to go to college. Maybe we could hire her as a nanny to watch Penny in our house on weekdays and do homework with Nick and Abby after school. It seems like the York City school district is always recruiting teachers lately. The recession is behind us, so it should not be difficult to find a job.

# Chapter 23

*September 2014*

The York City School District was hiring, and I was right. I found a job easily: sixth grade math. It was cheaper to hire in-home help than it would have been to pay for three kids in daycare, and we are thrilled Lindsay accepted a position as our nanny. She is with Penny all day and responsible for getting Nick and Abby to and from school.

The city pay rate for teachers is much higher than the county, so I am making more money here than I would anywhere else, but working in the city is challenging. Pennsylvania is a commonwealth and each small municipality is responsible for itself. We set our local school budgets according to property values and charging a percentage for school tax. The high tax bill that is still sitting on my counter waiting for this paycheck means that my own children can attend the highest-rated school district in our area. I do not have to buy Nicholas or Abby school supplies because every year their crayons and notebooks are supplied by their school. My district is the one that was able to continue offering Nicholas special education services, even when he did not qualify. Most districts would not have the funding available to offer services to kids who do not "need" them. There were no positions available in my home district because full-time job openings for teachers tend to only pop up if someone retires. When there is an opening, it is likely to go to a candidate already well-connected with the school board.

In areas like York City where property values are low or there are quite a few vacant lots, there is less money collected through the taxes and the schools are less desirable. Those neighborhoods are also the places that have the highest rate of students who need free and reduced lunch, and they have the lowest teacher retention rates (which is why they pay us more, it's an incentive to keep us here, despite the extra challenges), and lowest student test scores. Hunger and poverty make it difficult to do well on standardized tests. Low test scores lead to even less funding and lower evaluations for teachers, regardless of how well they actually teach. That means very few people want to work here, and it is easy to find a job. It also means there is no money in the school budget for supplies, so I purchase all of my own materials for our classroom right down to the pencils and staples, and I ask the church to donate copy paper.

September twelfth is my thirtieth birthday, and I am spending the morning doing the mandated district testing with the sixth graders in the computer lab. It's almost lunchtime. There's a throbbing pain my right temple and the florescent lights are killing me. Finally, the three hours of testing are over. On my way back to my classroom during my planning period, I stop by the nurse's office. It's only the second full week of school, and she doesn't know me yet.

"Hi. I'm new. Stephanie Giese. Sixth grade math. Could I trouble you for some Advil? I think I'm coming down with a migraine."

"Only have Tylenol."

"That's fine. Thank you."

"Take two. Sign here." She hands me a clip board where there is a line marked to account for each pill.

I don't remember ever having to stop at the nurse's office for medicine before. The pain in my head is blinding and it is only getting worse. The pills don't touch it. There are twenty-seven sixth graders coming back to me in ten minutes, and I consider spending the remaining time lying on the cold tile floor in the supply closet across the hall from my classroom. At least it's dark in there. I settle for just turning out my lights. Paula knocks three times on the open door before she enters. She teaches English two rooms down.

"You don't look so good."

"I'm not feeling very well today," I shrug. Teachers always work when they are sick. It's nothing.

"Well, hey, no offense, but I'm just going to stand over here then, okay? Could be that flu that is going around."

"I think it's just a headache," I wince. I hope I'm not pregnant. Dizziness was always my first symptom.

"Seriously, you should stop at the nurse."

"I did."

"Good. So, I just wanted to pop in and remind you to fill out the log in Justin's folder. I'm trying to see if he can earn a reward this week. Has he been doing his homework?" Paula asks.

"Their homework isn't due for me till Friday."

"Oh, that's right, you do that packet thing. OK, I'll leave you alone. You look awful."

"Ha. Thanks. I feel it."

The kids come back and file into the room. They are rambunctious, even though they are trying to be sweet. "She said she has a headache. Y'all can't shut your big mouth for five minutes? Hush." Their concern for me makes me smile for the first time in hours, which is how I discover that smiling hurts. A lot. I give up on my plans for the day and pass out a worksheet from the emergency substitute plans file in my cabinet, hoping it will buy me some quiet. It's too close to the end of the day to go home.

The room has started spinning. There are red spots in my line of sight, so I blink slowly to try to rid myself of them, but when I open my eyes again everything is black. I close them one more time, not sure if it's me or the room that is turning, and will myself not to vomit. Swallow it twice. I can't see. I can't speak. Maybe it's not just a headache. My body wants to fall down and go to sleep and I know that if I let it one of the kids would probably go to get help. I move myself to my doorway and stand there, leaning against the frame, hoping another adult will walk down the hall. No one does.

I try to whisper different words to myself, just to see if I can say them. It's taking much longer than it should for any sounds to come out. Maybe I should try to go to the phone and call the office. Maybe if I dialed a few times, even if I can't talk, they would send someone down to check. The other side of the classroom feels impossible. That's where the phone is. I could write a note on the board and tell a kid to call on our class phone or bring me my purse from my desk drawer. It has my cell phone in it. Or maybe I could write a note and put it on the closest student's desk, send them to get Paula. I don't do any of that.

I can't decide if I really need the help. What if it stops as quickly as it started? If I can still think clearly about all my options like this, then I must not need help yet. Besides, I don't want to ask for help. I am the only adult in the room with these children, and I don't want them to worry. I don't want them to see me weak. They have enough stress in their lives, they don't need yet another situation where they have no choice but to reverse their role and become the grown-ups. The children in front of me have enough scary memories, and I simply refuse to be another one. I lean against the wall to wait until it passes. Except it doesn't.

I think I'm probably pregnant. Eddie won't be happy about that, but if I am it's his fault. He's the one who never went back to the doctor for the follow-up appointment. We don't actually know if his vasectomy took. Vertigo was my first symptom with both of the girls. It felt just like this. Kind of. Okay, maybe not *exactly* like this. I don't remember blacking out before. The point is there a simple explanation both of those times. That must be it.

\*\*\*

Two weeks later I'm out of sick days and I'm going to have to make a decision soon. I don't want to think about it. I finally got back into the classroom after a five-year hiatus, and I also really don't want to have to fire Lindsay. The kids love her and I love having extra help around here. She's here today watching Penny so I can actually rest.

Who am I kidding? I don't even know if we can afford for me to stop working. That was the whole reason I went back. Unfortunately, I have nothing but time to think because I've barely been able to get out of bed all week. Every time I sit up the room spins and I'm still seeing spots. My left arm keeps going numb, but it's probably just because I have been lying here for so long. I'm going to get up to go to the bathroom. Maybe drinking more water would help, too. Or not.

Even after walking around for a while, my arm is still numb and now it's not just that one. There are pins and needles in both of my hands and my legs feel like they're falling asleep and burning at the same time. Numbness in extremities seems like a red flag. I dig through my purse and find my insurance card. There's a 1-800 number on it. I only want to talk to a nurse for a second. She'll probably tell me to take some Motrin and drink more fluid, but just to be safe I dial. After pressing a few numbers from the automated menu, someone answers. She asks for my account information from the card and I give it to her. I think I hear her cracking a piece of gum. Then she asks me what is wrong.

"Yeah, hi. So, I've been home from work for a few days

with pretty bad vertigo, but this morning my arms and legs kind of started going numb and that's not great, right? So I called you."

"Ok, Hun, I'm just going to ask you a few questions. You say you've been having vertigo. How would you describe that?"

"Feeling like I'm spinning and falling, except I'm not."

"Uh-huh. And do you feel like you are spinning or like the room is spinning?"

"Both. You know, like the teacup ride where the cup you are sitting in is spinning, but also the entire ride is spinning."

"Okay. And do you feel nauseated when this happens?"

"Yes."

"How often is it happening?"

"It's been happening for weeks."

"But how often, Dear? Would you say once every three to four hours, or?"

"Oh, actually it's more like it never stops happening. Sometimes it slows down."

"Have you vomited?"

"Not today."

"Any changes in your vision?"

"Um, yeah, I guess. I can still see right now, but there are some red spots in my left eye, sometimes they are white though, and the other day everything went black for a little while."

"Fever?"

"Yes. It's not that high, though. I'll live."

"What does 'not that high' mean to you?"

"It was 101 the last time I took it, but I don't have a fever every day."

"All right. And you say you're experiencing some numbness?"

"Yeah, it started in my left arm, but now it's in both of my arms and my legs."

"Have you ingested any drugs or alcohol?"

"Ha. No. I took an Advil yesterday."

"Ok, Stephanie, I need you to listen to me. I am going to send you an ambulance."

"Wait. Hold on now. I really don't think that is going to be necessary."

"With the symptoms you are describing, I must recommend you seek immediate medical attention."

"It's truly not that bad. I'm standing here talking to you, so..."

"Are you refusing medical attention?"

"What? No. I mean maybe. Look, I don't need an ambulance. Lindsay is here. I know you don't know who that is, but she can drive me to the hospital. If you really think that is necessary, we'll go now."

"Very good. I am going to call the hospital now and follow up with them again soon. If you haven't been there within the hour, then I will dispatch an ambulance."

"That's very thorough of you. I promise you don't need to do that. We're leaving right now."

We're leaving after I shave my legs. It only takes ten minutes to get to the closest hospital. I totally have time to take a shower.

I tell Lindsay to drop me off at the entrance and take

Penny home. Who knows how long I am going to be waiting in the emergency room and there's no reason for a toddler to be subjected to a bunch of germs in a hospital, just to keep me company. Walking up to the front desk, I start to check-in. As soon as I tell her my name the woman behind the half-moon counter points to the empty wheelchair sitting next to her.

"Oh, good. We were waiting for you, Honey. Go ahead and have a seat. I'll call somebody to take you back to your room." I'm not sitting in that thing. There are several other people in the waiting room, some with injuries, glaring at me. I have no idea how I walked in three seconds ago, but I already have a room and they don't. Maybe I was the only person who called that insurance hotline nurse all day. Maybe she was bored and looking for something to do, so I became her pet project. That's probably it. Or maybe she was right, and this is more serious than I thought. No, I'm going with the first thing.

Four hours later, I've peed and bled into every container they've brought into this room. I've been for x-rays and scans and done the physical exams. Eddie has come from the office and is sitting in the chair in the corner while we wait for yet another doctor. He's on his phone checking my website's Google Analytics statistics. One of my blog posts has started taking off this week. It's a rant about laundry, of all things, but it's performing better than anything I've ever written.

Apparently other moms are also extremely annoyed by how small our daughters' shorts are made by manufacturers. Why can't three-year-olds have functional pockets and longer inseams for climbing trees and sitting cross-legged on the floor? Why are girls' clothes cut tight and short when the growth charts show they are physically larger than boys until adolescence? I submitted it to *The Huffington Post* for syndication, and my own website has had three hundred thousand hits from it so far, which is one hundred times more than my normal Binkies and Briefcases traffic, so it would appear I've hit a nerve.

I'm flipping through the TV channels, trying to find one that isn't obstructed by lines of static. Finally, the doctor comes in, looking down at his clip board.

"Ok, so it looks like I have good news and bad news for you today, and they both come wrapped up in the same sentence: We can't seem to find anything here."

"That's good, right?"

"Certainly could be. We all hope so. But to be safe, with your symptoms, we are going to refer you to a neurologist. You need some more tests, and they are ones that I can't authorize here in the ER." Figures. "In the meantime, we can't have you working or driving like this, can we? I'm going to write a note to excuse you from work and give you a prescription for some anti-nausea medication. Then you are free to go." Yet again, it looks like my decision has just been made for me.

\*\*\*

Another two weeks have gone by, filled with more hospital visits and hours spent half-naked inside of machines. A young doctor rushes into the room, holding a file folder. This is my neurologist? His hair is frosted, and there are aviator sunglasses tucked into the V-neck under his lab coat. He nods in my direction, but he does not shake my hand. He does walk across the room to shake my husband's. He introduces himself to Eddie. Not to me. Before he comes over to the table where I'm sitting on crinkled white paper, he stops to take something out of a drawer. It's a safety pin. He opens it but does not clean it or explain what he is doing before he takes my arm and presses the sharp end into my skin several times.

"How does this feel?" I only stare back at him through narrowed eyes, proud of myself for resisting the urge to answer his question the way I want to, which is *it feels like I should ask what your GPA was because you probably spent more time playing beer pong than you did going to class.*

He continues up and down my other arm, then my legs. "Does this feel pokey?"

"Yes," I answer flatly. "It does feel pokey when you poke me with a safety pin."

"When the other doctors saw you could you feel what they were doing?"

"Yes. Those experiences were a bit different, though. They were using, you know, medical instruments." I'm not even trying to hide the contempt in my voice. He holds out his hands in front of him and tells me to push as hard as I can into them. I oblige.

Then he scans me up and down with his entire head, and I get the distinct impression that it's his favorite part of his job. For once I'm glad for the extra thirty pounds of baby weight I'm still carrying. He must not think I'm hot enough to touch further. Fine by me. The safety pin experiment seems to be the extent of his exam. He opens the folder and takes out several black and white photos.

We're here for the results of my MRI. I take deep breaths in through my nose and look to Eddie, whose face reveals nothing. My husband hasn't said a word. I wonder if I'm overreacting. Maybe Eddie likes him. Is that possible? The doctor turns around to hang a photo in a lighted box, and his lab coat fans out behind him like a tail. It cements the image I have of him in my head. I'm going to remember him as Donald Doc because, I don't care what Eddie thinks, this guy is a quack.

"So, these images are obviously of a lesion that has built up from scar tissue."

"I'm sorry." No, I'm not. "Can we slow down please? This is the first time we are seeing any of these images. Why obviously?"

"Look, I do this every day, and this is a textbook case. You've probably had migraines your whole life. They scarred your brain. It's not cancer."

"How can you tell?"

"The color."

Well, that's a relief, I guess, although we hadn't even been considering the possibility until he said that. "It's a small lesion. It won't kill you."

"That's good to hear. What will it do?"

He rolls his eyes. "You already know that. Aren't those symptoms why you came here in the first place? It's on the part of your brain that affects your vision and your balance."

"Do I need an operation?"

The doctor sighs at me. It is taking every ounce of his limited patience to put this in a way that I will be able to comprehend. "We don't just do brain surgery on every person who has a brain lesion. What we are looking at here is not life-threatening, but surgery could be."

"So, we don't do anything?" He's telling me to just live like this for the rest of my life?

"Are you an anxious person?"

"Only when someone walks into a room and tells me I have a brain lesion."

"I'll give you some medicine. It should alleviate the migraines and help you calm down. Do not drive while you are taking this."

I haven't talked to him about my headaches. Hysterical woman that I am, he writes me a prescription for Valium. I still don't know anything about brain lesions or atypical migraines, but I know the dosage on the prescription he just wrote me is ten times higher than the dose they gave my mother during her eye surgery. That can't be good news.

Eddie and I walk out of the office in silence. Apparently, that doctor was right about at least one thing. My anxiety is building trying to process the news we just heard, and I think Eddie feels it because he puts his hand on my shoulder. Once we are through the automatic doors and standing outside on the sidewalk, I turn to face him. I have to cup my hand over my eyes to block out the sun when I look up.

"That was weird, right? It wasn't just me?"

He laughs, "What's the matter? You don't appreciate

being prodded by douchebags with unsterilized office supplies?"

"Why didn't you say anything to him?"

"I was afraid I was going to hit him. Besides, you seemed to be handling yourself just fine."

I wrap my arms across my chest and fold in on myself, and Eddie leans his head sideways.

"Hey, Steph?"

"Yeah?"

"Does this feel pokey?" He mimics the doctor and taps gently on my rib cage until I smile.

"Okay, stop." It's hard to sound demanding while I'm trying to stop myself from giggling, but he listens. I'm not ready to laugh. His hands stay on my sides and pull me closer until my jacket is touching his.

"Come here," he whispers as he rests his forehead on top of mine. "We're definitely getting a second opinion."

"Those pictures, though," I start a sentence I don't know how to finish. The doctor might have been a jerk, but the photos didn't lie. There is a lesion on my brain.

"I know," He raises his arms higher to wrap them around my shoulders and kisses the top of my head. "I know."

My phone pings with a notification, so I twist out of his hug to check thinking it might be something about the kids. Instead it's the editor of one of the national news sites that have picked up my blog post about the shorts. Can I do an interview tomorrow with a crew from *Good Morning America*? They can come do it at our house.

"Um," I hand the phone to Eddie and let him read it. He scrolls down the list of hundreds of unread messages.

"That's some insane timing," he hands it back to me. "Did you see this one?"

Today we found out I have a brain lesion, *Good Morning America* wants to feature my writing, and apparently Glenn Beck is asking if I would fly to Texas to speak on a panel of women he is hosting on his show. There are also requests from local news channels. The American Psychological Association has reached out to thank me for raising awareness for an important cause. Thanks to the shorts post and the follow-ups I wrote documenting my experience shopping the aisles of Target and Kohl's, speaking to Public Relations reps about their design teams, and the further research I've done on child development since writing, my name seems to have found its way to quite a few people's lists. One of the op-eds I wrote won an award and I have been getting emails from college professors who are using it in their syllabi. It would seem I have accidentally managed to become a leading voice regarding the cultural sexualization of young girls in America.

Life is really, really weird.

I will do a few interviews and some fundraising because I truly do believe this issue is important, but I can't give it the amount of time it deserves because, in the understatement of the century, our family has a lot going on.

We drive straight from the doctor's office to my school so I can hand my resignation letter to the vice principal.

# Chapter 24

*February 2015*

Fall was a whirlwind of press dotted with hospital visits, and when I wasn't doing interviews I spent most of my time in bed. Thankfully, things have calmed down on the writing front, but my health is getting worse. I'm losing words and function in my extremities, and I have no sense of equilibrium at all. My legs gave out while I was picking up Nicholas' prescription at the pharmacy, and I sat on the floor for almost twenty minutes until they decided to start working again. At dinner last night I had to grab the table and focus on the picture hanging on the wall because I couldn't tell if I was falling or still sitting up. I've been to the Emergency Room twice since the first visit just to make sure I wasn't having a stroke.

I know a second opinion is necessary, but that doesn't make me any less nervous. Actually, I think I'm more anxious this time because I'm here alone, and so far I haven't had the best of luck with neurologists. I scan the waiting room because there's nothing else to do, and it occurs to me that I'm the youngest person here by probably at least twenty years. I'm also the only person sitting by myself on the scratchy upholstered chairs, waiting for my name to be called. Everyone else in this room brought someone with them for moral support. There's a soap opera playing on mute on a television across the room and a stack of magazines on a table next to me, but neither option is appealing. Instead, I just close my eyes and try to breathe. I can do this. *Please, God, help me do this.*

I need a distraction, so I pull my phone out of my purse and scroll through Facebook for a minute before my fingers find themselves on the internet typing my new doctor's name into a search bar. She's smiling in her picture. She looks friendly. Her biography says that medicine is her second career. Before deciding to become a neurologist, she was a social worker. She worked with children in foster care. She obtained her medical degree from Eddie's alma mater. I'm starting to like her.

"Stephanie?" A nurse stands in the doorway and calls my name. I put the phone away and let her lead me down a narrow corridor and onto a scale. The nurse doesn't say anything about the number staring back at me while she pencils it into my chart, but I'm not happy with it. As it turns out, spending hours every day in bed and being too dizzy to lift your head, let alone exercise, doesn't do a ton to aid weight loss goals. We go into a small room where everything is various shades of white, pink, and peach and she gives me the choice between sitting on the papered table or a regular chair. I choose the chair because from there it's easier to pretend nothing is wrong. I've been in rooms like this enough this year, and I'm already tired of feeling like a patient. She proceeds to take my blood pressure and asks me about all of the medications I have taken within the past year. I try not to take the Valium because I have to be able to drive. I do take Dramamine and Advil and Topamax, and some of the emergency room doctors wrote me other prescriptions. As I spout them off, she makes a list for the doctor, then she asks me to describe my symptoms. I feel like I must have said the same thing to a thousand different people by now, but I summarize for her.

"I've been getting really dizzy for a while. Sometimes it gets bad enough that I can't really walk or see. And sometimes my hands or feet go numb."

"Do you get headaches as well?"

"Yeah."

"Can you tell me more about those?"

"Um, I guess. I've had migraines pretty much forever. As long as I can remember. I was five when my mom started taking me to the doctor for them. They had her keep a food journal for me and change my diet for a while when I was a kid. The bad ones are almost always in my right temple and behind my eye."

"What do you do for them?"

"Nothing really seems to help, honestly. I take medicine occasionally, but mostly just drink water and then lie down with a wet rag on my head. Sleep. Although, I have three little kids, so that's not always possible."

"I bet," she smiles. Her acrylic nails click against the keyboard as she types my body's numbers and my verbal responses into the computer in front of her. "How old are your children?" she tries to make easy conversation.

"Two, five, and seven."

She looks at me expectantly like I am supposed to speak further, but when I don't, she accepts that maybe I am just not very good at small talk. "I'm sure you have your hands full. Okay, well, the doctor will be with you in a few minutes." She leaves me alone with the peach-painted walls and the medical brochures wilting in their plastic display case. There's a stack of coupons sitting on the counter offering a discount on prescriptions and I stick one in my purse with the intention of giving it to my grandfather. The knock on the door is so faint that I think it was just my imagination until it opens and three people in white coats walk in. I only recognize one of them from her photo on the website.

"Hi, I'm Dr. Jolly." She reaches out to shake my hand. "I have a few medical students shadowing me today. Do you mind if they sit in with us?" She used to be a social worker and now she is a teacher. I know I am home. I tell her that is fine.

The medical students actually stand rather than sit. As they lean against the counter and try to make themselves invisible, Dr. Jolly takes a seat in the extra chair next to me. "So, tell me all about what has been going on with you." She listens patiently as I recount my story one more time, stopping me at a few points for clarification.

When we have gone through my entire story, she explains why we are here today. "Okay, we are going to do some tests on you. I'm sure they are the same ones you feel like you have already done a million times. I just need to test your reflexes and see some things for myself." She goes through the same series of exercises the doctors did in the emergency room, making me bend and push and squeeze, and examining me with her little light.

"Great. That all looks good. Now tell me a little bit about the medicines you have tried so far." I walk her through all of the medicines they gave me, the ones for nausea and the ones for anxiety and seizures, which ones sort of worked a little and which ones didn't work at all. She asks what I think about every one, and she takes copious notes. Then she pulls up the photos from my MRI. She confirms everything the other doctor said, just in a gentler way. It has formed from migraine scar tissue and she can tell it will not hurt me, but it is terribly inconvenient to live with something like this. The best thing we can do now is try to avoid the migraines so it doesn't get worse. Maybe we can even help control some of the symptoms.

"It seems you do have a small lesion on your brain and you already knew that. Here's what I would like to do," she turns to face me. "I would like to have you keep a calendar until the next time you see me, and I want you to write everything down. Every time anything doesn't feel good, write it down. Anything at all. I want you to track your menstrual cycle on this calendar too. We're going to see if we can find any patterns." She searches my face for affirmation, so I nod. Dr. Jolly takes it as her signal to go on, "Sometimes symptoms we think are not related to each other actually are. Bring your calendar with you when you come back in a few weeks, and we will go from there."

She also asks once more how I feel on my current medication, and she listens carefully as I tell her about the side effects. I don't like taking medicines that make me tired when I'm the only adult in the house with my toddler, and I don't like being prescribed medicines that affect my already too low blood pressure. All of the male doctors I've had so far have brushed off those concerns and told me that unfortunately some medicines are going to do that. Doctor Jolly doesn't. She says that my concerns are understandable and decides that since my current medication is making me too tired to function properly, we should adjust the dosage or try a different option. Then she tells me about each one of the top three medicines she might try for me and lists a few pros and cons for each one.

"I heard from our nurse you have children?" she asks.

"Yes, three. Although I've been told my son should count as four or five just by himself."

"A handful, is he?"

"Well, yeah, I guess. He has some special needs. It can be a lot."

"I see," Dr. Jolly nods. "I was just reading some new research about mothers of children who have special needs. All that extra caretaking. It really can add quite a lot of extra stress and take a toll on your health. I'm glad you came in." No kidding. It's not surprising to anyone that I would have a lot of migraines. All moms do. Especially moms of kids like Nicholas.

As she gets up to leave, she shakes my hand again.

"It was great to meet you, Stephanie. I hope we can get you feeling better." Little does she know, she already has.

At home I pull out my laptop and start researching ways I might be able to change my diet or exercises that might help the vertigo. Two hours down my rabbit hole, I decide to try cutting out gluten and dairy, and I also find the study Dr. Jolly was referencing. A new paper has been published in Australia. Their research finds that women who are mothers to children with intellectual disabilities (ID) or Autism Spectrum Disorder tend to have their own serious health consequences. I scan the abstract and the numbers are terrifying. It says women like me are forty percent more likely to die of cancer than mothers of children who do not have neurological differences. Apparently, I am also one hundred and fifty percent more likely to die of heart disease, and two hundred percent more likely to die from something they categorize as "misadventure." A separate Google search tells me that misadventure is a catch-all for anything from an overdose, to suicide, to homicide, to an accident, especially when you know there is inherent risk but choose to engage in the behavior anyway. You know, such risky behavior as choosing to parent a child with unique health or neurological needs.

Another study, published a few years before, tells me that mothers raising children with autism and ID have measured stress levels similar to combat soldiers and tend to have lower emotional well-being than moms raising neurotypical kids, even though both sets of moms showed no difference in positive experiences with their families and completed the same workload both at home and in the workplace. Moms raising children with neurological disabilities had more childcare tasks, which continued well into their children's adult lives, and more stressful or traumatic experiences related to family life. I feel like I could have told the researchers that upfront and saved them years of trouble.

There aren't very many studies available online, but the ones I do find all prove the same thing over and over: the lack of help and resources for parents raising children with neurological differences is not only detrimental to the kids, it is literally killing the women who tend to be their primary caregivers. What the academic research does not do is offer a plan or any practical advice for how to stop it.

# Chapter 25

*May 2015*

Nicholas' full battery evaluation was finally scheduled for the Friday before Memorial Day weekend and after a full year of waiting, that day has come. It's a school holiday so he will not miss class, but that also means that even though the school psychologist in the special education building is testing, the staff from his school is off today. Special Ed is serviced by a branch called the Lincoln Intermittent Unit in our county, and they have their own calendar that does not always align with individual districts. This building is open, even though others are closed. We are here for a full battery evaluation in their neuropsychological clinic. It sounds very official, but I'm still unclear about what exactly that means.

Eddie stayed home with the girls so I could bring Nicholas alone. They said to expect we will be here all day and told me to pack a lunch for both of us. They also said that it is not unusual for families to need to come back and do this all over again if the child does not cooperate for the testing. There is a high probability Nicholas will burn out and melt down and they won't be able to finish. The examiners will be doing every test in their arsenal, so it will take at least six hours.

I have not been here since Nicholas was in preschool, but I lead him into the building and sign us both in at the front door. It feels like a lifetime ago, but I suppose it has only been three years since we would occasionally meet with his speech teacher here. The building somehow seems both outdated and too extravagant for the clinical testing and paperwork it houses. It harkens back to a time when quality took precedence in construction, with wide sprawling halls and ten-foot-high carved wooden doorways, some of them adorned with arches of stained glass. In a makeshift waiting area that has been created by arranging a circle of various-sized unmatched chairs and tables in the center of the hall I recognize a familiar silhouette. I only know one woman who can rock a buzz cut like that.

"Mrs. Haugh, this is a surprise," I say as we approach her.

"Well," she smiles. "With school closed, I knew it might not be possible for our administrators to come, and I wanted to make sure someone was here with you. This can be an overwhelming day. Besides, I want to be at that table to speak up when they write their report today. They should have some input from one of his teachers. Hi, Nicholas," Mrs. Haugh turns her attention to him.

"Look, I brought a Blue Angel." He shows her the metal airplane in his hand and she acts impressed when he explains that Blue Angels are F/A-18 Hornets and they are

different than Thunderbirds, which are F-16s. Blue Angels
have two engines. Thunderbirds only have one. That's why
he prefers the Blue Angels, although it's a hard choice
because he wants to be in the Air Force when he grows up,
and they don't fly the Blue Angels, the Navy does. He tells
her that he has been to several airshows with his dad and
Gramps. He saw the Blue Angels twice, but he has only seen
the Thunderbirds once. His uncle took some photos at the
Blue Angels airshow and blew them up onto a one-of-a-
kind full-sized poster as a Christmas gift, which now hangs
in his bedroom, high enough so he can see it from the top
bunk.

Since he was three years old, Nicholas has maintained
that he wants to be an Air Force fighter pilot when he grows
up. I've tried to be encouraging and always respond by
telling him I think he would be great at working on planes.
Driving them would be cool, but there are a lot of awesome
jobs at airports too, like helping to keep people safe doing
security, loading the luggage, working on the runway
waving the flags, or being a mechanic. Even so, I still wince
inside every time he mentions the Air Force, weighed down
by the guilt.

I won't crush his spirit, but I know my decision to get
him diagnosed has probably already disqualified him from
being able to serve in the military. I looked it up, and their
website clearly says that a history of mental health issues
can prevent people from being accepted. Plus, whatever we
find today is likely to strip even more options away from his
future, but it's still the only way to help him in the present.
I sigh and force a smile as I interject myself into his speech

about the planes.

"I told Nicholas we were coming here today to do some riddles and puzzles with teachers and doctors," I tell Mrs. Haugh. I try to never use the word *test* with him about these evaluations.

"That's right," she agrees. "They are probably getting some puzzles ready for you now."

It isn't long before someone appears to escort Nicholas into an otherwise empty classroom and begin his first session. He gives me his airplane for safe keeping. Mrs. Haugh and I take our seats in the hall, and I do my best to start a conversation.

"Thanks for coming, you really didn't have to. I know it's your day off."

She waves her hand dismissively. "Of course I am here, and happy to do it. Every family should have our support. Days like this are not easy for our kids." Then she looks at me and adds, "Or their moms."

"Do you have any plans for the weekend?" I continue the small talk.

"Oh, yes. My family does an annual trip to our favorite cabin on Memorial weekend."

"That's cool, are you all leaving tonight?"

"They left yesterday, actually. I'll drive up and meet them when we wrap up here."

An overwhelming sense of gratitude engulfs me. She is missing her family vacation just to sit with me for six hours in an empty hallway and make me feel less alone. I will never forget this kindness, but instead of jumping out of my seat to hug her like I want to, I swallow and keep talking.

"That sounds like it will be fun. So, what exactly are they doing with Nicholas today?"

Mrs. Haugh explains as well as she can how the LIU psychologist is testing Nicholas today. This level of evaluation is expensive, and she fought hard to get it for Nicholas. Because he does not have Medicaid, the cost will need to be absorbed by our school district and that is not an expense they take on willingly if there is any possibility it can be avoided. She has been pushing for Nicholas to receive this evaluation for two full school years.

Some tests are done on the computer, others are administered in-person by a psychologist. There is a second examiner in the room observing and taking notes. They are screening his intelligence, his motor skills, his memory, his attention, his emotional and psychological well-being, his speech and language development, and whether or not any other issues like dyslexia or dysgraphia may be an issue. They have also collected information from me about all of our therapies and specialists and reviewed all of his previous special education evaluations from every school. Before we leave, we will receive a report compiling Nicholas' entire health and education history, which has never been recorded in one place before. By the end of the day, if there is a diagnosis to be had, we should have it.

Periodically, I am called into the room to answer some questions, to clarify a date in the paperwork, or to simply let Nicholas see me and take a break. Otherwise, Mrs. Haugh and I sit quietly in the hall sneaking granola bars or small pieces of chocolate from the stash in our purses. After what seems like an eternity, they are ready to call us in for the results.

We take our seats at a round table that may have previously been used in a cafeteria, anxious to hear the results. I reach into my purse and pull out the airplane, returning it to its rightful owner. He flies it around the room while the adults talk.

"Nicholas was very cooperative today," the examiner begins. "He is a nice young man, and he had no problem participating in our conversations. He seemed to put forth a good amount of effort on each test. That helped make today go smoothly, and it also makes me confident these results are accurate."

I brace myself. I have been fighting for five years to have someone recognize that something was wrong, but now that we are here, I don't know that I'm ready to hear it if I was correct. Then again, I also don't know if I could handle yet another person telling me they cannot put a finger on what is going on with my son.

I nod along and try to keep up as he pulls out charts and graphs plotting Nicholas in comparison to where an average child his age should place. For once, I agree with Eddie and am glad I have a background in education because I cannot imagine how much more overwhelming this would be if I weren't bringing my own experiences with screening gifted students and teaching child development to this table.

"Are you familiar with how intelligence quotients are measured?" he asks me.

"Yes, I have administered the KBIT-2 quite a few times, screening for giftedness."

"Great. Today we used the Reynolds for Nicholas." He

seems relieved that he does not have to dumb this down for me. I wish I would have said no because I already feel like I am underwater, my thoughts gurgling incoherently.

I bob my head while he flips through page after page and throws out words like "Aphasia Screening," "Selected Subsets," and "Comprehensive Test of Phonological Processing." I do understand the IQ results, and a score in the 60's sounds like good news in terms of getting him a diagnosis. Occasionally Mrs. Haugh interjects to make sure they have a clear picture of how Nicholas performs in a general classroom and in her small groups.

Finally, we get to the summary. In conclusion, they tell me, as a result of today's tests Nicholas has been officially diagnosed with: ADHD, Sensory Processing Disorder, a mild Intellectual Disability, and labeled at risk for clinical anxiety and depression as well as a psychotic thought process. The results also suggest the possibility of a Pervasive Developmental Disorder and indicate constructional dyspraxia. His performance with his left hand was measured to function below the first percentile, so he has significant delays with motor skills. *It's no wonder he still cannot tie his shoes or button pants*, I think while the examiner continues to list the results. He says that Nicholas was observed during the testing making comments that indicated hallucinations and the "extreme elevation of the scores relating to his behavior does reflect the likelihood of severe psychological difficulties."

It's all there in black and white: confirmation that everything I have been saying since he was two years old was right. I feel justified, but also more scared than I have ever been in my life. What does any of this mean?

The recommendation is that Nicholas be removed from the general classroom setting and placed in a Neurological Support classroom. They want to put him in a different school in a small classroom full of kids who also struggle with their brains. I don't know how I feel about that. Between preschool, cyber school, Baltimore, and his current school, another transfer would mean starting the fifth different school in three calendar years. Plus, they want to bus him across the county to a classroom forty-five minutes away from home in a separate district because that is where the students in kindergarten through second grade who need neurological support are sent. I just need to sign here.

That's when Mrs. Haugh speaks up. She mentions a new possibility that until now no one has told me exists.

"There is a neurological support classroom in the Eastern district, less than five miles from the family's home. It is my professional opinion that as a team we must consider the option, due to the fact that the proximity will create less strain on the family and student, in addition to the financial savings to the home district."

"That classroom is not an option for Nicholas, unfortunately." The psychologist tries to dismiss her. He says that room only takes students from third through fifth grade. Nicholas is too young. The legal guideline says they are really not supposed to have more than three grade levels in one classroom at a time.

Mrs. Haugh does not budge and continues to push for the option closest to home. "Their teacher, Joe Shrader, has extensive experience with students like Nicholas. He comes from a background in the mental health field and has over a decade of experience in special education. None of that can be said for the K-2 class. The room is not full. Mrs. Giese can sign a waiver recognizing the age discrepancy. Surely, if Mr. Shrader is willing to take Nicholas, we can make an exception?"

She reaches over and squeezes my hand under the table. Her idea would mean Nicholas would avoid over an hour of travel time every day, make it easier for me to get to him in emergencies, and evidently that classroom has a more qualified teacher to meet his specific needs. The school she wants for him is halfway between home and Eddie's office, so his father could get to him just as easily as I could. The school the psychologist is pushing us toward would mean an additional hour and a half in the car every time I need to meet with a teacher or pick him up for therapy.

We end the meeting by agreeing to a vague phrasing in the recommendation saying that Nicholas would benefit from smaller class sizes and specialized instruction such as a neurological support room, but it still has not been decided where that is.

"So, this Mr. Shrader just needs to agree to take Nicholas now?" I ask Ms. Haugh when we walk out together.

"We don't have to worry about that," she assures me. "I know Joe and I have already been talking to him about Nicholas for a while. Nicholas can be a hard nut to crack, as you know. Joe helps me when I run out of ideas. I'm very confident he would be thrilled to have Nicholas."

Once we find our way home, I need to lie down. I don't

bother eating dinner. The vertigo is back and this day has taken all of the energy I had left.

# Chapter 26

Later, my eyes blink open into the darkness. There are twenty-seven pages of paperwork on my nightstand to review from Nicholas' evaluation. The red numbers on the alarm clock next to them tell me it is three forty-two. I didn't hear the door open, but a small head full of curly blonde hair is peaking over the mattress.

"I'm scared." She still can't pronounce her r's, not to mention her th's and I wonder briefly when I should start to be concerned about her speech. Not tonight.

Eddie pops his head out from the cave he has created under the blanket. "What is it, Penny?"

"My room is scary now. Nick said the blonde girl is in there. What if she gets me?"

"Honey, the blonde girl isn't real," I try to assure her.

"Nick says she is real and she is mean. He can see her."

"Can you see her?"

"No."

"Then you don't have to believe him when he tells you

237

she's there. She's not real. Let's get you back to bed." I pick her up and carry her across the house. Our bedroom is on the opposite side of the house from the kids' rooms. After she is tucked soundly back in bed, I give her a kiss and sing *Hush, Little Baby* while I stroke her hair. She's still awake when the song is over.

"Mommy? I'm still scared."

"You don't have to be scared. Your room is safe. I'm right here. I'll tell you what," I grab a spray bottle of water from her dresser that I usually use for detangling the girls' hair. "I'll leave this bottle with you. It gets knots out of hair, but it also makes great monster spray."

"I can't spray her because I can't see her." Fair enough.

"Well, I'll leave it with you anyway. Maybe it will make you feel better. But I don't think you are going to need to worry about it, because she's not real."

"I hope so."

"Do you know what else? You can always pray if you are scared. God will be here with you, even when Mommy and Daddy aren't."

"Mommy? I can't see God."

"I know, but he is here with you." For some reason, that makes her start to cry.

"What, honey?"

"Then the mean girl can be here too, cuz I can't see her." Oh. Shit.

"Penny, listen. Mommy loves you. In this family we believe that God is real and the girl is not. Do you understand?" Do I even understand? I rub her back lightly until her eyes start to get heavy. She is still fighting them every time they threaten to close.

"Mommy, why does my brother lie to me?" It's hard to see her little heart so heavy. I haven't figured out how to carry the weight of this yet, and I'm the grown-up. How is she supposed to know how to process it? It's not fair to ask this of a three-year-old, but it isn't like there is a choice. Exhaustion breeds honesty, and from my perch here at the foot of my youngest daughter's bed at four a.m. there is nothing to tell her but the truth.

"He isn't lying, sweetie. He does see the girl. It's just that sometimes he sees things that aren't real." Through the darkness her blue eyes pierce into mine as she considers my words.

"I don't like that."

I don't like that either. And I don't know what to do about it. Finally, her eyes close and I manage to sneak out of the room. Back in our bed I lie down next to him and Eddie asks if Penny went down all right. I shrug and say, "I guess so," but my tone tells him that the actual answer is no. He wraps his arms around my waist and kisses my shoulder.

"I'm pretty sure we are royally screwing up these children," I caress his forearm as I say it and he squeezes tighter.

"Nobody could do it any better," he sighs what is probably the only response I'm going to get from him tonight. I don't know if he means raise them or screw them up. Maybe there isn't really a difference. Whatever the end result is going to be, we are doing the best that we can. It doesn't take long for his breathing to change and his arms to get heavy. As much as I feel like we are failing, I want another baby, but Eddie doesn't think it's a good idea. I asked him to reverse his vasectomy as his birthday gift to me this year, but he refused. He doesn't think my health could handle it, and we have a lot on our plates as it is. He's probably right. My body is weary, but my brain is wide-awake now.

It's impossible to sleep, but I know tomorrow won't be made any easier if I'm tired, so I try to take deep breaths and count backwards from one hundred while I concentrate on the muffled whirring of the ceiling fan, laying as still as I can, trying not to disturb Eddie. How many rotations will the fan make by the time I count all the way down to one? I try to think of anything but things I cannot control. I bet a hamster or a squirrel would have a really hard time running along a ceiling fan while it was on. Can squirrels be allergic to nuts? They'd probably just die, right? Come to think of it, why don't we see more dead animals just lying around outside. It's not like animals bury their dead. I mean, sure, vultures and maggots get them, I guess, but they don't eat bones, do they? Do deer ever just have a heart attack or a stroke and keel over mid-frolic? They have to. Where are all the bodies? Where was I, again? Seventy-three, seventy-two.

"Are you awake?" Eddie turns over and props himself up on his right elbow, while he runs his left hand along my waistband.

"Mmmhmm"

"What are you thinking about?" He inches closer and drops his head down onto my shoulder.

I move only my head to face him and deadpan, "I feel like

there should probably be more dead animals. You?"

"Okay, well, I don't really know what to do with that, so I'm just going to skip to the part where I say that I was thinking I miss you." His voice is raspier and lower than usual as his hand finds my hip and I let him guide me over so that my body is facing his. "You know the good thing about sex?" he asks in that breathy whisper that makes the hair on my arms stand up.

"Is that rhetorical?"

I know he smiles because of the short little breath that comes through his nose. "It's basically free therapy, and you don't even need an appointment." Eddie lifts himself onto his elbow and kisses my forehead.

"It's not therapy. You should definitely go to actual therapy. We both should." My voice trails as my mind drifts to the way my mother frequently talks about the different kinds of health and how they are all equally important. I always thought creative or artistic health should be its own category, and I still don't know why it's not when it seems to be the outlet so many therapists promote as a coping strategy to help heal the others, but I know mental health and sexual health are two different things even though a lot of people tangle them together, although focusing on one can certainly be good for another. I also know I don't want to think about my mom right now. I roll my head and stretch to bring myself back into the moment.

He continues, "Okay, we'll put our own therapy on the agenda once we find an extra $600 a month and a day without four appointments already on the calendar. Deal? In the meantime..." By now my eyes have adjusted enough to darkness to be able to tell when wags his eyebrows and I have to laugh. The guilt comes immediately. He uses his index finger to trace a circle lightly around my bellybutton.

"I'm going to make another appointment at the church." Pastoral counseling is usually free, they just ask for a donation to the church if you are able to make one.

"Okay. I think that's a good idea. Hey," he pauses and locks eyes with me. "I love you a lot, but could we maybe put a pin in the dead animals and clergy talk and just focus on each other for a minute?"

"Yeah." I take a deep breath and try to ground myself, then reach out to him. This is the only time my mind gets quiet and shuts out all of the to-do lists and unwelcome chaotic thoughts. So many of my friends talk about how at the end of a long day of doing everything for everyone they can't stand to be touched. It just feels like yet another chore or another person needing to drain more energy out of you. I've been there before, but not now. I've come to appreciate using him as an off switch for my brain. It's the most effective way we've found to absorb the tension and the stress: don't think, just touch. For now, it is the only way out.

But the relief is only temporary. As I drift into a fitful sleep, I start to create yet another to-do list.

# Chapter 27

Before Nicholas can begin second grade I need to meet with Mr. Shrader, so I've made an appointment to observe his room. He said Nicholas should come too. On Tuesday I sign Nicholas out of school so we can drive four miles away to a different building. Immediately, this other school seems impressive. There are children playing outside on brand new climbing equipment. I press the doorbell on the wall and speak into it when a voice asks why we are here today.

"Hi. I have Nicholas Giese here to observe the Neurological Support room?" I offer. When they buzz us in we see that it's brighter and cleaner inside than the school he currently attends, and there is air conditioning. A plaque on the wall describes how they were one of the first ten schools in America to receive Leadership in Energy and Environmental Design registration. They have reduced water and energy consumption by over thirty percent and have a focus on health and safety for students and staff. In comparison to the school we left earlier this morning, which has not been renovated since the 1970's, this building seems lightyears more advanced. It must be twice the size of his current school. Nicholas looks so small standing in the lobby and holding my hand, staring wide-eyed at the gleaming white halls and looming staircases. He has never been in a school building with classrooms on more than one floor, but he does not seem intimidated, just mesmerized.

The school secretary buzzes us into the office, where she collects my signature and pages Mr. Shrader through the intercom.

"He'll be with you in just a minute," she smiles. "Oh, you know what? There he is." She darts out from behind the chest-high counter and hurries into the hall to grab a man's attention. When she returns, he is standing next to her wearing a salmon-colored shirt and a thin, grey neck tie. She leaves us to our own introductions and excuses herself back to her desk.

"Great, Nicholas is here." The teacher is calm, yet somehow also exuberant. He radiates a confident contentment that reminds me of a young Mr. Rogers. We are standing in a room full of adults, but he only speaks to my son. "Hi. I heard you were coming. Do you like to be called Nicholas or Nick?"

"My name is Nicholas but sometimes people can call me Nick, too."

"Great. It's nice to meet you, Nick. We've been looking forward to your visit. I'm Mr. Shrader. Is this your mom? Can you introduce me?" The teacher raises his eyes to meet mine.

"Yeah, that's my mom," Nicholas points to me.

"Does Mom have another name?" Mr. Shrader asks him.

"She's Mom, my name is Nick." Nicholas repeats.

"Well, hi, Mom." Mr. Shrader smiles at me.

"Stephanie," I offer.

"Joe." He shakes my hand. "Our room is on the second floor, it's a bit of a hike. Follow me."

The classroom is tucked at the end of the hall on the top floor of the school, as far as it could possibly be from the entrance. It looks like any elementary school classroom: desks, whiteboard, kidney-shaped reading table, other than the huge painted newspaper tree smack dab in the middle. There are four students working at desks and two others sitting at the table doing math with a female teacher, and one is up in the tree.

"This is Ms. Callahan," Mr. Shader tells us. "She is my assistant and she will help Nicholas work in small groups or give him additional attention when he needs it. We try to always have a familiar adult in the room, so one of us should always be here, even if the other is absent."

A third adult sits next to one of the desks. Mr. Shrader notices me looking and adds, "That's Ms. Jen. She is a nurse assigned to one of our students. Sometimes we have friends in our room with medical needs that require full-time care." He continues to talk about the curriculum they plan to use next year and how beneficial it will be for Nicholas to have a much smaller class, but I'm not paying much attention. My eyes are drawn to the gigantic structure in the middle of the room. A ten-foot-tall papier-mâché tree grows up from the floor and houses a fenced wooden platform in its branches.

"This is our tree house," Mr. Shrader beams with pride

and changes the direction of the conversation. "One of our parents helped build it a few years ago. This is where our students can do their silent reading, if they'd like. Nick, do you want to check it out?"

Before he finishes the question, Nicholas is up the ladder and chatting with, or really at, an older boy who holds a book in his hand. The boy's words come slowly, and he struggles to form a response to Nick's greetings and questions. When he finally talks it is in a robotic, broken speech indicative of his disability. My son stares at him, mouth agape, until his new friend finishes a short sentence.

"Cool, I like your accent," Nicholas gushes. "Why do you talk like that? Did you come from England? Or Mars? Can I go there, too? Sorry, I mean can I *please* go, too?" The other boy just stares at him, confused. Nicholas keeps talking. "Are you an alien? Mom, Mom, Mom, guess what? He talks like an alien." He hops and shakes with excitement, pointing at the other child. "My friend is an alien. I'm going to tell Abby I met an alien in the treehouse. This place is awesome." A few of the students look up from their work and start whispering to each other. *Is Paul an alien? Who is that little kid?* One girl starts to rock in her chair and groan.

"Oh my god, I'm so sorry," I apologize, just in general, to everyone.

Mr. Shrader laughs, "It's fine. Nick will fit right in." He excuses himself for a moment to squat next to the moaning girl and redirect her back to her work. Then he turns to look up at the boys, "Nick, I would like you to meet Paul. He is from Pennsylvania, just like you. Paul, Nick is thinking about joining our classroom."

Nicholas' interaction with Paul prompts me to ask about bullying and the school culture, and all of the adults in the room assure me that it's a very welcoming school. There has only been one instance of bullying in all the years they've been in this building, and it ended when they invited the bully to come volunteer as a peer buddy in their room. Once he got to know their students, the bullying stopped and he became protective of them in the cafeteria and on the playground instead. We only stay a few more minutes, the class is getting ready to head to lunch and we don't want to interrupt too much of their day. Mr. Shrader invites me to come back on my own after school to talk more and review some paperwork.

Eddie leaves the office early to stay with the kids so I can go back for the meeting. This time, after saying hello again, we move to a conference room located in the office to sit at adult-sized furniture.

"It's nice to see you again," Mr. Shrader starts. "So, what can you tell me about Nick?"

"Well, Nicholas was born in Tampa and almost immediately placed into foster care," I begin the now well-rehearsed summary I repeat every time we meet a new doctor or therapist. "He came to our family when he was thirteen months old." I see him hold up a hand and pause my story.

"We don't have to do that here. I know all of that stuff." He lowers his hand and pats the stack of papers in front of him. "I'm familiar with his background and diagnosis. I read all of the reports. I meant please tell me about your son."

I stare at him and blink. I thought I was doing that.

"Who is Nick? Tell me about him," he prompts. "I saw that he was wearing a superhero shirt today. Is he a Batman fan or Superman guy? What does he like to do for fun?"

"Oh. Um, he really likes airplanes. And golf, believe it or not."

Mr. Shrader smiles. "Really? That's interesting. Does he play or just watch on TV?"

"Both. He took a few lessons over the summer, and he likes Bubba Watson because he's a pro golfer who talks about adoption and because we also call Nicholas 'Bubba' sometimes, so he thinks they have the same name." Golf is also one of the few sports where it doesn't matter if Nick can't run as fast as his peers, he's not disappointing any teammates or their rowdy parents if he doesn't perform well, and it has helped his gross motor skills improve.

"Great. What else?"

He patiently pulls more information out of me about Nicholas' favorite foods, toys, and TV shows. I tell him how our son is a good swimmer now and he loves LEGO and Star Wars more than anything in the world. Mr. Shrader writes himself a note and says he will brush up on the movies so they can talk about them together. They don't have any LEGO in the classroom right now, but if I would be willing to send some from home, Nicholas could use them during breaks throughout the day. Sure, of course, I can do that.

He talks about the curriculum and how they will differentiate it for Nicholas to meet him where he is, and he also explains a program their class has in place. Once a week a psychologist leads a small group and works on emotional regulation and coping skills. They also do whole group occupational therapy and speech in addition to the small group instruction Nicholas will receive in those areas. In return, I tell him Nicholas will eat anything, he is not picky at all. No, he doesn't have any food allergies. You have to watch him, though, because he's been known to go through the cafeteria line twice and get a second tray of lunch or take every container of chocolate milk from the sharing table. That makes Mr. Shrader laugh.

"He's very sweet, but he can be a handful," I admit.

"No worries, we have plenty of extra hands around here. We are excited to have him." He pulls a sheet from the stack in front of him and I sign to acknowledge that I understand Nicholas will be in a room that serves children from multiple grade levels, along with a few more papers. Then he goes to the copier and scans the pages so I will have my own to take home.

It was a much less painful meeting than I expected, but when I return to the parking lot and get into the van I catch a glimpse of the phrase *mental retardation* in parenthesis on the paperwork and scan down to the words that say things like *emotionally disturbed*. A shaky breath breaks through the wall I've put up and my floodgates open. I fought for years to get those labels for exactly this: so that Nicholas could access classrooms like Mr. Shrader's and have his rights to services in writing, but now that the words are staring back at me the reality stings worse than I expected.

Nicholas is an eight-year-old little boy who loves light-up tennis shoes and just learned how to ride a bike. In so many ways, he is just like every other little boy, yet there is a forty-two-page report sitting on the front seat next to me as a glaring reminder that he's really not like most second graders at all. I feel horrible because in order to get him the help he needs I've agreed, not just at this meeting but at so many others before it, to assign him labels like "retarded" and "psychotic." That is my own signature staring back at me, and because of me those are words that will follow my son for the rest of his life.

# Chapter 28

*Summer 2016*

The hot July sun is burning my scalp, and my legs are sticking to the lawn chair at my in-laws' annual fourth of July barbeque. Their home sits on Sue Creek and the Baltimore Yacht Club's annual fireworks show will be visible from their front yard later tonight. The basement that served as our temporary home for a year now houses a discarded treadmill and some old computer equipment. Another mosquito lands on my foot and I smack it with precision. The bugs love the water. I'm going to have so many bites tomorrow.

Penny can't lick her popsicle fast enough and the sticky purple juice is dripping onto my dress. I lift her up and set her on the grass, and I'm rubbing more sunscreen onto my shoulders when Abby walks up to us with her head down. She's crying, but she's punching the tears away, angry. I know my middle daughter. She's embarrassed because she doesn't want the other kids to see her this way. The

251

neighbors are having a barbeque too, and between my in-laws' yard and the chaos next door there are at least a dozen children running between the houses, screeching and inventing games.

"What happened, Sweetie?"

"Those kids are being mean. They said I'm not allowed to play with them."

"Why not?"

"I don't know. Just to be mean." She crosses her arms and stomps her foot. Abby cannot stand any sort of injustice. I don't know those children or their parents and I have no idea what they are doing. For all I know they could be playing a game she is really is too young for.

"Well, we would be happy to play with you. Your sister's having a popsicle. Would you like one?"

"No, I just wanted to play with those girls," her tears start to come harder. She is shaking when her brother approaches my chair from the other side.

"Mom, can I have another hotdog? Oh, what's the matter with Abby?"

Abby stomps both feet again in protest of the idea that anything is actually the matter with her, but I turn to Nicholas and explain. "There were some girls who hurt Abby's feelings because they said they didn't want to play with her. Now she feels sad."

"And mad," Abby clarifies.

"And mad," I nod at her as I repeat her words then turn back to her brother. "Yes, you can have another hotdog, but eat ten bites of fruit salad first." The baby has finished her dessert and she puts the slimy stick in my hand so I can dispose of it for her. Penny is really too old for me to be calling her "the baby." She will be starting school in a month, but I'm not sure I'll ever stop calling her that, especially if we definitely aren't having any more kids now.

"I'll play with you, Abby," Nicholas shrugs, for once ignoring the prospect of food and taking me by surprise.

"Really?" Abby sniffles.

He nods at her and they start to run away together, but I call after them and ask them to take their sister. I need to go inside and wash my hands. Eddie is outside with them and so are his parents, so I take a few minutes inside to appreciate the air conditioning and finally fill a plate for myself. Staring out of the large picture window in my in-laws' living room, I can see down onto the yard. The kids have started playing tag in the grass, and every now and again Eddie motions for them to come closer to him. He's keeping them away from the creek.

By the time I step outside again, it looks like tag is over. Abby and Penny are tossing beanbags with Eddie and his brother, but it takes me a minute before I spot Nicholas. He's marching, or maybe stomping. That seems odd. He's moving from one child to another, stopping briefly to say something, and then moving on. My curiosity pushes me toward him and when he makes a move toward another child, I position myself to hear their conversation.

"Do you know Dakota?" he demands. The other child simply points. What is he doing?

"Nicholas?" When I call him over, he stomps to me with the same determination. "What's this about?"

"I have to find Dakota," he tells me, as if it is the most

logical sentence in the world.

"Is that a person or a place? Is this part of a game?"

"No, Mom," he says, exasperated. "Dakota was the girl being mean to Abby. And I'm gonna..." he lets his sentence drift as punches his left fist into his right hand. Dakota must be the bully.

"No, you most certainly are not going to do whatever that is." I raise my eyebrows and point to my son's pounding hands. From across the lawn, Eddie notices our conversation and in a few easy strides he is standing between us.

"What's going on over here?" my husband's voice is light.

"Your son was just threatening to punch a little girl for picking on his sister," I explain.

Eddie turns his attention to Nicholas. "Hey man, we don't hit girls, but I'm proud of you for wanting to stick up for Abby. You've got to think of another way to work it out."

"Ugh. Fine." Nicholas stomps away again, with the same determination he had in the first place, and he finds yet another child. "Are you Dakota?" She nods.

I start to step forward, but Eddie puts his hand on my shoulder. "Let them handle it."

I wiggle away from him and whisper, "What if he hits her?"

It's like my husband never bothers to think about the what ifs. Why is this always my job?

He shrugs, "Then maybe she'll kick him in the balls and he'll learn not to do that. Word on the street is this Dakota chick is pretty tough. Or we will punish him, obviously." I roll my eyes at him, but he keeps talking. "Besides, what if he doesn't? Just give him a chance."

So we stand there, against my better judgment, watching and wondering what Nicholas will do. Dakota is sitting cross-legged on the grass in front of the neighbor's porch, drinking a red liquid from a plastic cup that is leaving a mustache on her upper lip. Her blond hair is in a high ponytail and her entire outfit is pink, which stands out among the red, white, and blue most people wore to celebrate the fourth. She doesn't look very intimidating. I'm tempted to call Nicholas away because there are several adults I don't know congregated on the porch behind her. They must be Dakota's family, and they are all about to witness whatever is about to happen between my nine-year-old and their girl. He's standing there, silent, simply staring at her. When he doesn't say anything else she turns her attention to the plate of snacks sitting by her feet. Then, finally, Nicholas takes another step toward her and speaks.

With one hand on his hip, and another pointed directly at her, he raises his voice, but only slightly. "Excuse me. You need to stop being mean to my sister. Did you hear me? I said you stop." After that he turns and walks away. Dakota looks after him with wide eyes.

A man who must be Dakota's father walks off the neighbor's covered porch and follows Nicholas. Eddie shifts slightly so that he's in front of me now and I feel the pit of my stomach turn. I don't want to deal with another confrontation. There have been enough of them already at the park and at school and everywhere else. I'm dreading the peacemaking speech I'm going to need to give when I can see from behind my husband's shoulder that the man catches up to my son, but I can tell from his body language that this time I can relax. All he does is reach out and shake Nicholas' hand.

"That took a lot of courage, young man. Good for you. You are a fine big brother."

It's true. He is. My eyes have gone misty with pride in this moment and regret for the doubt that can loom ugly and loud, clouding my ability to trust.

After the fireworks we put the kids to bed on an air mattress in the living room, and Eddie and I return to our previous basement dwelling for one more night. In the morning we need to leave right after breakfast. The contractor is almost finished turning our basement into a one-bedroom apartment for my mother and I'm supposed to meet with her to pick out paint colors.

# Chapter 29
*November 2017*

Just before dinner Nicholas was watching an unboxing video on the computer. I don't know why the kids love seeing adults open packaging, but they can spend hours seated in front of the screen. Eddie told Nicholas electronics time was over, and Nick melted down, begging for just one more video. After a few minutes he was calm again. We went about the rest of our evening, got the kids fed and into bed. Around seven thirty I came into my bedroom to start writing. I think the kids are asleep.

My mother comes into my room without knocking, slowly lowering herself to perch on the foot of my bed, the floral quilt wrinkling under her. It takes a moment for me to notice the butcher knife she lay between us. Her breathing is deep and measured as she weighs how to begin the conversation.

"Everything is okay," she starts, stretching out the words in a state of exaggerated calm. Except it obviously is not.

"Mom? What is going on?" A tense panic begins rising in my throat, caught in a high-pitched question mark.

"Everything is fine. But there is something you need to know." It does not seem fine. She looks down in the direction of the knife, then up at me and says, "Nicholas came downstairs tonight." That is not unusual. The kids are in her apartment all the time, watching TV, or doing puzzles, or helping her bake.

"Okay?"

"He was very upset. Something about watching another video? But he was holding this," she picks up the knife that I recognize as the largest one from the wood block sitting on our kitchen counter. "He was crying quite a bit, and he said he needed to kill the whole family, then himself, but he needed to start with me."

"Jesus Christ," the panic starts rising in me, but my mother stays collected.

"I told him he seemed sad and angry and those feelings would go away soon, then I said to hand me the knife. He did give it to me right away. No one was hurt. He said he was sorry and he seems fine now. But after what the guidance counselor said, I'm very worried. And I am also glad it was me."

"Well, me too, no offense. He could have started with one of the girls. Are you okay, though?" I blink in rapid succession as if it will help to clear the thick, grey cloud forming over my mind. It does not.

"Yes, I think I am fine. Nothing actually happened. I do think we need to find another place to put the knives, though."

"Um, duh. And pretty sure your grandson threatening your life counts as a significant something happening."

She brushes my concern away with a wave. "The girls were my biggest concern also. I just wanted you to be aware."

"I mean, yeah. Thanks, I guess. Um, what do we do now? I need to take him to the hospital, right? Do I call 9-1-1? Is there another number? Do we just show up?"

She looks at me wide-eyed and raises her shoulders. My voice is louder than I mean for it to be. "You're the therapist, Mom. What do we do?"

"You're his mother. It's up to you and Eddie. Nick came back upstairs and went to bed. He's already asleep."

"Can you promise he will still be like that in an hour?" I ask, although of course I know she can't. Should we let him rest and wait until the morning or wake him up and risk another meltdown to take him now? Every choice when it comes to this child always feels impossible.

"I cannot promise anything. I wish I could. I have never worked with a ten-year-old in crisis before, and I'm not familiar with the resources here yet. I'm sure there is a local crisis line, but just like Mrs. Crowley said, they will tell you to take him to the hospital if he is a threat to himself or other people. Right now, I would not say that he is a threat. But my answer would have been different fifteen minutes ago." She works across the state line, in Maryland. I can tell she feels helpless and I want to tell her it's not her fault, but my brain is buzzing with fuzzy, unfocused options and right now I just wish we had a clear plan.

It has to count as an actual crisis if he is holding a

weapon and saying he wants to kill people, right? Mrs. Crowley told me to take him to the hospital if he was in crisis again.

I don't remember telling Eddie what happened, or driving to the hospital, but somehow my husband, my son, and I end up in the parking garage across town. The girls are home, still asleep. My mother is sitting with them. The last time we were here was when I delivered Penny. When I had my brain issues, we went to a different, smaller hospital closer to home. But that one doesn't have a crisis unit. Mrs. Crowley told us to come here. My tongue feels too big for my mouth, and my neck starts to sweat when I realize I do not know where the crisis unit is. Is it even a place? It's not mentioned on any of the signs. Maybe "crisis unit" is just a nickname for a team of people who specialize in these kinds of situations, like the Special Victims Unit on *Law and Order*.

We walk through the main entrance and up to the desk where a receptionist sits, directing foot traffic. I do not know what to say to her, so I just open my mouth and figure something will come out.

"Hi, how are you?" I start, as if this is a regular conversation.

"Fine, thank you, how are you?" she asks pleasantly.

"Uh, not great, actually. I think my son is in crisis. Where do we go?"

"Can you be a little more specific, ma'am? Is he in a room here in the hospital?"

"No, uh, this is him." I point to the child next to me, who seems completely fine as he smiles at her and waves. "He threatened to hurt himself and his grandma, and his guidance counselor told us to come here if that ever happened, so..." I let my explanation trail and spread my open palms in front of me.

"Okay, you're going to want the ER, then. They are on the other side of the building." It turns out the crisis unit is not a designated place after all, just a group of people who work in the regular emergency room. She points and gives us brief directions through the winding halls. Straight, left, up, left again, then right. The halls are painted in uncomfortable shades of pastel pink and peach that perhaps once felt clean and hopeful, but after decades of fading now only conjure references to stomach medicine or chipping fingernails. The marble floors have been polished and shined to the point of looking wet and I can see our distorted reflections looking up as we march our way toward the elevator.

When we reach the emergency department, another desk waits for us. I tell them the same thing I told the first receptionist. They take his name and have him sit in a chair immediately to measure his blood pressure and other vital signs. Eddie and I both receive bright orange rectangular stickers stamped with the word "visitor" to display on our clothes. The woman behind the desk gives me a clip board containing several sheets of paperwork and a pencil. She points us around the corner to a waiting area filled with more potential patients sitting on vinyl chairs and says when I finish filling it out, I should walk up to one of the exam rooms and knock.

The waiting room is filled to capacity, so the three of us

cannot find seats together. Eddie stands across the aisle and Nicholas and I squeeze together onto a bench between a moaning elderly woman and a sleeping bearded man. Nick asks to go to the bathroom and I look at Eddie. There is a bathroom we can see from here, but we haven't talked about if he should be allowed to be out of our sight alone. Eddie offers to take him, and I finish filling out the forms, balancing the thin wooden board on my lap. The woman next to me vomits into a bedpan while her daughter holds her hair.

I feel uncomfortable knocking on the heavy opaque door. For privacy reasons, there are no windows in these doors and I cannot tell if the rooms are occupied by other patients, although from the size of the crowd in the waiting area, I have to assume they are. What kind of a jerk do you need to be to cut in front of everyone else who has been waiting for hours, and interrupt someone getting stitches just to announce that your own son is now here? But that is what they told me to do, so I knock and try not to look at the patient in the room when I open the door and inform the nurse that the front desk wanted me to tell her our name.

She tells me it will only be a few more minutes, and I go back to my seat, where Eddie and Nicholas have returned.

"Gees-say?" I think I hear someone call, but don't yet respond because that is not how we pronounce our last name and maybe they are speaking to someone else? "Geesay? Nicholas?"

"Oh, that's us."

"Right in here, folks."

The woman seated to my right begins to wretch again. Her daughter glares at me and I don't blame her because who knows how long they have been waiting, yet we only walked in fifteen minutes ago and have no visible injuries.

The male nurse has greying facial hair and is wearing faded blue hospital scrubs. He directs his attention to Nick. "Hop up here on this chair, Buddy. Why don't you tell me why you are here today?"

"I tried to kill my grandma with a knife." Nick states matter-of-factly. The nurse looks at Eddie, then to me for clarification, so I repeat what my mother told me.

"Do you still feel like you want to do that?" the nurse asks Nick.

"No, not really."

"Do you ever feel like you want to hurt yourself?"

"Yeah, sometimes."

"Do you feel like that right now?"

"Nah."

"Mr. and Mrs. Geesay?" the nurse turns to us, but our son interrupts him.

"My last name is Giese. G-i-e-s-e," Nick says without emotion. "It rhymes with rice and ice."

"Ok, thank you," our nurse smiles. "Mr. and Mrs. *Giese*, I will need to take Nicholas back to talk to the social worker and see the doctor alone. You both can just stay right here. It shouldn't be long." His tone is warm but firm, and he is not asking for our permission as he escorts our son out a back door and into a separate hallway.

Alone in the sterile room with my husband, the terror of what is happening hits me in another wave. Eddie must see my eyes widen or sense my breathing change because he lowers me into a chair and hands me a tissue from the counter. We only speak in whispers, and although I know it is completely irrational, I wonder if we are being watched through a two-way mirror or secret microphone and judged on our parenting by what we say and do now.

"What do you think they are doing?" Eddie asks, shaking me out of my paranoia.

"I think they are probably questioning him about our house and checking for signs of abuse, don't you? I don't even know if he has any bruises."

"Probably. He's an eleven-year-old boy." Eddie sighs, resigned that some bicycle bump that got past us could potentially change our fate.

"How are you so calm?" I ask with genuine curiosity, although it comes out sounding more like an accusation.

"I wasn't aware I had another choice. Seems like any other reaction wouldn't do a lot of good right now." In an act of condemnation disguised as kindness, he hands me yet another tissue with yet another exaggerated sigh.

"Are you mad at me right now?"

"I'm just frustrated with the entire situation, and I don't want to be here," he starts, but before I can ask if he has changed his mind about coming to the hospital or point out that it's a bit late for that now if he has, a woman we have not met enters through the back door at the same time she is knocking. Her badge identifies her as a hospital social worker. Nicholas is with her.

"Hello, Mr. and Mrs. Giese. It was nice speaking with Nick tonight. He is so friendly and talkative, he made my job very easy. I know it's been a long night, but please come with me. I'm going to take you to our crisis room. This is John," she opens the door wider to reveal an armed security guard standing behind our son. I think he's armed, anyway. There's a holster on his belt. I don't know if he's carrying a gun or just a taser, and I don't know if I'm thinking clearly enough to tell the difference. "He will sit with you while you wait to speak with the counselor." Then she turns her attention to Nick.

"Guess what?" she whispers. "This room has a TV in it, and you get to control the remote. I'm pretty sure we get Nickelodeon." She waves goodbye, and we follow John down a winding corridor to a small cluster of empty rooms. There is a small couch sitting across from an old box-style television, a desk where John takes a seat behind a computer, and a separate room with more sofas and chairs we can see through large glass windows.

"If they have SpongeBob, am I allowed to watch it?" Nick asks, bouncing with the question.

"Sure." He has never watched a full episode before, but what is the point of keeping your child from cartoons where the characters speak to each other disrespectfully if it has proven to do nothing to stop him from becoming a potential threat to the people in your own house?

As we wait, I use the time to make phone calls and arrange for a friend to pick up Abby and Penny for a sleepover and keep them at her house tomorrow. The hospital says we can only have two visitors with him, and I refuse to leave my son, but Eddie and my mom want to take turns being here with Nicholas. Three full animated shows later, I know it has taken ninety minutes for the door to open when another woman we don't recognize walks in. Upon her arrival, the security guard excuses himself, which strikes me as odd. I suppose he was only there to guard us while watching television. She introduces herself as the counselor on call tonight and apologizes because it has been an especially busy shift.

Separately, she takes turns inviting each of us into the windowed room to sit and talk her through what happened tonight. During my turn I'm distracted by the fact that Nicholas and Eddie are still in the waiting area, in the exact same position that needed an armed guard two minutes ago, but now apparently doesn't. I must seem like a cornered chipmunk as I half-answer her questions, constantly turning to look at the guys and then back at her, wondering if she's concealing a taser of her own. When I finish retelling my mother's version of events, she leans back and asks more questions. It's the same interview we've had with every therapist and examiner.

"What can you tell me about his experience in foster care?" Hardly anything.

"When did you notice the behaviors begin?" When he was a toddler, but no one ever believes me when I say that, so I tell her it's been a few years.

"How does your husband typically handle stress?" Fine. Probably better than most people, really. He's not the problem, I promise. Thank you, no, I don't have a need to discuss him. I take the number for the domestic abuse hotline just to be polite, knowing I'll throw it away when we get home.

"Are there any weapons in your home?"

"No. None."

She pauses and looks directly into my eyes, "It's very important that if there are guns in the home, they are stored securely."

"We really don't have any guns," I promise. "What about kitchen knives and stuff? Should we get a lockbox?"

"That is up to you, but it would not be a bad idea. Do you feel comfortable taking Nicholas home tonight?"

This is where I pause.

"I don't know how to answer that," I tell her honestly. "What is the alternative?"

"Well," she begins, "I would love to help you apply for a classroom aide to work with him in school, or a home-based therapist to come into the house, or a partial placement program where he could receive treatment services during the school day." I would also love all of those things, but not one of them is realistic for our family.

"What are the options for families without Medicaid?" I ask, defeated and exhausted. Her face changes. She moves to the computer and clicks a few buttons, reviewing his file.

"Nicholas is not enrolled in the Access program?" She clicks her tongue. Access is what our state calls their Medicaid program that serves children with special needs. It is aptly named. Without it there is simply no access to most services. We do not have it, so we cannot receive any of the services she is listing.

"Not for lack of trying." My shoulders slump further. I filled out the application again after he received the latest evaluation. The ADHD diagnosis alone should make him eligible, but all I have to show for it is another rejection letter.

"We will send you home with the application tonight. I see no reason he should not qualify." I don't bother telling her how many times I've filled out that same application. She continues, "Without being enrolled in Pennsylvania's Medicaid Access program, we only have two options at the moment. He can either go home if you are comfortable, or we can get you a room here at the ER and attempt to find him an inpatient bed."

We call Eddie and Nicholas back into the room and explain our situation.

"Is the inpatient program here in York?" Eddie asks.

"Unfortunately, no. Not for someone his age with his background. Nicholas would likely be taken to Hershey or Philadelphia. He would stay here in a private room in our Emergency Department and be monitored while we do a bed search."

"I'm sorry, but I don't understand."

She explains that a bed search is simply the term for their hospitals calling others, looking for an empty bed anywhere that can take on a new patient and accept our insurance. There are very few psychiatric hospitals that serve children, and those that do have the option to turn down his case for many reasons. They might not feel they can appropriately serve a child with his particular diagnosis, they could have other patients who would not respond well to having a roommate, our insurance could deny the request, or any number of reasons. She is hopeful but warns it is not unusual for a bed search to take several days, sometimes much longer. Because it is before midnight, they can begin the search immediately, then start again in a few hours if he is denied. Apparently, the process starts all over again from the beginning every time the clock strikes twelve, like a perverse game of Cinderella.

"He needs help, and it sounds like this is the only way to get it," Eddie offers.

"I'm not sure I'm comfortable taking him home without any sort of plan in place to prevent this from happening again," I add.

"That's completely understandable, I will begin the process to get you a room and start our search. Also, please take my business card. This is the crisis line for the hospital," she says circling a phone number in black pen under the hospital logo. "If you call this number, you can speak directly to me or whichever counselor is on staff at that time." I wonder briefly if the school and the therapists know this number exists. If they do, no one told me about it until now. There are only a few days before Thanksgiving, does this mean he will spend the holiday without any family? From what Charlotte has told me, parents are not allowed to see their kids as much in psychiatric hospitals as they are in, what do I call the kind I am standing in? Regular hospitals?

"I'm going to a different hospital?" Nick asks. "Do I get to ride in an ambulance?"

"We think so." I tell him, then turn back to the counselor. "Can you see if they have a bed at Johns Hopkins? Maybe Kennedy Krieger?" I ask, a tiny spec of hope rising in me for the first time tonight. "My sister works there." Although it is across the state line in Baltimore, Kennedy Krieger, a Johns Hopkins affiliate for children with developmental disabilities, is more of a long-term solution and not really a crisis management strategy, and I know that, but their parent hospital, with a psychiatric ward of its own, is one of the best in the world. It is geographically closer than almost any other option. Charlotte could be with him even when I can't, and if we go to Baltimore we would have a lot of other family just minutes away. But it's an extremely long shot to take.

"I can try Hopkins," she looks at me with sympathy. "But I should tell you I've never had a patient successfully admitted there." Like I said, it's a long shot. A very long shot. "The Kennedy Krieger waitlist can be up to a year-long, and it might be a fight with your insurance if there are other options available in Pennsylvania." She shakes her head in a way that lets me know it will never happen. Certainly not tonight.

She moves us to a private room within the emergency department where Nicholas can be under 24-hour surveillance. There are cameras fixed on him and a desk just outside his door that is always staffed. They say we aren't allowed to close the door, and if he needs to use the restroom, they will send a guard. He changes into a gown and hops onto the bed, where he is hooked up to the machines by a nurse so they can monitor his heart rate and stress levels. They check his vital signs and put stickers on his chest and belly to run an EKG. Then we are left alone to wait. Eddie and I sit in the pair of chairs against the wall and since it is now three hours past his bedtime, it isn't long before Nicholas falls asleep.

After what must be another hour I'm surprised to see the newest pastor from our church enter the room, but now that he is here, I think I do remember texting him earlier to ask him to pray.

"Pastor Dan? I'm surprised they let you back. They said we couldn't have more than two visitors here at a time." My voice sounds flat and lifeless.

"Oh, they make an exception for clergy if you ask nicely," he winks.

Nicholas' eyes pop open and he sits straight up in his bed, as animated as ever. "Huh? Oh. Wow. Hi, Pastor Dan. It's me, Nick. I'm in the hospital."

"I see that, Pal. I was worried about you."

"Yeah, I tried to kill my Pumpkin, that's my grandma, but I'm not going to do that anymore. That was not a very good idea. They took my clothes and now I have to wear this polka dot dress. I got to keep my underwear, though, don't worry." Nicholas rushes through his story.

Pastor Dan laughs, "You know, that wasn't really the part I was worried about, but you seem to be doing much better now. I'm glad to see that." Then his face is more somber as he turns back to whisper to Eddie and me. "How is he really doing?"

"Weirdly all right, I guess?" is all I can offer, still seated with my arms clutched tightly around my stomach, which is betraying me by making all sorts of loud gurgling noises and sending the taste of sewage into my mouth.

"We are just supposed to wait here until another hospital can take him, whenever that might be," Eddie adds.

I read an article online about a family that had been waiting a month in another state for an inpatient bed and still hadn't found one at the time the article was published because the facilities near them couldn't serve a child with intellectual disabilities. I wonder if that will also be our fate. I should probably stop reading stories about families like ours. They always seem to be full of despair, and they never offer any real hope or solutions. Tragedy porn, I've heard other friends call it.

Nicholas is so perky and pleasant now that I am second guessing everything. Is it even necessary to send him away? I can't leave him here like this for a month in the emergency room like that other family had to do, that would be insane if he isn't even showing signs of aggression, and it would also cost a bajillion dollars. But if we don't get him help and something worse happens when he comes home, then I will never be able to forgive myself. What if he hurts himself or one of the girls? We still have to do this, right?

Eddie stands and puts a hand on Pastor Dan's shoulder. "Thanks for coming, man. We really appreciate it. I know it's late." Pastor Dan brushes a hand against the air to show that it doesn't matter how late it is, and Eddie leans closer and tries not to let me hear him. "Would you mind staying with Steph for a few minutes? We've been here for hours and I need to go find some food she can eat. I know she didn't eat dinner and she's not looking great."

I stopped eating dairy, gluten, eggs, and meat a few months ago to deal with my headaches. It has worked miracles for the migraines and the vertigo, but there is nothing here in the hospital that fits that menu plan. I must look even worse than I feel, because a few minutes before Pastor Dan arrived a nurse brought Nicholas some Jell-O, left, then came back and handed me a huge Styrofoam cup filled with ginger ale.

Pastor Dan sits next to me and makes awkward conversation until Eddie returns twenty minutes later with a vegetarian burrito bowl and some chips and salsa from the Chipotle a few blocks down the street. I'm surprised they were still open until a glance at the clock tells me it's only slightly past ten-thirty. I don't know how that can be true when it feels like we've been here for a hundred years. Then Pastor Dan leads us in a short prayer and says goodbye, and our little family is alone again. Nicholas and Eddie share the chips while I eat my dinner and sip my ginger ale in silence from the chair at the foot of my son's bed.

I think Pastor Dan also offered to set up a meal train for volunteers to deliver food to our family before he left. A friend has gone to our house to take the girls. I know my mother has been here with us in the hospital tonight, too, and given her story to the counselors, but everything starts to blur together in a foggy haze like a dream sequence from a movie.

A strange new cloud of unease descends upon us because we have no idea where or with whom our son will be living by this time tomorrow. It could be only a matter of hours before we are transporting him. Do we do that, or will he go in an ambulance? How much does all of this cost? If Nick is in a psychiatric hospital, where do Eddie and I go? I cannot start booking hotels without knowing where they are sending us, and even if I did, we would not be able to check into one until the afternoon. What happens if we roll into an unfamiliar city, hours away from home, at 9 am?

At midnight, from our private room, I start texting college friends in the Philadelphia area with vague messages asking if we can stay with them if Nick is admitted to CHOP tonight. *Of course*, they respond. *Hope everything is ok.*

*Thanks*, I text back, suddenly freezing and beginning to shiver. It doesn't make any sense. The hospital is heated and I'm dressed to brave a Pennsylvania winter because, even though we've been here for ages, I never thought to take off my parka. Within minutes my body is shaking so uncontrollably that Eddie takes his winter coat and slips it on top of my own. I believe he's talking to me, but I can't fully understand him because my teeth are chattering so hard now that it's impossible to hear over the noise.

"I think you're in shock." My husband stands and pushes our chairs together, laying me down across them and rubbing my arms roughly for a few seconds before stepping back and leaning his own body against the wall. I feel stupid. My trembling is moving the chairs in a rhythmic thumping against the wall. This is so dumb. Nothing even happened to me. My mother and Nicholas both seem fine, and they are the ones who actually went through their own near-death experiences tonight. Why am I the one going fetal like a drama queen? Maybe I should say trauma queen? I have no control over my own body, but I feel my husband standing over me insisting, "It's okay. It's okay."

Eventually the shaking stops, and I sit up again, still unreasonably cold and now weaker and more exhausted. It's not okay, but at least we have a semblance of a plan. That is, until a nurse enters our room and announces they've found a bed in Allentown. I have no idea where that is.

# Chapter 30

The ride to the hospital is engulfed in a silent, nervous energy. Nicholas has been at KidsPeace for almost a week. We visit every day, but they only allow parents to come for one hour. Because today is Thanksgiving, they've extended the holiday hours and we can have some extra time, depending on how Nicholas reacts. It won't do any good to push him. For the two and a half hours it takes to get there, Eddie and I sit in the front of the blue Chevy pickup and try to make small talk by telling each other things we already know.

"We got a Christmas card from your cousin," I offer.

"Yeah, I saw it on the counter," he responds, fidgeting with the heating vent. After a few more minutes of silence, he reaches out with, "Do you think we should stop for milk on the way home?"

I shrug. He doesn't see me, but it doesn't matter because we're both too exhausted to pretend to try for normalcy anymore. It feels like there should be more important things to talk about, but what else is there to say? I vaguely remember Eddie suggesting that I sleep, but adrenaline and anxiety reject that idea entirely. He turns on the speakers and I'm thankful that he took the time, although I'm not sure when, to create a playlist of worship music. We don't have the energy to pray, but we can repeat the words we know by heart. The remainder of the trip is sprinkled with our sporadic singing and occasional sobs. Eventually we are silent once again. It might be a beautiful drive through the rolling hills of Allentown if I were allowing myself to feel. It's easier to go numb. Just like ice on a wound makes the pain go away, but only temporarily, hearts work the same way. People still bruise, regardless of the ice. I suppose the brief relief from shutting down and choosing to be cold seems worth it when it gives us a minute to breathe, but it also shuts out the warmth that fuels our relationships. I think the ice that numbs the pain is the same coldness that makes relationships die. I don't want that to happen to us, but I'm just too tired to stop it if it does.

Every time we pull in for gas, I think how hard this journey must be on families who don't have the resources. There isn't a direct bus route or a train, but at least we have a car. Not everyone does. Not everyone has a job with a flexible schedule, paid time off, and the ability to work from home if necessary, but Eddie does. Who knows how much the insurance company will be willing to pay, especially if he needs to stay longer than the measly ten days covered in our plan. Thankfully, the staff told us that the average length of a first stay is about five days, unless he exhibits any dangerous behaviors that would extend that timeframe.

Still, how does anyone afford this? But then what choice is there? The gasoline alone costs three hundred dollars every week. How do struggling families find the money, not to mention the time off work?

The empty waiting room that greets us day after day during the one and only visiting hour tells me that they probably can't. The kids are suffering for it, alone and scared, living with strangers in a residential psych ward. Some of them are only seven years old. Eddie and I asked if we could split our visit and take turns talking to the other patients, or have them join us to play a game with Nick. It's heartbreaking to see these children so alone. The answer was no. We aren't allowed to talk to any of the other children because of confidentiality and safety rules.

The hospital is the size of a small college campus, sprawling over several acres of land in the middle of nowhere. We park and sign in at the front desk, waiting to be escorted to the appropriate wing. I wander to the bathroom and notice the angel tree sitting in the middle of the hallway is still full of tags saying things like *Sarah, age 11 wants socks, pony tail holders, and puzzles*. Every piece of paper represents a child who won't be getting a Christmas gift this year unless someone takes it off the tree and returns the tag attached to a present. I want to take all of them, but I don't know if we will be able to afford to fill them all, and the sign propped up on the table says the deadline is next Wednesday. I don't want to risk removing the tags and keeping someone else from trying. I know I'm not supposed to do it, but I take out my phone and snap a picture of each tag before I slink back to the waiting area. As we wait, I edit the names and ages out of the pictures and post them into my writing group. They have been asking how to help our family, and this seems like something I know these ladies would be happy to do.

*We've got this*, they respond immediately. *Every one of those tags is getting filled.* They start sending money to my PayPal account and making Amazon orders. I post the tags on my personal social media account as well, and I ask our local friends if they can help. It feels good to take control in a positive way and be able to do something. Eventually, a nurse holding a clipboard stands in the hallway and calls out, "Parents for Nicholas." She's ready to take us back to him.

Before we knew better, I think I thought it would be more sterile. Maybe I expected hospital gowns or the harsh kind of neon light that hums and takes your eyes a few minutes to adjust, or the clean, artificial citrus smell of antiseptic. In reality, although the facility is clean, everything smells like old urine and most of the spaces are empty. Heavy wooden furniture, purposefully too big and bulky to move, randomly punctuates otherwise vast carpeted areas. It's the same kind of solid, pine and plaid utilitarian furniture used in dorm rooms and elementary schools, built for function and cost efficiency. There are chips in the paint, and I don't have to touch the cement-colored carpet to know that it might as well be sandpaper. The stains that dot its surface could be from yesterday or ten years ago and no one would know the difference.

We're standing in the center of a web of hallways and common areas. The largest rooms are completely empty in a way that makes it obvious that aesthetics and objects are secondary here. No one has bothered to make it feel like a home. The only color comes from the windows in the common area. They look like stained glass, but on closer inspection it's easier to make out the seasonal paintings and sketches done with window markers. Children have drawn snowmen with crooked smiles and rainbow flags with the letters LGBTQ inside of them. I see a few Santas and flowers. Briefly I wonder how many of those artists are here for the same reason Nick is. I don't think any of the drawings are his, I would recognize his work, wouldn't I?

Patients walk through the common area in sweatpants with socks on their feet. It looks like a group of kids headed back to the locker room after gym class more than anything. A few are friendly and ask if we are here to visit Nick. Others avoid us and are silent, still more only speak to the staff. Adults easily identified by their matching polo shirts are sprinkled throughout the open space. The only thing unusual is the lack of furniture. A burly man donned in the royal blue reserved for staff brings over a few chairs he's retrieved from a closet. They're the same kind of hard plastic I remember from my elementary school cafeteria. "I'll go get him for you. We'll be right back." He smiles.

In the meantime, we need to check our coats, phones, wallets, and car keys with the desk. Everything else stayed locked in the car. Eddie and I wait as the nurse in her standard blue polo shirt distributes evening doses of medication and Dixie cups filled with soap and shampoo to patients ready for the shower. When she's finished, she takes our coats and disappears around a corner. I called ahead and asked if we could bring Uno cards for the visit, so I have the red box, fraying at its corners, in my hand and nothing to do but fidget with it as we wait.

My mind drifts to my sister. Nicholas loves his Aunt Charlotte and she can connect to him in a way that no one else can. My sister has always been the wild, uncontained, unpredictable one in our family and she has a gift for seeing diamonds when other people see coal. She's the fun aunt who takes a week off of work to follow her favorite band, bring the kids to Go-Kart racing, or stays up with them eating candy and watching movies we probably wouldn't allow at home, but she's also strict in a way kids respect and respond to. She has a slender build, but over twenty years of competitive soccer experience have her muscle-toned. Ink is scattered on her arms and back, and she has never been afraid to tell anyone exactly what is on her mind. Charlotte is like a tattooed, punk rock military captain. If she ever met the singer P!nk in real life, I imagine they'd become fast friends because my sister shares the same vibe: power laced with mischievous approachability, all in a tiny little package.

Charlotte works in a similar facility in Maryland, but her focus is on autistic youth. I can't remember her exact job title, but I think it's something along the lines of Personal Care Assistant. Her patients aren't as high-functioning as the ones here on Nick's unit. She has scars on her arms from showers and diaper changes gone south, but she loves her patients, especially the difficult ones. If she were here she would be wearing one of the blue polo shirts. I wish my sister were here. Well, actually I guess I wish no one were here, but if Nick has to be in a place like this I wish my sister were with him. She'd dive right into conversations about video games and Star Wars movies with enthusiasm and not bother to sit here overthinking the way I do. She would know the right questions to ask the staff, and she'd probably make fast friends with all of them as well. She'd leave with five phone numbers and still be texting with one or two of her new friends this time next year.

"Oh, Uno. We used to have that game," a different male employee pulls me out of my head so I have to acknowledge him. My smile is a reflex, once I put it on it feels out of place, but there doesn't seem to be a more appropriate facial expression for the occasion, so I leave it on my face.

"No more? What happened to it?" As soon as I ask, I realize it's a stupid question.

"Things don't seem to last long around here," he's also smiling and friendly. All of the staff is. The older, muscular man has a cadence that reminds me of my uncle. He introduces himself as George and I tell him we are Nicholas' parents. He nods.

"You know, we aren't supposed to have favorites, but I like that Nicholas. He's a real good boy." George winks at me. He probably says that to everyone, but his kindness chips a hole in the wall I'm trying to keep up, and a lump in my throat threatens to release a deluge of tears before I'm ready for them. Not yet. I need to look calm and upbeat during this visit. I swallow hard and nod at him. I want to ask him if it's all right to leave the Uno cards as a donation, but before I can find the words he starts to walk away.

"Here he comes. My man." George sees Nicholas enter

the room before we do and crosses the space between them to give our son a high-five. "You've got visitors today."

Nick stiffens his arms and shakes his entire upper body while he smiles. He's already stimming more than usual.

"Yep. I do." We sent clothes, and we were careful to be sure they met the criteria (no draw strings, no violent scenes or weapons on t-shirts), but he's wearing plain grey sweats I don't recognize and white socks. None of the patients wear shoes. The borrowed white t-shirt is stained with food from some previous meal, but at least he looks comfortable. There is masking tape on his glasses, and his hair is jutting out in every direction. Patients don't receive haircuts. I asked. Sometimes stylists will volunteer their time and come in, but that hasn't happened for the past several months.

Eddie and I stand up to hug him. When my son walks toward me slowly I have to fight against my instinct to flinch. When we hug his hair tickles my nose. I wonder what happened to his glasses, but I'm not sure I want to know.

"You look good, Buddy" Eddie's voice sounds so normal and even. I don't know how he does that.

"Yeah, thanks. You guys look good too," Nick hops and shakes his hands in the air. "I'm glad I can see you today."

"We're glad too. Are you having a good day?"

"Well, it's mostly good and a little bit in the middle. I didn't get restrained today." He's sitting now, bouncing in the chair. He seems as much like himself as I could have hoped to see. Yesterday we received a call to inform us that he was put into an isolation room for about an hour after attacking a member of the staff. He was mad at her because she gave him three check marks on his behavior chart, which meant he would receive an early bedtime. He earned the check marks by writing "Help! These losers are killing us" on the wall with a marker he was given for a craft project.

"That is good. No one wants you to need to be restrained."

"Yep. I don't really remember the rest though. Mom," he changes the subject, "why does your face look like that?"

I'm not sure what my face was doing, but I raise my eyebrows and smile in an exaggerated way. "I'm just a little tired. It was a long drive. What did you have for lunch today?" I can always count on Nicholas to be willing to talk about food.

"I didn't eat lunch yet. Yesterday I had spaghetti, and salad, and applesauce. I put ranch dressing on my salad, but they don't have any croutons. The spaghetti tasted different. I like the one at home better, I ate it all, though. Did Uncle Trey come for Thanksgiving?"

"Not yet. We are waiting until you're home to celebrate." There's a boxed meal from a Bob Evans restaurant waiting at the house for us later today. The church delivered it. They budget for several catered meals each year and deliver them to families in need. This year that was us. I'll cook our real meal when my son is back where he belongs. Today's dinner will be charity microwaved on paper plates.

"Did you go outside today? It's pretty sunny out there," I ask. It's funny how people always resort to talking about the weather when they don't know what else to do.

"Not today. I went outside on Sunday, I think?" He offers. Sunday was five days ago. Eddie is much better at filling the silence. They talk about Star Wars and new movies that are expected to be released next year. After a bit, Nick changes out of the blue. He stops bouncing and starts darting his eyes in different directions, distracted by both the kids in the hallway and the television in the lounge. He's finished.

"Well, thanks for coming to see me. Can we be done now?" He's pleasant, but we agreed to let him lead this, so Eddie and I agree to say goodbye. It's only been fifteen minutes. We hug goodbye and retrieve our coats from the nurse. George walks by once more and nods at me. "He's a good boy." He repeats. "One of my favorites. He'll be home before you know it." Today I can add George to the list of things I'm thankful for.

# Chapter 31

*November 2018*

George was right, Nicholas only stayed in the hospital for a week. We celebrated with a second Thanksgiving feast when he returned, and this time I actually cooked. But what we didn't understand was that being released from a psychiatric hospital is not the same as being released from other hospitals. I expected him to be healed, just like when he broke his arm falling off his bike, and the doctors made it better. Instead, we learned that the goal of inpatient treatment is only stabilization. They adjust his medication and keep him under observation until he can go few days without hurting himself or anyone else, then they send him home in order to open a bed for all of the other children who are waiting in emergency room beds all around the country.

He came home and we added more medicines to his schedule, switched to a different psychiatrist, and worked with Mr. Shrader to put more supports in place at school. Nicholas now has prescriptions for four different pills, which we administer three times a day. I meet with the school nurse to go over what he needs at school, and I schedule more psychiatrist appointments and blood work. One of his medications is a controlled substance, so I have to pick up the script in person every thirty days and hand-deliver it to the pharmacist. The insurance won't cover that one, so it becomes another three-hundred-and-fifty-dollar payment each month. When his medication costs are added to the therapy, psychiatry, pediatrician, and hospital and insurance bills, the cost to keep Nicholas stable averages out to well over a thousand dollars every month.

The medication is keeping him alive, and the rest of us by extension, but they have nasty side effects for Nicholas. He has gained over fifty pounds in the last few years, going from an underweight seven-year-old to a clinically obese pre-teen since starting them. His triglyceride count is so high that we are worried he may have a heart attack before entering middle school. Despite their negative effects on his physical health, the medicines worked for a while to subdue the violence and the hallucinations, but they don't account for the fact that he picked up even more unpleasant behaviors in the hospital.

Until he went there, he didn't know what the f-word and the b-word were, but he picked them up from other patients and now he screams them at me every time he gets upset. When I send him to his room for a time-out now, he strips off his clothes and pees on things, the same way he saw his roommate do at the hospital. He has also learned how to escape out of his bedroom window. Sometimes he streaks naked through the neighborhood. We put an alarm on the window, but it doesn't stop him. He will still run naked and barefoot through the snow. We are weighing if it is more dangerous to have this behavior continue or glue the window shut, knowing that it would be harder to escape in a fire.

Despite those behaviors being hard to deal with, at least they aren't life-threatening. That is, until recently. Just like last year after October came, things all went downhill quickly. The anniversary of his adoption seems to be a trigger, or at least that's what everyone on his team agrees is probably the case. This time he attacked me, screaming about how and where he wanted to stab me, and the only reason no one was hurt is because the sharper knives were already locked away. He is spending Thanksgiving in the same inpatient hospital where he spent the holiday last year.

I can't think about it without my breath getting short and my fingers beginning to shake, but it still plays clearly in my mind.

The girls playing with stuffed animals in the living room while Nicholas is pinching two LEGO bricks together. Me making dinner, cutting vegetables with a paring knife when the next thing I know, he is lunging at me, screaming.

"I need that knife now, Mom. Give me the fucking knife. I need it. I am going to put it in your tummy, and your face, and your eyes." I throw the knife toward the front door, trying to get it out of his reach before his fists flew into me. We are almost the same size now, but he doesn't have the motor skills he would need to fight me. I can tackle him to the ground. He spits and bites and scratches, and I already feel my arm starting to burn from an area his finger nails caught on the way down. I'm bleeding a little bit, but none of the kids are hurt and from the floor he can't do much more damage. I don't know what else to do, so I sit on him and hold his wrists in each of my hands to try to keep him away from the girls, and I tell him I can't get up until he calms down.

"Abby," I try to keep my voice calm. "Take your sister to the playroom and lock the door, please. I need to talk to your brother for a few minutes."

My nine-year-old guides the first-grader past me and to the bonus room above our garage as I crouch over her brother. We've practiced this with the girls before. There is a box waiting for them upstairs with their favorite things in it: coloring supplies, Play-Doh, and Shopkins figurines. Their job is to hide themselves away and do things they enjoy until they hear me say the code words "oatmeal with bananas" and know it is safe to come out again. I wait until I hear the door close before I address my son.

"What are you doing? Like, what is happening in your head that makes you think any of this is a good idea?"

He just spits at my face and pushes his pelvis up, trying to knock me off of him.

"Look, man. I want to let you go. I have stuff to do, and I don't think you like acting this way, but you have to calm down. I have to be able to trust you to be safe. Can you do that?"

His face is turning red, and he only grunts. It's not really an answer, but I don't want to be making it hard for him to breathe. I let go of his wrists. Immediately, he digs his nails into my thighs and scratches, hard. "Dumb shit bitch, let me go. I need the knife. Give me the knife."

With his hands free it is easier for him to fight back, and he escapes me and runs toward the front door. Toward the knife. It's a tiny kitchen tool that can barely cut through the skin of a tomato and shouldn't do much damage, but as Nicholas picks it up, he mumbles to himself, "Good. Now I can cut out my eyes."

Before my brain can think to tell my body how to react, the front door opens, and I scream three words at my husband, who is just returning from work. "Take him down." Eddie tackles Nicholas to the floor once again and secures the knife, while I grab the kitchen phone to call 911.

My mother walks up the basement steps and asks, "Why is everyone screaming up here? I heard a bunch of yelling." I shake my head at her and point at the phone so she can listen to me recount the past five minutes to the dispatcher.

They send an ambulance and two police cars. It takes an hour before the ambulance crew calms Nicholas down enough to be safe for them to transport him to the hospital.

We leave the girls with my mother again, and Eddie and I follow in his truck. An unexpected snow storm is starting to coat the roads with ice.

Arriving at the hospital, we are directed to the all-too-familiar waiting room in the ER, where we stay for over an hour before we receive any news about Nicholas. Finally, a woman wearing a light pink sweater arrives. A hospital badge is clipped to the waistband of her pants.

"Mr. and Mrs. Giese? I am the social worker on staff tonight. Can you come with me for a few minutes?"

"Where's Nicholas?" I don't bother with any

pleasantries.

"You can see him in a few minutes. Our nurses are helping to get him settled in his room. In the meantime, can you walk me through your version of what happened tonight?"

I tell her everything. I know I didn't handle it well. I should not have sat on top of him like that, and I should not have thrown a knife across the room, but I still don't know what I should have done instead. Eddie interjects to describe his own involvement when I reach that part of the story. I hope offering complete honesty will work in our favor, but I'm terrified that it could backfire and make her launch an investigation into whether our girls are safe at home. I don't know if Nicholas is old enough to be considered a perpetrator, but once he is if this behavior is not under control then the social workers could force us to decide between removing him from our home or losing our other children. Without access to other support programs, as a child with an intellectual disability and a history of violence, our house is Nicholas' only option. No one else will take him.

Hospitals don't hold people indefinitely. Residential programs tend to reject cases like his because they don't have the resources to handle him, and without state funding they won't even consider admitting him in the first place. Not that we have any resources to handle him ourselves, but it falls to us to deal with it at home anyway. If we can't handle it (and apparently do so better than the professionals, since they have the option to give up and we don't), we could be charged with child endangerment for knowingly subjecting our girls to his behavior. The only thing preventing that from happening already is his age. Until now, he's always been young enough to not be too scary. We have to get him access to Medicaid or else this is going to get very bad, very quickly. Without the funding that will get him access to other programs, the only other realistic option, especially as he gets older, will be to press charges against Nicholas and send him to jail. There, he would be monitored and receive medical care, everyone else in our family would be safe, and we would not face bankruptcy from medical bills. But we would be purposefully choosing to have a child with special needs incarcerated just for having a disability he can't control. How is a parent supposed to make a choice like that? How has our country allowed itself to get to the point where that is even an option?

"That sounds very similar to what Nicholas told me." The social worker is friendly and pleasant, but she reveals nothing and sends us back to our seats in the waiting room.

Eventually someone comes to lead us to our son. Once again, he's wearing a hospital gown, hooked up to beeping monitors.

The social worker leaves and we sit with him, quietly leaning against the wall from our space on the twin chairs as Nicholas tosses in the bed. Sometimes Eddie tries to make light conversation about a Star Wars movie or share a memory about a time he and Nicholas went fishing together. Nicholas is not acting like himself. He's much more agitated than the last time we were here. He doesn't want to talk to anyone about anything. After a few hours lying restlessly in bed, it all becomes too much for him. He bursts out of his bed and throws himself at Eddie, screaming profanities.

The attack only lasts a few seconds. Before we realize what is happening, the tiny room is filled with five additional people wearing scrubs and lab coats. One of the men turns to us and says with authority, "I need you two to step out into the hall. Now."

Shaken and confused, I follow Eddie out the door, feeling like we have been sent to the principal. Did we do something wrong? Are they mad at us? What happens now? What are they doing to our son? Will there be handcuffs or a straightjacket? Will they ever let us back in the room? We walk without purpose through the hall and find ourselves at a dead end. Eddie sits on a window ledge and gives in to the emotion he's been carrying. In the twenty years I have known him, I have never heard him sob like this. His entire body shakes as tears and snot fall through his hands and onto his lap, leaving small dark marks on his jeans. Until now, I hadn't realized that I was crying, too.

A young nurse approaches us, and I brace myself for her to tell us more bad news about our son. Instead, she smiles sincerely at my husband. "I just have to tell you that you are good parents. I know this is hard. But we have cameras in that room and we have been watching. We can see how much you love him. This is not your fault. We are going to do everything we can to get your boy some help."

The movement in Eddie's shoulders slows as he brings his head up to look at her in stunned silence. She nods at him and turns to face me, "Is it okay to give you a hug?" I blink and bring my chin down, then up again, just once. She wraps her arms around me tightly for a brief moment, then tells us she needs to go check on some patients, but we will see her around, and to holler if we need anything before she walks away.

Eddie wipes his face with his hands and inhales, looking back toward Nicholas' room. The extra staff seems to be leaving. "Well," my husband prompts me. "I guess we should be getting back in there."

Nicholas stays in the Emergency Room for three more days waiting for a bed. As we wait, Eddie and I take turns staying with him at the hospital. Sometimes the nurses encourage us to go home and get some rest for the night. Finally, a bed opens, and he is admitted back to the same inpatient program he attended last year.

Before the ambulance arrives to transport him back to Allentown, I sit next to his bed in the Emergency Room. I don't like crying in front of him, but the tears spill out too easily. He is going to miss Thanksgiving again. Two years in a row. Nicholas always said Thanksgiving was his favorite holiday because "It's a whole day to eat as much as you want and be happy about all the stuff we have." Now it will be forever associated with hospitals.

"Don't be sad, Mom." It seems so backwards that my fifth grader, donned in borrowed clothes on his raised bed with the paper-thin sheets, should be the one comforting me. "I have to do this. I will try to be good this time and ignore the bullies. But I have to go. I have to learn how to stop hurting people. I'll try to be back for Christmas."

I take a deep breath and reach out for his hand. He lets

me hold onto him and wonders out loud, "Do you think Santa understands how brains work? Like, does he know they can get sick? Because I promise I'm trying really hard to be on the nice list, but I just don't think it's working. Do you think he will still bring me any presents, even though I did that bad stuff?"

"Yes, Baby," I pat his hand. "I'm sure he understands."

"Nicholas?" A nurse I don't recognize pokes her head into the room, after knocking just once. "Your ambulance is ready for you. Time to say goodbye to Mom." She helps him out of bed and hands him his shoes, and he gives me a hug and says goodbye.

"Wait," I stop them as the nurse leads my son away. "He needs his glasses." I take the case out of my purse and put them on his face, then pull him into a long, final hug. "Be good, try hard." I whisper into his hair.

"I will, Mom. I have to go. Tell Abby and Penny I said bye and I love them. Dad, too."

And then he's gone.

At home, we continue to fight with insurance companies and collect huge bills, which seem to be piling up more each day.

"I don't understand how they can do this, he has like six different eligible diagnoses. We literally mailed the application from a hospital where the billing department helped us fill it out," I slam the latest Medicaid rejection onto the desk in our home office. The inpatient psychologist added Intermittent Explosive Disorder, also called IED, to our ever-expanding list of labels during Nicholas' first stay when the hospital staff observed how his reactions seem to come out of nowhere, with no identifiable triggers. The disorder is exactly what it sounds like, it's just a name to give some sort of rationale to the fact that our son sporadically explodes with rage for no apparent reason. For what it's worth (which isn't much) the inpatient psychologist said it was her professional opinion that Nicholas was most definitely on the autism spectrum, but that's not a diagnosis they make in-house.

Regardless of if we can get an autism label, now Nicholas has several eligible diagnoses that should qualify him for government insurance. Simply having ADHD is supposed to be enough, and we have a general mood disorder, IED, and an intellectual disability in addition to that, yet all of our attempts to apply for Medicaid are still being turned down.

We have reached the limit of what the insurance company is willing to pay. There are ten different bills labeled "Explanation of Benefits" spread out on the desk, and between them they tell us their company is charging thirty thousand dollars in the "Amount We Owe" category. He has only been there for a few weeks. If they reject further treatment then there is no other option that private insurance covers. He might not even be able to go back to an inpatient hospital without Medicaid and their additional funding, it could just become a cycle of us taking him to the ER and them sending him home because no one will pay for him to receive treatment. If he continues to be dangerous at home and our insurance won't allow him to receive treatment, then we won't have any other options but to surrender our parental rights to get him help. At that point, the only option is to place him back into foster care because the state will be forced to do what the doctors recommend if he is a foster child.

I hate that it is a business decision for the insurance companies, whether or not the life of a fifth-grader is cost-effective to attempt to save. Sorry, little boy, you've reached your quota for suicide attempts this year. If you simply must continue to suffer from mental illness, then please come back to us again in January when the deductibles re-set and the timing is more convenient. Until then, best of luck.

The insurance company, to their credit, did assign a case manager to our family. Thus far her one and only suggestion has been that Nicholas needs to receive Medicaid and an insistence that he qualifies, but she doesn't know why his forms won't go through, so that has not been super helpful.

"We can file an appeal," Eddie tries to find something positive to say, but he can read just as well as I can. The date to appeal the decision has already passed. They had ninety days to get us the letter, and while it is dated within that timeframe, we received it in our mailbox several weeks later than the date stamped on the letter, and there was a short appeal window. We didn't even get the notice saying Nicholas was rejected until the time to reverse the decision was behind us. Now it's too late. I will try again of course, but as I have been on the receiving end of these rejections almost every year since our son was two, my hopes are not very high.

"It would just be nice if one damn thing would go well for us, this is insane. There has to be some other way to get him help. Why is their entire system based on sending written correspondence through the postal service like this is 1873?" I grab my laptop off the desk and stick it under my arm along with a tangled pair of headphones, then march myself to our room and hide in our bed with my computer. Eddie sighs and leaves me alone. He shuts himself on the other side of the door to take care of dinner and bath time. He knows I won't come out until I have formed a plan for our next step.

# Chapter 32

I call every one of Nicholas' providers. Most are sympathetic, but they do not have any useful advice. His new psychiatrist's office, however, does offer some practical support. There's a Medicaid specialist downtown. They give me her name and help schedule an appointment. The rules have changed recently, and we can apply again. They say Nicholas is more likely to get accepted if she helps to fill out the paperwork. I wish someone would have told me about this option eight years ago, but I'm grateful to know it exists, and now I have a bit of hope. If he qualifies, it will be retroactive for ninety days, and they will cover the most recent hospital stays and ambulance bills. About thirty-five thousand dollars' worth of our medical debt would disappear, he could have access to therapy in our home, or more time in the hospital or residential placement if he needs it, and they would also start to cover the cost of his medications.

Not a single provider mentions it, but in my frenzied

internet searches I discover something else. Pennsylvania apparently has a program called MH-IDD, which stands for Mental Health, Intellectual and Developmental Disabilities. It was created to serve people exactly like Nicholas. Their website says they offer respite support to families, provide funding, and have resources for adults so that as Nicholas grows, he could receive job training or help with appropriate housing. Why, after an entire decade of seeking help for my son through five schools, multiple therapists, psychiatrists, doctors, and hospital stays, did no one tell me this? Do they just not know either? Did they assume I already knew? Whatever. At least now we have the information. I print that application, fill out most of it, and mail what we have, then ask Eddie to handle a few more forms that need doctors' notes. He promises to handle it.

I walk into the kitchen to get dinner started and freeze when a knife stares back at me from the sink. That knife. Someone must have casually used it recently to chop a carrot or a potato, but all I can see is a would-be murder weapon. That's the knife that could have killed my children or my mother, and now I'm supposed to just squirt some Dawn on it and wipe it off as if nothing ever happened? My heartbeat races in protest, and my hands forget how to work. None of my thoughts are coherent. I don't have any idea how dinner got itself on the table. I think I ate, but who could know?

After a few days of walking around the house like zombies, Eddie stops me in the hall outside of Nicholas' bedroom.

"Hey, I've been thinking." He stands close enough to

rest his chin on the top of my head. "We can't bring another baby into this house."

"All right, you made your point." I pull away. He's right, but I still resent it.

"But. Let me finish."

I look up at him. "But?"

"Maybe it's time to think about fostering again."

"What? Are you serious?" There's no way that is happening. "No one is going to give us another kid right now." I am an emotional mess. That is a terrible idea.

"Maybe, but I'm not so sure. Think about it," he says. We have always said we wanted to foster older children once the three we currently have are grown. "Why not? There's no such thing as a foster family who is not dealing with trauma, and we basically have a PhD in it. There is a huge need for homes for older kids, it wouldn't affect your health like another pregnancy, it might help Nick to have someone else in the house who relates to his feelings about his bio family, and we have a ton of experience dealing with navigating therapy." I take a deep breath. It's a lot to think about. Eddie goes on, "I think the social workers might actually see how we are dealing with Nick's issues as a positive. We know where the resources are now, and we've shown we will fight to get our kids access to them."

I want a baby, but he's right. It wouldn't be a responsible decision for me to go through a pregnancy that puts my health in jeopardy or for us to have a vulnerable infant in this house while Nick is acting out. But, certain extremes notwithstanding, most of our son's behavioral issues are pretty run-of-the-mill for older kids in care. Any social worker whose focus is on foster care and adoption will understand them. We could request an older child, and it would be seen as a positive. Most people want to adopt babies. Homes for older kids are few and far between, especially with parents who are already practicing trauma-informed care. Nothing we are going through with Nicholas will scare a caseworker away from our family. If anything, they would see it as proof that we know how to handle a behavioral or mental health crisis and that we are more than willing to stick with an adoption, even when things get tough. We also have the added benefit of a third adult who is a licensed therapist living in our home. They would look at us as a potential home for their most difficult cases.

"I guess it wouldn't hurt to get re-certified. You know we are insane, right?" Things have changed quite a bit since we were trained the first time. New laws are in place, and this is a different state. We will have to do the entire process over from the beginning.

"Well, yeah, I thought that was a given."

"We doing this?"

"I think so, as long as Pumpkin is on board."

# Chapter 33

It has only been five days since he came home, but the lump of anxiety in my chest and the logical part of my brain are starting to become allies in a way that feels unfamiliar. I've spent years worrying about things that hopefully would never happen, preparing for the worst, but using logic to talk myself down and build hope. I can't do that anymore. They are on the same team now, reason and worry. Anxiety is supposed to be unfounded fear. All mothers worry about what ifs and lack of control. This is different. The fears have manifested into reality.

The doctors said he can't go back to school, but the appointment with the partial program isn't until next week. I'm not sure what to expect from a partial, but we were told it's just like the hospital, except he can come home at night. He will only be partially hospitalized, hence the name. There are doctors and therapists on staff, and they will be able to observe him and make changes to medication, but at the end of the day he can come back to us and sleep in his own bed. Even then, once the intake meeting is complete, we still have to wait until they have a spot for him and the insurance clears. For now, we're stuck in limbo. He can't live in the hospital forever, but he's not safe enough to go to school or stay home without help. But since it takes time and paperwork to establish the help, we need to deal with it by ourselves at home until all the proper channels have been followed. No one knows how long that will take. Every day the hospital or the insurance or the therapists call to follow up and make sure we are going to our appointments and reiterate that it's not safe to have him home without resources. Except, for the time being, that's exactly what we are being forced to do.

I feel like a soldier in my own house, always scanning our surroundings, looking for things that could be used as weapons, whether to remove them or position myself to use them first. Earlier, I moved the toilet brush out of the kids' bathroom. It was metal. I couldn't take that chance. I also packed the trophies from ballet and the Pinewood Derby into keepsake bins. My eyes look at anything sharp and hard differently now. As I walk in front of him down the stairs, I realize I'm leaving myself too vulnerable and move aside to let him pass me. I flinch reflexively as he brushes past. He smells like pre-teen body odor and a unkept public toilet. He calls that smell "buttery pee" and for some reason, he's developed an obsession with it.

"I'm not going to hurt you, Mom." He reads my body language correctly and rolls his eyes. I nod back at him, with purposeful eye contact and force my tightly closed lips to smile, afraid any other reaction might set him off. He gets upset if I breathe too heavily. I've made a habit of sucking in and biting the inside of my cheeks to stay quiet, and every time I do it aggravates the open wound. I don't realize I'm doing it until I can taste blood. Every cell in my body is screaming at me to retreat, go to another room, calm down. Whatever you do, don't sigh. I can't risk setting him off again, I'm the only adult here, and there are other children who have only me to protect them.

It was easier when he was gone, and I hate myself for admitting that truth. I want to want him here, but honestly, the person I want back just doesn't exist right now. My son is standing right in front of me, yet somehow he's gone, and I hate this. I wish there were a stronger word than hate. I try to convince myself that I can hate a situation and still love the person who caused it. That has to be true, or what is the point?

Yesterday won't stop playing over and over in my mind, like an awful movie, and I resent everything about my reality. Yesterday was the day he tried to attack the younger kids. There wasn't a reason, although I wish we could find one because if there were a cause it would be so much easier to find a solution. There never is, though; all they did was have the nerve to exist. Penny was sitting on the sofa and Abby walked from the hallway into the living room. Nicholas' mood turned on a dime and he lunged at them, cussing and screaming that he was going to kill them. He swung as hard as he could and tried to punch Penny, but she is small and fast, and she ducked out of his way. I still don't know why. Maybe he heard Penny breathe or he didn't like the speed at which Abby was walking. Who knows? He went from zero to a hundred million in a millisecond. Intermittent Explosive Disorder on full display, he exploded without warning for absolutely no reason at all.

Adrenaline and a primal need to protect my other children gave me the strength to tackle Nicholas to the floor and hold him there before he got to the girls. I sat on top of him as he thrashed and kicked and tried to bite me, but I put his own arm in his mouth and held it there. I shouldn't have done that, but I couldn't risk letting go of him for enough time to get a kitchen towel or something else for him to bite. He chewed a chunk of skin off his wrist while he squirmed on the floor. Abby shut herself into her room, and Penny curled into the fetal position, hugging her knees and screaming at her brother to just stop it. After five or six minutes, he did. His demeanor changed, he started taking deeper breaths, and he was calm again. He apologized.

It would be so much easier to just go. Or not. I wouldn't get far. I know I couldn't live with the guilt, and there's nowhere to go even if I did. I don't have a job and I'm not healthy enough to get one. I have to actively push away the fantasy of driving to the bank, taking half the money out of our joint checking account, ditching my phone and my minivan, and taking a cab to a hotel. Maybe just for a few days. I'd come back. Eventually. Probably. I can't let that play out too long in my mind because I'm afraid if I actually think it through, then I'm likely to do it.

The smell snaps me back to reality. He needs a shower, and I can't think of a single thing I'd rather deal with less.

"Ni-ick?" I force a sing-song quality into my voice. "In five minutes, it's time to get ready for your shower. Or a bath. You decide." I hope by giving him some advanced warning and a choice about the mode of cleanliness, I can head off some of the push-back I know I'm going to get.

"Ugh. Whatever." Indifference is something I might be able to work with. After five minutes, I try to continue to give him choices while I direct him toward the shower. What shirt will you wear? Can I get you a towel? He enters the bathroom without fighting, and I try to give him as much privacy as I can by stepping out into the hall and pulling the door almost closed. I'm really not supposed to do that, someone should always have eyes on him, that's been made very clear, but he's eleven. There's no eleven-year-old boy in the world who wants his mother to watch him shower.

Five minutes pass, and the water still isn't on. I peek through the crack and I can see his bare feet standing on the grey and white tile. His legs are so hairy it would be easy to mistake them for a grown man's.

"Nick?" I raise my voice an octave and try to keep it perky. "You need to get into the water."

"No, I'm not doing that." His tone is flat and lifeless. It sounds completely different than a few minutes earlier. I'm not talking to my son anymore. I don't know who this version of him is, but it's becoming too familiar and I wish I knew how to make it leave.

"Do you need some help? I can help you. Here, I'll come turn on the water." I straighten my shoulders and hold my head up, trying to project confidence and control as I go in.

"Get out." He's using the same emotionless tone, standing stark naked in front of the bathtub.

"Here, Honey, we'll do a super quick bath." I walk over and reach out toward the faucet. Before I realize what's happening, he lunges forward. I hadn't noticed until now that his right hand is covered in shit. As in literal feces. He holds it high and attempts to smear it on my face, but he's clumsy and it's easy to dodge him. That makes him angry and I resign myself to another battle. I step backward so I don't have to take my eyes off him and use my leg to shut the door quickly, then reach back and lock myself in with him to keep the other kids out.

"Nick. Just get in the shower." I am calm but trying to maintain some semblance of control. It might be nice to at least pretend I'm in charge.

"You're a dick bitch, Mom. Fuck shit bitch." He repeats a nonsensical string of curse words he learned from other patients at the hospital and a small laugh escapes me in a puff of air because this entire situation is so far beyond ridiculous.

"Ok. Just move. You smell, and I'd like to get this over with." That's when he snaps. It's my fault. I knew as soon as it came out of my mouth that I shouldn't have mentioned the smell. He snarls at me, grabs his penis, and pulls it in a twisting, violent way that seems like it should be extremely painful. He isn't feeling anything. He seems completely hollow, except for the desire to cause hurt in any way he can. Nick lunges at me again and I really don't think he even knows what sex is, but is my own son actually about to try to rape me? It's a thought my brain can't even process before he slams his full 165-pound weight into me, and I'm pinned against the wall. He is still a few inches shorter than I am, but he outweighs me by about 20 pounds and he has momentum and gravity on his side while I try to push him away. I need to get behind him to do the safe restraint techniques we saw online.

He holds his filthy hand to my face while his naked body pins me to my own wall. It smells putrid. There is a thick layer of poop under every fingernail, and I bring both hands up to twist his arm away from me. He's still holding onto his crotch and tugging with the other hand. I don't know if he's trying to jerk off or pee on me. His eyes are empty. I think I feel a part of my soul float away.

This is not happening. I look into his eyes to search for my Nicholas, but I don't see any sign of him as I plant my feet firmly. Then I knee him in the groin. He finally backs away a few steps, and before I know what I am doing my instincts take over. I slap him in the face and start screaming.

"I am your mother. I am your fucking mother."

Hot tears pour down my cheeks and I can barely get the words out, I'm so angry and sad and scared and ashamed. He just stands there snarling and spits at my face. I slap him again, not sure if it's because he's being so disrespectful or just because I need to prove to him that he knows how to feel. Instantly I feel even more guilt and shame. I'm supposed to be the adult. I'm supposed to know how to stop this. I can't hit and swear at him or I'm just modeling the exact same behavior I want him to stop. It's my fault. But I don't know how to make it stop and neither, apparently, does anyone else.

I don't have time to continue my pity party for very long

because he lunges at me again, still tugging at his penis, but this time I don't stop to think before my reflexes take over and I grab a hairbrush off the counter and swing it with my full force directly at his crotch. The hollow crack when it hits his knuckles forces my eyes to widen. What did I do? I'm a terrible mother. But what if it had been one of the girls instead? Maybe I did the right thing. What even is the right thing? He straightens, but continues standing there, naked and smelling like a sewer, with no expression on his face. There's already a red mark starting to form on his hand. I expected him to have a bigger reaction. He doesn't seem to be able to feel. How am I going to explain that bruise? His bruise. I have no idea yet if I'm going to have any of my own.

My legs are starting to shake, and I am ready to curl up and sleep for a day or seventeen. I grit my teeth, hard, and steel myself to be able to continue to parent him.

"Are you ready for your shower yet?"

"Yeah, okay." He drops his hands, turns, and steps into the shower, closes the curtain, and runs the water as if nothing happened.

That night Eddie and I sit on the overstuffed black leather sofas handed down from Bobby, Eddie's brother, when he outgrew bachelor pad décor. I don't know if we'll ever quite reach that phase of adulthood. Our house is cute, but it's pieced together with hand-me-downs, Craigslist finds, and IKEA. Although the couches aren't my taste, they've been easy to clean with just an occasional swipe with a baby wipe, and they hold up well to daily beatings from the kids and the dog. The TV, perched up on a dresser we spray-painted after finding it on Craigslist, is on because we are trying for the third time to get through the latest episode of *Last Week Tonight*. We don't have cable, but adding HBO to our Amazon account is one of the few adult indulgences Eddie and I allow ourselves. The fireplace remote is resting on the cushion next to him, and Eddie reaches over and turns it on. Between the fire and the Christmas tree in the corner, it almost feels like a normal December night. Almost.

"What did he say?" I sigh and keep my eyes on the screen, resolved to at least pretend I'm listening to John Oliver.

"Honestly, I have no idea." Eddie responds with a similar defeated exhale. "Did we fill out that Google doc today?" By "we" he means me and no, I didn't even think about writing the incident from the bathroom in our behavior log until he asked. We should, I should, because two doctors and a therapist have all recommended keeping a record. Maybe we could see some patterns. I can't see much of anything. I can't feel anything either. I've gone numb.

My brain is on autopilot and I'm not sure I am thinking at all so much as I am reflexively walking through the steps of being a person. Sit. Stare. Say a word or two if someone talks to me. I don't have more than that in me, and I don't know if it will ever come back. I glance over at Eddie and notice, that quickly, his eyes have sealed shut and his head is titled back. I empathize with his exhaustion deep into my bones, and I can't fully explain why it feels a bit like a betrayal to see him give in and let himself rest, but my own jaw clenches as I stare at his now-open mouth, and an equal part of me wants to curl into his lap and fall asleep with him.

His hair is greying at the temples faster than I realized, and his facial hair is growing in patches since he hasn't taken the time to shave in days. I wonder briefly if he locked his razor away with the kitchen knives, as I absent-mindedly reach into the pocket of my robe and run my thumb across the smooth screen of my cell phone. It's there. Just in case.

We managed to get through dinner and bathe the other kids, but bedtime is the part of the day that I dread the most. We've installed a video monitor in Nicholas' room and hung the Christmas jingle bells around the girls' door knob to alert us if the door is opened in the middle of the night. Who knows if it will ever be enough. We are used to walking on eggshells, but for whatever reason, those eggshells are extra fragile and paper thin at night. It feels like waiting for a bomb to go off, and in a way it is. Intermittent Explosive Disorder, IED, has the same abbreviation the military uses for their Improvised Explosive Devices. It feels like a minefield because it is.

"Why is he here?" His voice is a low growl, and his fists are clenched as he stands shirtless illuminated by the dim light of a distant bulb. I hadn't heard a single sound, but Nicholas is standing in the archway that separates the living room from the hall where his bedroom is located. Eddie snaps upright and opens his eyes.

"Who?" I try to ask gently. "Dad? He lives here, just like you."

"No, get him away. Get him away."

Eddie rolls his eyes and mumbles, "Awesome, here we go again," sarcastically under his breath but doesn't move from his seat on the sofa as Nick walks into the room with a heavy, dragging gait and leads with his shoulders. His arms drop down, fists still clenched, and he reminds me of a primate. His previous attempts to smear me with feces only add to this picture. I squeeze the phone in my pocket, on purpose this time.

"Get out," our son continues to growl and drag himself toward Eddie, who is trying to fight his own instincts and stay patient.

"Hey, Buddy," my husband's tone is friendly, but guarded. "It's nighttime. Time for sleeping. Did you need something?"

"I need you to get out," Nicholas seethes, and lunges, the same way he did in the bathroom. I dart up from the couch and across the room, pull my phone out, and start recording a video. Standing here on the sidelines makes me feel useless, but we need the documentation so the therapists can see his at-home behavior first-hand and also, I imagine, because it might be necessary one day to show to an officer or social worker if our parenting abilities were to come into question.

He tries to punch Eddie, but Nick is slow and clumsy and Eddie is bigger, faster, and stronger. Eddie grabs Nick's wrists and wraps him in a bear hug, holding him from behind so Nick's arms are crossed in front of his own body, like we saw on YouTube. Nick continues to buck his head back, stomp, and twist violently in Eddie's arms. "I'll kill you. I need to kill you. Let me kill you! Why won't you let me fucking kill you?" Then he sinks his teeth into Eddie's forearm. Eddie winces and lets go of one of Nick's hands so he can pry our son's jaw away. Nick punches him with the free arm, then scratches a huge gash into his father's arm. Eddie is bleeding, and he's the biggest, strongest one here. There are younger kids in the house, and my mother who is recovering from a hysterectomy and walking with a cane, is asleep downstairs in the basement in-law suite. I don't have a choice anymore. I hit the red emergency icon on my phone.

"9-1-1. What is your emergency?" I always find it jarring when the operators sound like they are smiling when you call them in the middle of a crisis. Most people are probably comforted by that. I wish, just once, I would get an operator who transformed into an angry friend on my behalf during these conversations. *He did what now? No, he did not. Girl, smack him upside the head twice, once for you and once for me.* Obviously, that never happens.

"Hello, I need an ambulance transport for my son," I try to sound calm and authoritative, and simultaneously wonder if maybe I should be more upset. "218 Meadow Grove. He was receiving in-patient treatment and was just released from the hospital on Tuesday. They said if there were any homicidal threats he needed to be readmitted....Yes, he is being violent...Yes, that is him you hear screaming....Yes, my husband is bleeding. No, well, let me check, Eddie, do you think you need stitches? Ok, no, we don't think he needs medical attention. Just my son. Nicholas."

"Ma'am, because your son is currently being violent, I have to send officers to assess the situation. It's standard procedure. You just stay right here on the phone with me and confirm when they are at the door."

"I understand. It's not the first time."

"Ok, well, we are going to get you some help. What can you tell me about your son?"

"Uh...he's eleven. He likes LEGO and Jurassic Park. He has an intellectual disability and a mood disorder. I don't know how much your computer is telling you, but this sort of thing happens a lot."

"That's okay, Honey. This is what we do. I have a son about that age. He likes dinosaurs, too."

She makes small talk for a few more minutes until I can see the flashing lights in our driveway. It never takes long for our officers to respond, one of the benefits of living in "the biggest small town in central Pennsylvania." That's our Borough's actual motto. Hallam Borough is less than one square mile in total, has a population of under 3,000 people, and a crime rate so low it's listed as "not applicable" every time I've ever tried to look it up. Responding to us is likely to be the highest priority call our officers get this week.

"The police are here. And the ambulance is pulling up behind them. We're okay now." I tell the operator.

"That's good, Sweetie. When the officer comes to the door, please hand him the phone."

They came without their sirens, which is a small blessing, but the neighbors must still be wondering why our driveway is lined with emergency vehicles at midnight. Again. There's a heavy thud on the door. My first thought is that I wish I would have changed my clothes. What would a competent person be wearing right now? Probably at least a bra, and not faded floral pajama bottoms, a tank top and a pink used-to-be fuzzy robe that is caked in my own snot from using the sleeves to wipe my face during countless ugly cries.

There's another knock on the door, and I open it to a fully uniformed officer whose partner is just a few steps behind, navigating the way to our front porch through the snow. I realize I forgot to turn the porch light on for them, and I ignore my grandmother's voice in my head telling me to make sure to offer them something warm like coffee or hot chocolate. Opening the door, I hand him my phone and he talks briefly to the 911 operator to confirm they've arrived. Then he hands me back my phone.

"Thank you for coming, Officer." I focus on not smiling, not that I want to, but it's reflexive to diffuse these situations, and I don't want him to think I'm happy right now. Should I shake his hand? I start to reach out, but stop as I'm in the middle of over-thinking, and just let my arm hover awkwardly for a few seconds before putting it back down.

"Ma'am, I'm Officer Justin." I know. His son goes to school with my girls. He's not letting on if he recognizes me from years of back-to-school nights and Trunk or Treats.

"Yeah, hi, come in. I'm sure you remember Nicholas. He is in the living room. Just follow the screaming."

The living room is easily visible from the front door and it's obvious that Eddie is still struggling to control him.

Officer Justin and his partner make their way in, and I stand in the foyer to talk to his partner, whose name I've already forgotten, while Officer Justin tries to calm the chaos in the other room. I can only catch blips of the living room side of the conversation, although my eyes are fixed there. I'm not even bothering to glance at Mr. Partner while we speak.

"Can you tell me what happened tonight?" he is all-business, and his brashness sounds unintentionally accusatory. I immediately wish they would've sent a woman, although I don't know if the tiny seven-person police force in our Borough even has a female officer.

*Hey, Buddy. I'm here to talk, but I need you to calm down and step away from your dad. I hear your name is Nicholas.* Justin's words float in from the other room.

"I can show you." I'm still holding my phone and I look at it long enough to pull up the video before I hand it to his partner. It's basically exactly what he's seeing now: a pudgy, shirtless child thrashing violently and screaming that he wants to kill his dad.

"What happened just before he started acting this way?" the officer asks, as he hands me back my phone. He has a notepad out now.

"Nothing." I will myself to look away from the living room and stare him in the eyes.

"Ma'am, would you prefer to step outside and talk to me privately? We don't need to have this conversation near your husband."

"That's not necessary. I honestly mean nothing. We were just sitting on the couch watching TV, and Nicholas had been asleep, then he woke up and came out of his room like this. He was just discharged from inpatient treatment last week. He's not doing very well."

The Christmas ornaments crash together under the force of Nick's flailing feet hitting the tree, and the collision snaps our attention to the living room, where his partner and I both see Nicholas charge at Officer Justin. Before I know what is happening, Nick is on the floor, with his hands cuffed behind his back. His partner reacted more quickly than I did, and it was he, not Officer Justin, who took Nicholas down. Officer Justin now kneels beside him, still talking in a calm, patient voice. I wish we had gone for the fuzzy handcuffs after all. The cold, hard clicking as Nick pulls against the metal, burning his bare chest as he scrapes it on the carpet, cements how awful the situation truly is. My fifth grader is lying handcuffed under his own Christmas tree, the one where just two days ago Santa left new LEGO and a Stretch Armstrong doll. I did this to him, I told them to come.

"Nick, man, I want to let you go, but you can't act this way. I need you to calm down." Officer Justin tries to reason with him as Nicholas continues to scream and thrash on the ground.

Nick's yelling, "You're hurting me. You are all hurting me. Why won't you just let me kill you?" and crying now. Something physically breaks inside of me, the final link in a chain reaction, as if I'd been walking on weak ice all along and one last step caused the widening crack that took me under. I can't take seeing my son on the ground, half-naked, with his arms twisted behind him bound by metal, and a uniformed officer towering over him. Like this, it is so obvious that he is just a child. My legs give out completely, and I fall to my knees and wail in a way I thought mothers only did in movies. I'm fully aware that it's not helping, but I have no control over what my body is doing.

Officer Justin glances up at his partner and shakes his head, but neither of the men bother asking me to stop. I couldn't, even if they did. The officers both turn to us. It's out of our hands now, and whatever they say is what is going to happen tonight.

"So, Nick, you are not being safe right now, and we all want you to get some help." Then Officer Justin turns to Eddie. "Since you are the one he attacked, and we were here and witnessed it, you can press charges if you want. I don't like to recommend it in these situations. But it's your choice." It is somehow comforting when he references similar situations. We aren't the only ones. I have to cling to that.

I look at Eddie's arm, where a new gash is dripping blood. My husband is six feet tall and has the muscular build that got him named Senior Athlete of the Year for being the only person in our high school class who played five varsity sports. He's the biggest person in this room, yet he looks so small and defeated.

"No, I don't want to press charges," he whispers, eyes closed, turning his head away from us toward the wall.

"Ok, well, here's what we are going to do." Officer Justin continues. "I think it's pretty obvious that we are going to the hospital. If he calms down, I could ask the ambulance crew if they will take him, and I can follow. But here's the thing: if they take him, it's going to cost you three grand, even if you have decent insurance. So, I'm going to go out and tell them he's being too violent, and I'm going to transport him myself."

In the police car? Like a criminal? But he's right, we can't take on another huge bill. I suck in a few shaky breaths and try to think straight, then I rub the tears and snot off my face with the sleeve of my robe for probably the fiftieth time this week. Nicholas seems to have realized this situation is serious, and now he's looking at me through his own tears, begging me to help him with his eyes.

"Can he get dressed?" I don't recognize my own voice, it's gone completely hoarse.

"Sure. And we can lose the cuffs if you promise to calm down, Man. Deal?" Nicholas nods. Justin continues to talk to him while he unlocks the handcuffs, "I've got a kid about your age. You go to school up there?" he tilts his head to the left, in the direction of the school.

"He is in a special education class across town," I interrupt.

"Ok, cool. You play any sports?"

"He likes dinosaurs," I interject again. "Jurassic Park, Star Wars, Superheroes," I sigh and hear my own voice trail off. Eddie offers to start packing a bag. The last time we left for the hospital we didn't return for a full twenty-four hours. Thank God my mother is here to be with the girls.

We follow behind the police cruiser, but we are separated at the hospital entrance because they head toward the ambulance bay and we need to find a place to park. By now we are familiar with the sign-in procedure, and Eddie and I make our way to the waiting room yet again. Fifteen minutes later, Officer Justin finds us. It's disconcerting to see a fully uniformed officer heading straight toward you in a crowded space, and the other patients don't even try to disguise their eavesdropping when he starts to talk to us.

"That's a good boy you have there." He tells us. I don't know how he can possibly say that after what he witnessed tonight, but suddenly I'm flooded with gratitude that he took the time to find us. "He said he couldn't watch the Jurassic Park movie until he read the book. Is that true?"

"Um, yeah. We try to do that if something is rated PG-13. It wasn't the original book, though, it was a shorter version they had at the school book fair," I tell him, not knowing why those irrelevant details seem so important now.

Officer Justin laughs. "I like that rule. I think I might try that one on my kid." He pats Eddie on the shoulder and tips an imaginary hat to me. "Well, you all try to have a good night now. Call us whenever we can help." Then he is gone. Nicholas is admitted once again.

# Chapter 34

"We finally got Medicaid Access for Nicholas," I say to Pastor Bob, attempting to start this appointment with something positive. We received an acceptance letter.

"That's wonderful. I know you have been trying for that for a long time. Certainly something to be thankful for." Then he changes the subject.

"So, I've been wondering something. Can you tell me why you choose to come to me for counseling?" Pastor Bob looks at me expectantly and I have to cock my head to the side to indicate that I don't understand what he's asking. Isn't it obvious from our story why I would need to talk to someone?

He elaborates. "You could have gone anywhere. You could have chosen to see a therapist or a life coach, or you could have tried talking to your own mother. Isn't this her area of expertise? And now that you have Medicaid Access, you will have therapists coming into your home as well, correct? Why do you think you found your way into a pastor's office?"

I honestly don't know. "I guess you were just the first person who came to mind, and it always helps to have a spiritual perspective," I attempt to answer him. Plus, his time is cheap, but that would be rude to say out loud.

He smiles, "Well, as flattering as that is, why do you think that might be?" I just sit and stare at him silently. I have no idea. He's not really the first, I suppose. I sought countless experts for my son. But he is right about one thing. He's the first person I came to for myself. There has to be a reason for that. Am I supposed to be the one who knows what it is? I think I thought that's why I was here, so he could offer these kinds of insights into things I don't understand about myself.

After a few minutes of letting me stew in my own thoughts, Pastor Bob leans back casually in his chair. I don't think he intends to pierce me with his questions about Eddie or my childhood or my faith, but the words feel sharp today. Or maybe that is exactly his intention, to finally break through the armor and get me to bleed. Is it strange that we've had so many sessions now, and I haven't cried at all while I've recounted our story? Should I cry? Do most people who sit in this chair? It feels like I'm running out of tears.

As if he's reading my thought about how to seem normal, Pastor Bob says, "Most people who have been through these kinds of traumas tell me they have struggled quite a bit with faith, and especially with doubt. Do you find that has been an issue for you?" He's asking if I've been questioning God's existence. I guess that might be a logical thing to do, if I had ever been a logical kind of person.

"No, not really." I tell him the truth, but he looks skeptical.

"People are disappointing," I shrug, as if that is an explanation. He nods and writes something on his legal pad, but I don't think he understands what I mean. It makes perfect sense to me. The people in my life kept leaving when I needed them. Or maybe that's not a fair assessment, maybe it's fairer to say they weren't showing up. I needed a friend, and the ones I had from high school or college didn't work particularly hard to stick it out. Although, I do have my friends from the internet, real life personal connections have been hard to maintain.

Some of that is on me, I could have reached out further, stretched longer, tried to do more, but I already felt like the captain of a boat that wasn't just sinking, it was capsized, and my entire crew was drowning. I didn't have time to remember birthday cards and phone calls and eventually most of them silently drifted away. Some not so silently. Some made it clear that they weren't comfortable with their own children being around a kid like Nicholas. Yeah, I needed a friend, and Jesus seemed like a good one. I figured if I had the choice to go through this completely alone or do it with Him, then the latter seemed like a much better option. I clung hard to my faith because it felt like it was the only thing I had to pull us through this. And I *was* going to get us through this. I don't know how to say that out loud without sounding ridiculous.

"I suppose I've been fortunate that doubt has not been one of my struggles." I know these one-sentence answers aren't helping, but for now I just hope he has been doing this long enough to be able to read my mind.

"Hmm." He touches his fingertips together so his hands form a pyramid under his chin. "Then what do you think has been a struggle for you recently?"

"Just life in general, really."

He smiles. "I may need you to be a little more specific than that." Apparently, he's not as good at mind reading as I'd hoped. That's unfortunate because it means I'm going to have to say it all out loud.

I don't know if I can do that. I know I should. I have to, eventually. But I can't. Not today. I can't talk about what the real problems are, not here, not anywhere, because I'm terrified that if they learn the truth in its entirety someone will haul my son away from me. He doesn't deserve to lose another family. I have to fill the time with half-truths and hope Pastor Bob reads between them. Eventually someone has to figure out what I'm trying to say. I can't spend another decade letting the truth fester inside of me, slowly smothering tiny pieces of my soul.

My shoulders slump and I can't bring myself to make eye contact while I pick at my thumbnail. "I know God is here with us. We've seen Him do incredible things for Nicholas and through Nicholas already. But it does feel like I'm left doing an awful lot of the grunt work. It's just, well, it's...it's a lot. And I'm tired."

"I'm sure that is definitely true." He pauses and waits, comfortable in the space of the silence. We are delving deeper, which is in theory what I'm here for, but I can also feel myself fighting back against the way he's trying to gently pry me open. It feels unnatural to say these things out loud when you've been building a fortress around yourself for years just to keep them in. He switches gears.

"Let's talk about Nicholas. He's been with your family for a few years now."

"Yes."

"And you have never considered the alternative?"

"I'm sorry?" I raise my eyebrows at him, forcing him to give voice to what he was hoping to only imply.

"I've counseled other families in similar situations. Some found the stress was more overwhelming than they anticipated."

"I see. And?" I am not making this easy for him.

"Unfortunately, many were forced to seek another placement eventually." Adoption dissolution is more common than many people realize. Children can be legally adopted and then placed right back into the system by parents who felt ill-prepared for the challenging task they faced. All the warnings and all the classes in the world don't compare to the reality once it is in front of you. Some people cannot handle it. And sometimes there is no choice. It's not always a parent's decision if they get to keep custody.

"That is not an option here," I state emphatically. I will never consider it. Not once, not ever. "Nicholas is our son." I do not differentiate between my son and my daughters in this area, and I never really understood why other people do. If Abby or Penny came out of my womb struggling with a mental illness, I could not decide to cast either one of them aside and make them someone else's problem. I will not abandon Nicholas either. I don't know why anyone assumes

I would just because he is adopted. The thought of tearing our family apart and forcing another trauma on a child just to ease my own burden is soul-crushing to me, but I know there might come a day when that choice is taken out of my hands. As long as it is mine to make, I choose to keep my family together.

I continue, careful not to break eye contact. "I can't imagine not being there to see his high school graduation or his wedding, let alone waking up every day with one of my children missing. What would it do to my daughters to see us rip their big brother out of the family, after he has been a part of it for their entire lives? Why would I ever do that on purpose?"

I will spend the remainder of my life fighting with my entire being against those who try to tell me that dissolution is an option. It's hard for other people to understand. Someone once tried to argue with me that I needed to stop judging it, and I simply needed to look at it like a divorce, but it isn't like a divorce at all. I am a child of divorce. If there is one thing that was pounded into my head over and over while my own parents were getting divorced, it was the phrase "children are not divorceable." Divorce is a mutual decision made by two consenting adults. I see dissolution as a decision adults try to justify with adult-centered arguments, and frankly I'm not at all interested.

Although, "I do know it happens," I admit. "We have several friends who have had to terminate their rights just to get help. I'll do everything I possibly can to make sure that isn't us." I remember specifically when my friend Jane's daughter started getting aggressive. She has severe autism and, like Nicholas, is the oldest of their children. They had to make the choice to find an alternative placement or risk losing custody of their other kids. Since there weren't any services for adults with special needs in their area, Jane and her husband ended up buying a second home they couldn't really afford and renting out rooms to other families in similar situations. Now their daughter lives in that second home with three roommates and a hired nurse they also can't afford, but they have to anyway.

"Eddie and I have already talked about the maybes." I assure Pastor Bob. "We understand what we're dealing with. Maybe one day we will need to sell the house and get two smaller apartments or townhomes next door to each other so we can separate Nick from the other kids. Maybe one day we will need to make decisions about jail time or residential treatment. But not today."

"He is a very lucky boy," Pastor Bob responds. I hate when people say that, but I smile at him anyway. Nicholas is anything but lucky. There is no such thing as an adoption that does not start with trauma, but my son has had his fair share of additional battles. Losing our family will not be one of them.

"Oh, no. We are the lucky ones." It's what I'm supposed to say. It's easy for people to hear, plus it ends the conversation. I read once on a blog run by another foster mother that she responds to the "I don't know how you do it, I could never" comments by saying, "You'd be surprised what you would do for someone you love." I think she's right.

He's looking at me the way I used to look at foster

parents like Debbie, and I don't know what else to tell him. Everyone keeps expecting me to rise to every challenge, soar over every obstacle. As if I have a choice. Nicholas needs me. Besides, someone has to prove that hard does not mean impossible. Prove it to whom? Nick, I guess. Or maybe I need to prove it to myself, or maybe everyone in general. Somehow, I have become the example and I need to show that it can be done if I want other people to be willing to do it. I'm trying, really trying. But whatever this is that I am doing, it doesn't feel an awful lot like success. It sure doesn't feel at all like flying. It feels like falling. Like failing. It turns out I am only human.

"Well," he moves on, "I imagine all of that must take a toll on a marriage."

"It did at the beginning. I think we have learned how to lean on each other."

"And are you making time to focus on the relationship?"

"Yes." Now I'm being vague on purpose. My time with Eddie is mine and I am fighting to protect it, even now, when it is not threatened.

"How so?" I know this trick. He's trying to push me past my reservations.

"We try to give each other space to do our own stuff. He has his music, I have the blog. But then we spend a lot of time doing things together."

"Such as?"

Does it matter? It must because he's asking, and so does everyone else, but I don't know why they are always curious. The honest answer is I don't care what we're doing, I just really like hanging out with my husband. He's been my best friend since we were fifteen. Every time I tell the truth, people get disappointed. I think they are hoping we have some sort of secret spark they can take and use to jumpstart their own relationships, but our solution is not anywhere close to ingenious, and it is not one that is going to work for everyone.

"We put our kids to bed early and we stay up late. Sometimes we eat dinner together after everyone else is asleep. That's really it. Like the other night when he had a 9pm volleyball game and brought back Taco Bell afterward. The only secret we have is that we don't sleep a lot. And we happen to like each other. We stay up until one or two in the morning several nights a week to eat takeout, watch TV, and, you know."

"I do, but you can say it here."

"Sex, we have sex." Obviously, all these kids did come from somewhere.

"Have you managed to keep intimacy a priority?"

"I think so." I don't know how much detail I'm supposed to give him, so I don't give any. It's strange that I feel shy today, I usually don't mind talking about it when people ask. We're married. It's normal. And it seems to be the one thing people wonder most about us, but are afraid to ask. Most people assume that stress ends your sex life. Maybe it usually does, I don't know. I can't speak for anyone else, but that just isn't true for us. The more I feel drained and depleted by all of the stuff that is weighing on me, the more I need some sort of emotional and physical release. Our bed is the one place where I don't have to be strong anymore. Eddie will let me need him.

"And yourself?" He is still talking.

"I'm sorry, what?" I wasn't listening.

"What are you doing to prioritize yourself?"

"Oh. Um," an image from the other night sneaks into my head uninvited and forces me smile. "Writing. And reading. And taking bubble baths, I guess." The last one is new.

"Those are things you enjoy? You know, you remind me quite a bit of my daughter-in-law, Chelsea. She's about your age. She and my son have one little girl and are hoping to adopt one day. They are moving to our area soon, I bet you would really get along." I already know Chelsea a bit through Facebook. She follows my blog and we've chatted online because of my connection to her family.

"Mmm," I nod, but I'm not here anymore. I'm still thinking about Saturday.

We weren't fighting last weekend, but I wanted to be. Eddie was just letting me yell at him, or rather onto him, because, as usual, none of it really had anything to do with my husband. And I wasn't yelling so much as I was whisper-seething because the kids were asleep and my mom was in the basement and I had a lot of anger and no place to put it because there were too many people around me that I didn't really want to disturb.

"Honey, you are allowed to be mad."

"Oh, really? Well thank you so much for your permission."

He won't respond to that. Nothing I say right now is going to bother him. We learned a long time ago that in order to survive we have to take turns being angry, and we know now how to get angry without getting mean.

"Talk to me."

"About what?" I am spitting words at him like weapons.

"Talk to me, girl." He does a terrible and exaggerated Justin Timberlake impression that makes me laugh in spite of myself. I give up.

"You already know about all of it. I'm just fucking exhausted, and it's never going to be over, is it? There's always more."

"Sure seems that way, lately."

I know that our problems are no worse than other people's problems. I've never lost a child or battled cancer or been to war. I know there are people who have seen all three of those things in one lifetime. I know that the weight we are carrying is no heavier than anyone else's, it is just different. But damn, different feels lonely. I feel like I could stand in the middle of a crowded football stadium and ask all of the people to raise their hands if they were diagnosed with brain lesions in the same year that they found out that their seven-year-old son may or may not be schizophrenic as well as intellectually and physically disabled, but in a crowd of a hundred thousand people my hand would probably be the only one raised. There have been a dozen doctors and the thing they all had in common was that none of them offered any hope that I am going to get any better. And Nicholas probably won't either.

Not even Eddie can really understand. I try not to complain too much in front of him. It hurts him to watch me be in pain, and there is no point in letting both of us suffer. And, if I'm being honest with myself, I need him now. He knows that. It's the pressure to provide for us that comes out when it is his turn to be angry. Someone has to have the career that will pay the mortgage and carry the health insurance. My body has rendered me useless and it can't be me anymore. Not that it was truly me in the first place, but at least I used to be able to hold on to the possibility that it could have been.

"If you could do anything tonight, what would you want to do?" he asks. I don't know if he's trying to get me to do some sort of visualization exercise or if he wants to see if I'm going to say something he can actually offer.

"Do you know what I want to do right now?"

"Well, no. Hence, the question."

"What I would really like to do is just shut everything off. I'm tired of my brain giving me problems. I want to turn off all the lights and get in the tub with candles, a bunch of scalding hot water, and vanilla-scented bubbles, and put The Head and The Heart on Pandora."

"This sounds like something that can be easily arranged." He starts to laugh gently but stops himself when he sees the daggers that are shooting out of my eyes.

"I'm not done yet," I continue. "I want you to do it with me, but don't you dare expect anything out of it because this is not about that." He holds up both of his hands in mock surrender and shakes his head, smiling. I don't scare him at all when I'm angry. That is irritating. "Actually, what I would really like to do is try smoking pot to see if it helps, because I've been wondering if I qualify under that Medical Marijuana Act, and also I want to eat chocolate cake." My arms are crossed now and I'm huffy, like Penny, except she's expected to throw tantrums. She's five. I'm thirty-two.

"You want to eat the cake in the tub?" He's humoring me.

"No. I want to eat cake in bed after that. But we don't have any cake. Or pot. And it's midnight, the stores are closed. Not that you can buy pot at a store. I don't have any idea where to buy that. But we can't buy cake and we both know you're not baking one. And I'll be damned if I am going to have to do any work to make this happen. So it doesn't matter anyway."

"Well...you're right about the cake...but as far as the other stuff..."

I raise my eyebrows at him. He nods.

"How? Where is it? Where did you even get it? How long has it been in my house?"

"Do you really want to know?" No, I probably don't.

"We can't actually smoke right now."

"Why not? Who is going to stop you? You're not a teenager, there are other responsible adults in your house, you're not driving anywhere, and you don't have to work tomorrow. You just said if you could do anything tonight, this is what you wanted."

"I did say that."

"Yes, you did."

"I'll get the candles."

# Chapter 35

It just never seems to stop. If he is awake, he is violent. There are scars on Eddie's arms and his back, and I woke up with a black eye because Nicholas punched me in the face yesterday. He was angry because it was someone else's turn on a video game. We've tried to monitor the electronics. We only allow video games on weekends, and then only games that are rated "E for Everyone." We have a strict No-Active-Shooters-in-Video-Games policy. It doesn't seem to make a difference. Today is just like all the other days, which have started blending together under the thick, dysfunctional haze. The only reason I know it's Tuesday is because we were supposed to have a therapy appointment. I had to cancel it because no one will serve a violent child outside of the hospital. The liability is too great for them. No one seems to think about what the liability is for me or my other children.

I called the hospital's crisis hotline earlier when Nicholas opened the second-story window and started pulling himself onto the roof. Talking to the counselor over the phone calmed him down a bit, and he has stayed indoors since. They gave me a number for the mobile crisis unit, which I remember from his incident with the scissors in school in the first grade. It is a group of crisis counselors that comes straight to you in a mental health emergency.

They advised that they could send a team to the house if he were only talking about scary things or having thoughts, but just like our usual therapists, they will not come if there is any sort of violence or risk to their team. Because he is already trying to climb out of windows at those heights, it is doubtful they could help. I took the number anyway and wrote it on the list of emergency numbers hanging on our refrigerator, right under the Poison Control Hotline. Yet again, I have to wonder why as a society we have prepared parents to know what to do in physical emergencies, such as your child swallowing poison, but no one told me how to handle these mental health issues until we were smack in the middle of them. The crisis counselor's only other advice for me was to call 911 if there were another incident tonight.

Nicholas was moody throughout the afternoon, but everything has been relatively uneventful since he managed to calm down. Or at least calm down enough to refrain from jumping out of windows. He's been sitting on the playroom floor, vacillating between playing calmly with his LEGO and breaking down into inconsolable sobs.

"Nick, do you want to talk about why you're sad?" I ask for what feels like the millionth time today. "Dinner is downstairs whenever you are ready." I gesture toward the kitchen, where a paper plate sits waiting to serve him more reheated fast food. Eddie's co-workers pitched in together and bought us a large event catering-sized tray of nuggets from Chick-Fil-A. It's been serving as dinner for the kids for more days than I'd care to admit. Although I did dump some unsweetened applesauce onto the plates to ease my own guilt, just a bit. The card that accompanied the nuggets is still sitting on my dresser. It's filled with thoughts, prayers, and well-wishes from the entire office, which, like the chicken nuggets, are also condensed into bite-sized pieces as each person struggled to write a sentence or two. What could they say? Hallmark doesn't make an I'm Sorry Your Kid Went Crazy card.

I hate that we phrase it that way. We say people go crazy, like mental illness is a desirable destination or something within their control. We do the same thing to women who miscarry, as if they did something incorrectly. It's a thing that happens to you, not something you actively do, but for some reason our language always either puts the victim in the driver's seat or makes your illness define you.

If a child gets cancer, we don't say Johnny is cancerous. That would be callous and cruel. Yet, if someone develops a mental illness, it suddenly becomes the defining characteristic of what they are. Susie is bipolar. Jeffrey is schizophrenic. *I have depression* is a different narrative than *I am depressed*. We think they are saying the same thing, but they aren't. Only one version of that sentence places ownership solely on the suffering and reduces an entire disease to the level of a fleeting, temporary emotion.

"I just, I just," Nicholas holds his knees and rocks back and forth. "I wish I had a gun."

"Why? What would you do with it?" I prompt, and immediately regret it. There can't be a good answer.

"If I had a gun I would put it in my mouth like this," he mimes with his fingers. "And I would," he lets the sentence trail as he pulls an imaginary trigger with his thumb. "Mom, you don't understand. I don't want to hurt you, but I have to. I just have to."

"Nick, that's the thing. You really don't. Your brain is telling you things that aren't true. We need to take you to the doctor again." I try to be discreet and keep Nicholas unaware as I text Eddie at the office *Leave. Now.*

"Yes, I do. He said if I don't listen to him, he will hurt me." Nick crumples onto the floor and gives into heavier sobs. My shoulders straighten and the hair on my arms stands at attention.

"Who? Who said that to you? If someone hurt you, you can tell me. I will keep them far away from you."

He sniffs and sits upright again.

"You don't get it, Mom. You can't make him go away. Nobody can. He's The Boss. He's mean, and he lives here with me." He exhales one long, shaky, resigned breath and bumps his palm into his forehead three times. "He's in here and he says he is in charge now. He says I have to hurt you, or else he will kill me. I don't want to listen to him because I love you guys, but I'm scared of him. I wasn't supposed to tell you, and I think he is going to hurt me now."

"Nick," I fall to the floor and take his head in both hands while I look into his eyes. "The Boss is not going to hurt you or anyone else, but we are going to need to go back to the hospital."

"No. No no no no no no." He shakes his head and then his entire body. "Don't send me back there again. You can't do this to me."

The house alarm dings and alerts us that the garage door is open. Eddie must have left the office before I texted if he is already home. I call down to him that we are upstairs.

"Why is he home? You told him?" Nicholas yells and scrambles to his feet. "I have to get out of here."

"Nick, come on, bud. Let's just talk about this," I sigh, knowing it's useless. He is already fumbling down the stairs in a too-fast panic. I follow behind him, trying to fill Eddie in as much as possible. My husband is not interested in calling the police again, but it's obvious our son needs to go back to the hospital, and I have no idea how we are supposed to get Nicholas into the truck by ourselves.

Nicholas runs into the still-open garage. I hadn't considered until this moment that it's the most dangerous room in the house. I try to stay calm and keep my voice even while I take note of the potential weapons around him. Hedge clippers, shovel, axe. I am careful not to let my eyes linger on any of them, afraid that if he follows my gaze, he will pick one up. I walk toward him with my hands raised in front of me, not for the first time a hostage in my own home.

"C'mon, Bubba, we're going to take a ride," Eddie says lightly. "You can pick the radio station." He advances a few more steps.

"You can't take me back there," Nicholas strips off his shirt and runs half-naked into the yard. Eddie starts after him, but first calls back to me to tell my mom to stay with the girls and for me to meet him at the truck.

I didn't see what happened, but three minutes later Nicholas is in the back seat, clothed once again, and there is a new gash on Eddie's arm when I open the door and climb in. Eddie is staring straight ahead, gripping the steering wheel so tightly his knuckles are white. Nicholas glares at the back of his father's head.

"Hon, I really don't know about this, they said we should call," I whisper. If he can hear me, Eddie ignores my protest and puts the truck into drive.

After a few long moments of silence, other than Nick's low growls, Eddie turns to me and whispers, "I won't take the highway." It's a small peace offering, at least we will be able to pull over if necessary. When necessary.

I'm more surprised than I should be when, just a few blocks from home, Nicholas' fist makes contact with my cheek. The yelp that comes out of my mouth is more from shock than pain. Eddie reacts quickly and is able to pull over and stop the vehicle as Nicholas tries to climb into the driver's seat, wildly flailing his fists. It doesn't seem to take much effort for my husband to push our son back into his seat. The hot tears that start to flood my face are not because it hurts, they are purely from shame. Shame that I raised a boy who would act like this, shame that I can't protect myself from him, shame that one day I won't be there anymore, and he will probably continue to do it to someone else.

"Sit down and be quiet. Hit my wife one more time, and I swear to God I will break every bone in your hand, don't test me." My husband bellows, twisted to look Nicholas in the eye. Nick only seethes through flared nostrils and mumbles to himself.

"Eddie," I start to scold him. Nick's behavior is not okay, but this isn't helping either.

"No." Eddie looks at me hard. "He needs to know there are real consequences for this bullshit. You don't deserve this, and the next person he hurts isn't going to be as nice as his mommy. We have done everything for him. And if the therapy, and the medicine, and the hospitals, and even the fucking police aren't going to work on him, then he can deal with me. Better for him to learn now with his dad who, believe it or not, actually cares, than for him to cross some gun-toting redneck one day and end up dead. You want to be a tough guy, asshole?"

He turns again to face Nicholas. "All the times you attacked me, I've never fought back, have I? Not once. But that is over now. The next time you come after me or anyone else in this family, I'm not holding back."

"You can't do that," Nick laughs. "It's against the law. You can't do anything to me."

"You want to find out?" Eddie says flatly. "You attacked me in front of a police officer, gave your mother a black eye, and were restrained four times the last time you were in the hospital. I'll let them interview every social worker, police officer, and show them the paperwork from all the doctors we took you to. Nobody would do jack shit to me. They'd probably take you away, though. Is that what you want? You want to end up in a residential home where there are bigger kids who are meaner than you are?" Eddie's tone is taunting.

"Fine, just put me back in foster care," Nick screams.

"Look, you two, can everybody just be quiet? We will be

there in a few minutes." I plead, sniffling.

Eddie sighs heavily, but he relents and starts driving again. After a long silence he offers, "Look, Dude. We love you, but the way you are acting lately is not okay, and I don't think you like acting this way either. We need to get your brain straightened out."

I close my eyes and rest my head on the window, barely starting to notice the throbbing in my cheek. I run my tongue along my teeth, checking to make sure none of them are loose. A clinking sound makes me turn around.

"Pull over again right now," I try to stay calm. Nicholas is holding a huge metal chain and snapping a small section of it like a belt.

Eddie looks in the rearview mirror and goes pale. "I completely forgot that was in here." He must have used it to hook up the trailer or tow something earlier this week. It was in the side panel of the back door. In our hurry to leave, neither of us checked the back seat. Nick lunges forward, trying to hurl the chain at us, but it is too heavy and awkward for him to maneuver the way he wants. It slumps onto my arm, but barely registers as a contact. When I don't react, Nick is less than pleased.

"I'm going to kill you tonight, Mom."

I don't know whether to be relieved or offended that no one bothers to stop and help when we pull over again, and Eddie wrestles the chain away from him. I know what it must look like, me sobbing in the front while Eddie towers over a child and they crash together, Nicholas trying to hit him with the chain. I wonder if I should call the police myself before someone driving by calls to report us, but we'll be at the hospital soon enough, and it will all be on record there once we tell them what is going on.

Finally, Eddie secures the chain and throws it in the back of the truck. Nicholas' mood turns on a dime, and he becomes a different, more pleasant child. He returns to the back seat willingly, where he sings Christmas carols and talks a mile a minute about the latest episode of *Henry Danger*. He doesn't understand why we still look sad and don't feel ready to sing along with him yet.

We make our way through the Emergency Room door, where the staff now greets us by name. He is admitted once again. Between November of 2018 and February of 2019, Nicholas bounces in and out of hospitals so much that he spends less than three weeks at home.

When he returns around Valentine's Day, our son is walking around deflated and empty. He has gained more than fifty pounds in the last three years because of medication side effects and lack of physical activity, but he is alive. The violence doesn't exactly stop, but it is not directed at people any longer. He focuses his anger back to less harmful outbursts, like throwing toys or punching walls.

During his latest hospital admission, they switched to a hands-free crisis management technique called Ukeru (based on the Japanese word for "receive"), which aims to eliminate the use of restraint and seclusion. Instead of being held down or confined to a room alone when he was having an outburst, the way we had all been taught in the past, the staff now uses padded mats to protect themselves and block his aggressions, the same way I've seen football players practice shedding a block by running into padding. Just like when he was young and we switched from time-outs to time-ins, this gentler approach proves to be much more effective for Nicholas. Although once again, there do not seem to be any trainings on this technique offered for parents. Through internet searches, we try to take from it what we can and plan to use Penny's purple vinyl gymnastics practice mat as a shield if necessary.

Because he is finally eligible for Medicaid, we have been assigned a team of therapists to offer wraparound services for our family. They come to the house several times each week to meet with Nicholas alone, once a week to his school, and once to do a family session with our other children and my mother. Sometimes his new therapists take Nicholas out into the community, to places like fast food restaurants or trampoline parks, so he can practice his coping strategies in public spaces. They also come once a week after the kids are in bed to offer a couple's counseling session to Eddie and me. There is no charge for any of their services, beyond our regular taxes. The bills have stopped.

The entire team would like to see Nicholas go to a partial placement program during the school day, where he could continue to receive treatment from doctors monitoring his medication, group therapy, and spend those hours with trained staff, and still come home to his own bed at night. Unfortunately, because we already have the wraparound our insurance will not approve it. It is considered a duplication of services, even though wraparound and partial placements do completely different things. For now, he has transitioned back to school, where he is still in Mr. Shrader's class, for the fourth year in a row.

During Nicholas' hospitalizations, his teacher became one of the most supportive friends our family could have asked for. The entire class made *Thinking of You* cards for Nicholas, and hand delivered them to our home, and Mr. Shrader checked in more often than anyone else we knew. Now that Nicholas is back in class, Joe texts me updates every day, spends his lunch breaks communicating with our therapists, and is also working to fix a years-old mistake we found in Nicholas' IEP paperwork, which has blocked us from receiving community-based services from the MH-IDD program.

Slowly, Nicholas starts to seem like himself again. One day I catch him in a good mood and ask him how he is feeling.

"I feel happy, Mom. I like being home with you guys and my LEGO. I didn't like being in the hospital. I felt sad all the time there."

"I'm sure it felt very lonely."

"Yeah, I cried a lot."

"Did you?"

"Uh-huh. Mostly, I cried my tears in my heart, though. Sometimes I cry my tears here," he says, pointing to his chest. "They don't always come out of my face. But that is still crying, right?"

"You know, Bubba, I never thought of it that way, but that makes a lot of sense."

"Don't worry. I feel better now. But, Mom, do you think the other kids in the hospital are going to be okay? I think their hearts were still crying."

"I hope so, Nicholas. I hope so."

He nods, then holds up a small toy dinosaur. "Hey, Mom, check out my velociraptor."

"Very cool, Buddy. Very cool."

# Chapter 36

There are five social workers seated in a circle around our living room. Nicholas has been in inpatient treatment four times in the past eighteen months, but that's not what we are here to talk about today. After a few months of Saturday trainings, background checks, finger printings, and completing checklists around the house, our profile has been approved. We had a few home interviews already, and today is more of a match meeting. Briefly, my mind drifts to Dana, the first child we were presented with as a potential match. She must be at least fifteen by now. The county sent two caseworkers, our agency sent two of their own, and a separate agency has been working with the children and sent a transition specialist. We have been warned the siblings we are discussing are an especially difficult case.

"Ana and Donny have been in care for a little over two years," the brunette seated cross-legged on the fireplace explains. She introduced herself earlier as Nicole. "Their case is a hard one. The trauma is severe. We are seeking a placement that is up to that challenge." The last four homes the county has tried have fallen through. Ana is seven and her brother, Donny, is nine. The caseworkers do not have access to their current file yet, but they tell me to imagine the worst reason a child could be placed in care, then add a bit more. Then pile a bit more onto that. There absolutely will be behavior challenges. Can we handle it?

"We have experience with trauma, and we already have established relationships with therapists and resources in our area." I begin to tell them a bit more about Nicholas and Eddie interjects.

"Nick was hospitalized for a while last year. He has some behavior concerns of his own." We want to be honest, so we tell them in depth about some of Nicholas' issues. He is home and has been stable for a few months. The white board calendar in the kitchen shows his daily dose of medication and multiple appointments every week. By now the list of medications is long: Risperidone, Sertraline, Abilify, Clonidine, Topamax. There have been others on and off, and we have been looking into trying CBD. We don't know if that will keep them from thinking our home is a safe enough environment for additional kids. On the contrary, they seem to find it encouraging.

"Great, so you are comfortable taking the kids to therapy and getting services? And it sounds like you are not strangers to the behaviors our kids can sometimes exhibit. They are good kids, just processing hard things."

"Of course. Would you like a tour of the house?" A few of the caseworkers excuse themselves and leave for other appointments, but the woman named Nicole who works for the county stays. Eddie and my mother stay with the kids, and I walk with Nicole around our home, pointing out which beds and dressers would belong to Ana and Donny. Our last stop is the playroom, a recently finished area that sits above our garage.

"Oh, I'm sure the kids will love this," she says.

Now that we are alone and out of earshot of my other children, I take the opportunity to ask her the question that's been on my mind.

"Are you considering other families?" I need to gauge my expectations. I remember how soul-crushing those rejections can be.

Nicole looks straight into my eyes and is somber and serious when she says, "There is no one else. The decision is yours at this point." It is good news in that I am relieved there will not be competition, but I feel heavy as her response sinks into me. They have been trying to place these children for years, working in two different counties. Ours is currently the only home within fifty miles qualified and willing to have them. It's in my hands now whether to accept the challenge and become a mother of five overnight. Both of our new additions will have behavior concerns very similar to what we already see with Nicholas. Can I really handle going through all of this all over again, if we have to? If I say no, the most likely next step will be for them to go to a local group home, the modern-day version of an orphanage.

I nod at Nicole, "We will take them." Eddie and I have already discussed it with my mother. If the caseworkers said yes, our answer was also yes.

"Take a day to think about it and call me tomorrow."

We don't need more than fifteen minutes, but we oblige her anyway and call our agency the following day.

"That's great news," the voice on the other end of the line is smiling. "Let's set up your first meeting. How about Tuesday at McDonald's?"

# Epilogue

*Spring 2019*

"I'm excited, but nervous," Chelsea confides. Our new neighbors, pastor Bob's son and daughter-in-law, moved into a home less than a mile away from our own. I invited her over for tea during Nick's second hospitalization, and we became fast friends. Only a week after meeting us in-person, she organized a group to do our yardwork for the summer and set up a meal delivery chain for our family. We made a standing appointment to get together every Tuesday, but she never gives me a hard time when I need to cancel for some emergency that has popped up. Chelsea and her husband, Nate, have just completed the training to become a licensed foster home, but they have yet to receive a placement.

"What do you wish you would have known when you were getting started?" Her eyes are wide as she smiles, eagerly awaiting my response.

A flood of memories rushes back all at once, and there is so much I want to tell her, but it's hard to find the balance I want, one that will leave her encouraged but still contain the amount of honesty she deserves.

"If I could go back and talk to my younger self, I think she'd be relieved to see we are still here, thirteen years into our marriage, and everything is fine. I do wish we would have been more prepared to handle trauma and known how to access help." I tell her. "There just wasn't as much information about it available when we were getting started, so that will be a huge pro for you. People are starting to become better educated about it now."

She nods. I'm confident she will be an amazing foster mom. She walked with us through the darkest parts of our story and came out wanting to jump headfirst into the same universe. Her question deserves more attention than I can give it in a single conversation. I could fill a book with all of the things I didn't know back then, but wish I had understood. There are so many things I wish.

I wish trauma were recognized as its own category for educational and mental health services.

I wish lawmakers had a better understanding of the implications of their decisions.

I wish mental health services were more accessible, affordable, and easier to obtain. I wish people in America had a better understanding of how integral Medicaid access is to this process, regardless of a family's income.

I wish more people would share openly about their own experiences with brain health and treatment. The shame that clouds these conversations is harmful and unnecessary. I think I would have been a better mother if more people had been talking about this ten years ago.

I wish insurance companies, hospitals, and private practices treated mental health with the same quality of care they provide for physical ailments. I wish there were other options that did not involve our country's most vulnerable children being held in Emergency Rooms indefinitely, denied treatment based on neurological differences, and denied insurance money.

I wish teachers, doctors, and community leaders

received more training about trauma and mental health.

I wish community centers, libraries, hospitals, schools, and religious institutions published and distributed more information about how to obtain local mental health services. I wish free parenting courses were more widely available. I wish there were more books, movies, television shows, and other media centered around the reality of mental illness. Representation matters. I wish people like my son were not painted as simply scary, bad, and villainous as much as they were pictured as normal, complex, human, and suffering. I wish I saw parents of children with neurological differences represented more often in positive ways as well.

I wish as a country we were better at providing healthcare and pre and post-natal support to women. So much of Nicholas' early trauma was caused by circumstances that were purely economic. It seems arbitrary and unfair that I am the one who received financial support in the form of Medicaid or community-based therapies to help him and manage my own mental health, whereas his birth mother lost custody simply because she did not have access to similar supports. It would cost so much less pain and money to simply support birth mothers in the first place.

I wish people understood just how much we could change if we simply acknowledged and treated the trauma. Do they know that incarceration, homelessness, addiction, domestic violence, and teen pregnancy all have extremely high correlation rates to childhood trauma? The fastest, easiest, and least expensive way to start addressing all of those issues at once is simply to give people access to the treatment they need to begin healing.

I wish there were more facilities that offered help as our children grow. I wish we did not have areas in our country where mental health services simply do not exist. I wish we were not relying on prisons on the back end to address the problems we did not take the time or spend the money to solve up front.

I wish people understood that not all therapy is created equal, and I wish that more clinicians and first-responders were trained in trauma.

I wish we prepared ourselves as well for mental health emergencies as we do for others. We teach children how to "stop, drop, and roll" if they ever spontaneously catch on fire, not to take candy from strangers, and how to hide from school shooters, but so often we do not do a single thing to prepare families for the much more likely possibility that one day they or someone they love will experience a brain health crisis. Suicide is the second leading cause of death for teens and children over the age of ten in our country, yet as their parents, most people in my generation have no idea how to pro-actively fight against the forces that lead our children there.

I wish there were more foster parents, respite placements, CASA volunteers, and social workers. And I wish those of us in the trenches were better prepared to parent through trauma and the behaviors that may come with it.

"I'm going to miss you so much," Chelsea tells me.

"We are going to miss you too, but we will still just be a

text or Facetime away." The corners of my mouth curl up. There is a For Sale sign on our front yard. Eddie has a new job offer that will pay him well, and we are headed back to Florida in hopes things will be better for all of us there. The weather will be good for Nicholas' health, and he will be close to his biological roots. It will be a fresh start for the rest of us as well, a chance to start over. Between selling the house, Eddie's new position, the lower taxes, and Nicholas finally having the Medicaid Access which paid this years' medical bills, we have climbed out of the hole and are on-track to pay off all $128,000 dollars of our debt within the next six months. But it means we have to leave.

I wish this story had a happier, more hopeful ending, and maybe it will, but we don't know how it ends because we are still in the middle of living it. For now, Nicholas is still home and doing well. Looking at all five of my children playing in the living room as I answer Chelsea's questions, I wish I had the power to fix all of it, but I'm only one person, so I need to stop focusing on what I wish and start concentrating on what I *will* do.

What I will do is keep moving forward, especially on the days when I would rather curl up and give in. I will educate myself, discover the resources available to us, raise my family to the best of my ability, and continue to share our life and our knowledge of available services with every person who will let me. I will give my children space to share their stories, and when they ask to use my voice, I will gladly lend it to the conversation. It doesn't feel like enough, but I believe that if just one person who had lived through similar experiences had been sharing openly with us at the beginning, it would have been everything.

What I will do is keep working and hoping that our story has the power to touch hearts and open minds. What I will do is push shame and embarrassment aside and ask for help, always.

And I hope that you will too.

# Letter to the Reader

Dear Reader,

I'm happy to say that as I am typing this letter, it is 2021 and Nicholas has been home full-time for over two years. His aggression has significantly decreased. Only time will tell if that continues, but he has benefited greatly from techniques like Internal Family Systems therapy, learning coping strategies to regulate his emotions and behaviors, and medication. Ana and Donny joined our family and our adoption was finalized in the spring of 2019. We are now a family of seven. We became debt-free other than our mortgage in 2020, but unfortunately, we also lost Nicholas' access to Medicaid when we relocated to a new state.

The reason that there are no dates included for the last few chapters of the book is because in real life many of those events were happening concurrently, between the spring of 2018 and the summer of the following year. For the sake of simplicity, I chose to present them in a linear fashion.

Over the past two decades, there have been huge strides made to understand trauma and how it affects the brain and to help children like Nicholas, Ana, and Donny, but we have a long way to go.

Because Nicholas was a child when he began to experience brain health issues, as his mother it was important for me to share this story from my perspective so that it could benefit a reader as much as possible by showing how families can obtain access to help and resources, and also show the obstacles that parents can face trying to do so.

However, I wanted to be sure that Nicholas' voice was included in the telling of this story as much as possible. The remainder of this book is filled with interviews with Nicholas and other family members as well as resources for you.

I want to acknowledge that as a neurotypical person, my voice should not be the leading voice in this conversation. I encourage you to seek out neurodiverse voices and listen.

I will never be able to thank you enough for investing in our family and our story. Writing this book was the most difficult undertaking of my life, and we appreciate the time, money, and emotional investments you made to get here with us. Our story may have made you uncomfortable. That's okay and we understand. Our hope is that you will feel moved to act.

By purchasing this book, you have already begun to help. As a family, while we believe their stories are important and respect their willingness to share, we have no interest in profiting financially from our children's trauma, so proceeds from this book will be donated to organizations such as The Heart Gallery of Tampa and The National Federation of Families.

Further action might look like passing a copy of *All I Never Knowed* on to another family so that they feel less alone in a time of crisis. It might mean taking a minute right now to add a crisis line phone number to the list of emergency contacts on the side of your refrigerator. I hope you will also add that number to your cell phone contacts and to your teenagers' phones. This book is not a substitute for professional counseling. Please make an appointment with a licensed therapist or healthcare provider if you or a family member need help.

I hope you have been given ideas through our story about how to access mental health resources in your own area. Maybe you will write or call your local government representatives, or maybe you will enter a field like social work or psychology as a profession. More information about how to access emergency mental health services as well as a list of coping strategies that have helped Nicholas can be found in the "Resources" and "Coping Strategies" sections of this book. However, those strategies should also not be considered a substitute for professional advice.

We welcome you to join the effort. Every child and family deserve the chance to access mental health services and receive the help they need without the fear that it will lead to bankruptcy or social stigma. All children deserve access to appropriate services in school and in the community.

Thank you again. And if this book found you because you are in the midst of a similar story, please know you are not alone. You are valued. You are worthy. You are loved. You are worth the fight.

Love,<br>
Steph

# Family Interviews

## In Their Own Words:
## Interviews with Giese Family Members

*Transcribed from audio recordings and edited for clarity.*

### Nicholas, age 13
Conversation #1

**Stephanie:** I'm here with Nicholas today. It is July 27<sup>th</sup> in the year 2020 and Nick's going to talk to us a little bit today about brain health and about when kids' brains get sick. Okay, can you tell your story?

**Nick:** Okay, so what happened when I was in the hospital was I was eventually transferred to a hospital called KidsPeace and it was very hard for me. People were beating me up and it made me upset, and then I came home and I gave my mom and dad a hug and it made me very good inside. My feelings were very hurt once I got there, but once I came home I gave everyone a hug and everyone cheered and yelled, "Yay, Nick's here! I'm glad you're here, Nick." And that was pretty much it.

**Stephanie:** Can you talk about why you were in the hospital?

**Nicholas:** Yeah, sure. I was in the hospital because I did some very physical things, I was punching people, kicking people, throwing a fit with people and, like, not getting what I want. And, like, that's pretty much it about that too. And most of it was the medicine that can cause that. Most of it was my actions, too. So, it was mostly all of that.

**Stephanie:** And why were you on medicine?

**Nicholas:** I was on medication so that can help me. One reason why they can help me is because it helps me stay on task, and it hits me very well to, like, get my mood back on for the medicine to help. And there's been some fear times for me that I've been having some issues with impactions, sometimes with impactions with one of my meds. You don't have to worry about that. It's pretty much nothing, that's just impactions and stuff.

**Stephanie:** Can you talk a little bit more about the fear times?

**Nicholas:** Well, the fear times that I used to have were like when I have anxiety, a lot of anxiety about my birth parents and all. A lot of anxiety about some other people, my family and friends in case this Coronavirus doesn't get all mixed up in all that. I wanted this Coronavirus to end, and sometimes I have anxiety about the Coronavirus and I really wish it could end, but...

**Stephanie:** Okay, but what were you having anxiety about when you had to go to the hospital?

**Nicholas:** I was having anxiety about when I went to the hospital, I was having anxiety about people beating me up, I was having anxiety about, like, people.

**Stephanie:** That happened in the hospital?

**Nicholas:** Yeah. I was also afraid people were gonna say that and do that before I was going to go in the hospital.

**Stephanie:** Where?

**Nicholas:** Well, not in the hospital. I mean I was thinking about that before I came in the hospital. I was afraid people were gonna do that.

**Stephanie:** Okay. But you talked a little bit about how your actions made it so you needed to be hospitalized. Can you talk a little bit about what was going on in your brain and your actions that made us have to take you to the hospital?

**Nicholas:** Um, yeah. Yes, my brain and actions weren't that very good. The reason why they weren't very good is because they were very messed up and my brain couldn't handle it. My brain just needed help because sometimes my brain doesn't work the right way, and I don't know why the reason why is, but I just can't figure it out.

**Stephanie:** So, what are some things that you do when you feel like your brain's not working the way you would like it to?

**Nicholas:** What do you mean?

**Stephanie:** Like coping strategies.

**Nicholas:** Oh, what coping strategies I do is I usually play LEGOs, play my guitar when I get upset, or build something creative out of my LEGOs or whatever. Play with clay, play with Play-doh if I get upset.

**Stephanie:** Okay, what would you say to kids who feel like maybe their brains aren't working the way that they would like them to? What's your advice to kids who are struggling with their brain health?

**Nicholas:** Well, I would probably just say be careful out there and just make sure that you're doing your coping strategies, and make sure your medications are really doing well. Make sure those doctors are taking care of you very well. Make sure the doctors are protecting you. Make sure your mom is protecting you from any harm. Just to make sure your moms are protecting you from any harm, just in case you get physicalated or anything.

**Stephanie:** I think that's very good advice. So, what did you ask me to do so that kids could have more information about hospitals, do you remember? Do you remember asking me to write something?

**Nick:** A book?

**Stephanie:** Yeah, that's what you asked me to write. Do you remember that?

**Nicholas:** Yeah, I remember.

**Stephanie:** Well, this is part of that. I'm gonna try to type up part of this conversation to put it in the book. Would that be okay with you?

**Nicholas:** Yeah, that's fine.

**Stephanie:** All right, thanks, Nick.

**Nicholas:** You're welcome. Did it record or is it...?

**Stephanie:** Yeah, it recorded.


Conversation #2


**Stephanie:** Today is July 28th, 2020 and I am here with Nicholas today, and we are recording about brain health, and specifically brain health issues. And Nick's going to share his thoughts today about what happens in his own brain when he's struggling with some brain health issues. (To Nick) Can you just explain what happens in your mind when you're having what you call "an incident?"

**Nicholas:** Um, yes. When I have incidents, when my brain says I have incidents, explain that I usually have this incident and some incidents and that usually causes we already know, you already know what it causes, but um, I just don't know why. I just don't know why the reason is, but I just can't think of it any, but I don't know why my brain works that way.

**Stephanie:** What happens in your brain when you do have an incident? Even though you don't know why, what does happen?

**Nicholas:** When I do have an incident, I like I said, I punch people and kick people a lot, and like maybe thrash on the floor a lot. I kick the dog a lot, my dog. And my brain is telling me to do all those things. It wants me to do all those things because it just wants me to react to that behavior because it's, um, I just don't know how to explain it. But I guess it's just kind of hard.

**Stephanie:** Okay, and what would you say if a kid is having an incident like that and they don't understand what's happening or why it's happening, what could they do?

**Nicholas:** They could talk to someone, as in a therapist or, like, a social worker or someone like that. Or maybe not a social worker, maybe someone like a social worker or whatever. Maybe someone more like a therapist, or someone more like a person who wants to take care of you very well.

**Stephanie:** Okay, great. I think that's an important answer. So, you think kids should know that they should ask for help if they need it?

**Nicholas:** Yeah. Yeah.

**Stephanie:** Yeah? That's what I'm hearing. Okay,

awesome. And do you remember when you started going to therapy how you felt?

**Nicholas:** Yes, I felt pretty scared in therapy at first, but then I got through it and it felt and my brain felt scared at first in therapy. But then my brain felt and then I felt "Wow, this is very interesting, I like it now." And I felt very shy at therapy at first, but then my brain was changed a lot in therapy and talking about my feelings a lot, it made me express my feeling a lot, and it changed a lot more.

**Stephanie:** That's awesome. So, you feel like it helped you a lot?

**Nicholas:** Yeah.

**Stephanie:** Very cool. Who do you think has helped you the most to have coping strategies for your brain?

**Nicholas:** My therapists. Mostly my mom, and my dad, and my grandmother. Not my grandmother, but my mom's mom. And that's pretty much it.

**Stephanie:** Ok, great. Is there anything else that you would like to share with kids who might be having some problems with their brain health?

**Nicholas:** Not really.

**Stephanie:** All right. Thank you.

**Nicholas:** You're welcome

**Stephanie:** Good job.


Conversation #3


**Stephanie:** Today is July 29th, 2020, and I am Stephanie Giese, and I am here with my son Nicholas Giese to do our third interview. So, Nick, do you want to say hi?

**Nicholas:** Hi.

**Stephanie:** Okay, so I have two questions for you today. The first question is why did you want to write a book for kids with brain health [concerns] and talk about your own brain health stuff?

**Nicholas:** Um, just to let them know about some advice and some things, just to let them learn about some new things that I haven't told them yet.

**Stephanie:** Okay. What are those things?

**Nicholas:** I can't actually remember, but it was what I told you when I told you and what I told the other people, too.

**Stephanie:** Okay, so are you talking about, like, years ago when we would have conversations about this and when you would talk about how you wanted to write a book?

**Nicholas:** Yeah, yeah.

**Stephanie:** All that stuff? Okay. My last question for you, I think, is can you talk a little bit about what you call "The Boss" in your head? Can you explain what that is and how that works for you?

**Nicholas:** The Boss is a technological brain problem in my head that he likes to control me a lot, and he likes to control me with my brain a lot, and he likes to mess with my brain. And he likes to connect with me and say mean things to me when we sometimes we agree and sometimes we don't. Today we did so...

**Stephanie:** What did you agree about today?

**Nicholas:** We agreed about, today we agreed about not

doing mean things. I don't remember what those mean things were, but we just agreed not doing mean things.

**Stephanie:** Okay. So, do you feel you have conversations with him at the beginning of each day?

**Nicholas:** Yeah.

**Stephanie:** Yeah? And you decide how your day's going to go?

**Nicholas:** Uh-huh.

**Stephanie:** Interesting. Okay, what are some examples of mean things that he might ask you to do?

**Nicholas:** He might ask me to punch, kick, and some other stuff. He might ask me to swear at people, cuss at people a lot and just not behave, so.

**Stephanie:** Why do you think that is?

**Nicholas:** Cuz sometimes me and The Boss can't agree and I can't talk it out myself with him cuz I seem a little scared when I talk to him, cuz he's pretty rude to me a lot and I don't know why the reason he's mean to me is. I just can't figure it out.

**Stephanie:** Hmm. So, who helps you to deal with The Boss and how to talk to him?

**Nicholas:** My therapist and some of my other parts in my brain help me with that.

**Stephanie:** Okay. All right. Is there anything else that you want to share with kids who might feel the same way?

**Nicholas:** Uh, no, not really. Just tell them to stay safe and just what I told them before, like to learn what I told them today. And to stay safe for their health and parents and stuff.

**Stephanie:** Okay. Thank you for doing this with me.

**Nicholas:** You're welcome.

## Perspective from a Sibling:
## A Conversation with Abigail, age 11

**Stephanie:** I am here on August 3rd with my daughter Abigail Giese. And we are recording to talk a little bit about brain health in kids and Abby's experiences with her brother, Nicholas, and inpatient treatment, and his behaviors. So, Abby, do you remember, well let me say, what's the first thing you remember about maybe realizing that Nick was a little bit different than you and his brain worked differently? Loud, please, so I can hear.

**Abigail:** Oh, okay. I don't know, but I remember sitting in like an office at our old house and I asked why Nick acted the way he does, and then you went into this entire conversation about um....

**Stephanie:** You can use whatever words that you're comfortable with. What do you mean by "he acted the way he did?" Like what behaviors?

**Abigail:** It was just, I don't know, it just seemed weird to me for some reason. I don't...

**Stephanie:** What was weird about it? Like the way he talked, or the way he acted, or?

**Abigail:** It wasn't the way he talked. It was just like...he's just kind of...he's...this is hard. Okay, it was just I can't explain it. Like, it was just, okay, so imagine a line full of giraffes.

**Stephanie:** Okay.

**Abigail:** And then they all have the same neck height except this one kid, this one giraffe, has a neck longer or shorter than all the other giraffes. And, like, you might not

369

notice it until you look a little farther, like a little closer or whatever. And then you just kind of realize that.

**Stephanie:** Okay, so I think that's a really good analogy. Um, so he just seemed different when you compared him to all the other kids around you?

**Abigail:** Yeah. Like if he was the only one I knew in my entire life I'm pretty sure I wouldn't have noticed anything. But, yeah.

**Stephanie:** Okay. What's your favorite thing about your brother, Nicholas?

**Abigail:** I like his LEGO sculptures. He's very dedicated to his LEGOs.

**Stephanie:** That's true, he is. If you were going to describe him to someone who had never met him, what would you say?

**Abigail:** Not your average type. Like, well not in a mean way, but like one that's kind of stands out, but also fades in the background? That doesn't make any sense and that sounds like I'm being a brat.

**Stephanie:** (laughs) No, it doesn't.

**Abigail:** But like, I would describe him as friendly. He likes talking to people at our church and school. He talks a lot. Yes. Talks a lot. Yeah. I mean, friendly when he wants to be.

**Stephanie:** All right. Do you remember when Nick had to go to the hospital?

**Abigail:** Yes.

**Stephanie:** What stands out to you about that time?

**Abigail:** Three things. One, I was in the girls' bedroom with Donny, Penny, and Ana, and they were sitting on the bed trying to tell jokes. And I was just over here looking out the door into the hallway just like, "Again?" because it had happened before. And I remember sitting on the couch and I remember a police officer, a big buff police officer, at our door and you and dad talking to him. And like I don't remember where Nick was, but that's another thing. And then I remember the office and I remember sitting down. We were all talking to Nick on the phone and he, someone accidentally hit the hang up button and then you started crying. I don't mean to make you feel uncomfortable.

**Stephanie:** No, I'm not uncomfortable.

**Abigail:** And then you called him back. I don't know why that's so vivid. And then I remember my siblings who weren't Nick sitting on a fireplace, oh this is four memories, okay, and I remember me sitting on the carpet of our living room. And lots of swearing. And then...

**Stephanie:** Who was swearing?

**Abigail:** Nick. And then I got mad and I swore, which I regret doing. It was my first time swearing. And I was like nine, so that's not good, but you know, that's okay I guess. Not really, but whatever. You know, it's fine.

**Stephanie:** I'm not mad at you at all about that.

**Abigail:** But those were the four but I don't know why. Oh. One other thing I remember. This wasn't when he was in the hospital. I remember trying to talk to him, like a lot. Trying to talk to him about getting his feeling and trying to explain what was happening without making him feel, like, uncertain if that makes any sense.

**Stephanie:** Mmm-hmm. He likes to talk to you a lot as a coping strategy. He says you're one of the people who helps

371

him the most when he's having what he calls an incident. Do you have any strategies that you use to help him, or is there anything special you do with him to help with that?

**Abigail:** I don't act as if it's like this humongous deal. I stay calm. I try not to get mad, and I make him breathe in for five seconds, hold it for six, out through seven, which I learned through a book. And then I try and talk about feelings and emotion because men are sometimes unclear about emotions, and yeah. And especially middle school boys, like you know. Like, there isn't anything wrong with him, and sometimes I feel like people would [think] that. So I try to make him feel like there isn't anything wrong with him, 'cuz there's nothing really wrong with him. Makes sense?

**Stephanie:** Yeah, absolutely.

**Abigail:** And then I just talk and I try, yeah. That's that.

**Stephanie:** I think that's a great answer. Do you remember the name of the book that you learned that from?

**Abigail:** No. It was just a book.

**Stephanie:** That's okay. What has been the hardest thing for you, being a sister to someone who struggles with their brain health?

**Abigail:** [There are] not a lot of people my age that I can talk to about it because the only other people that I know relate to this are my siblings who are close in age, but they also have [brain health issues]. And so, it's kind of like I feel like I'm making them feel uncomfortable. Or just that kind of thing. And then Penny, I don't know. She's not like young, but she's not...I feel like she won't understand. And I just don't like talking to parents about that stuff. No offense.

**Stephanie:** (laughs) I'm not offended. I appreciate that you're being very honest with us.

**Abigail:** And most people in your school can't relate to any of this kind of thing.

**Stephanie:** Sure.

**Abigail:** So......

**Stephanie:** So, it feels lonely sometimes?

**Abigail:** Yeah.

**Stephanie:** I can understand that. I feel the same way as a mom sometimes. What is some advice that you would give to kids who are either struggling with their brain health or might know someone who is struggling with their brain health?

**Abigail:** To the people who are struggling, like I know it's hard but talk about it with someone. If it makes you feel uncomfortable talking to your parents, or a sibling, or even just a friend, if you have a therapist talk about it with them. Or if you don't have one just even talking to stuffed animals helps. Same for people who are, like, feeling stressed who don't have [brain health issues] or are struggling, talking about it even if you're just talking to like a stuffed animal or a wall.

**Stephanie:** Okay.

**Abigail:** Or if like a fictional character. I do that sometimes. And to those people who are struggling with having someone struggling... that makes so much sense. (Both laugh)

**Stephanie:** We know what you mean. Have a family member struggling or a friend?

**Abigail:** Yeah. If they don't feel comfortable telling you everything that happened right away, just be patient with them. It may seem very annoying that you have to be very patient and just waiting. Just be patient. Be trustworthy. Listen to what they have to say. Don't pretend you're listening when you're really not. Like actually listen to what they have to say. Because sometimes you can learn something from what someone has to say and they don't know that they're helping you, and you're trying to help them. They could also be helping you at the same time.

**Stephanie:** That's very mature and very profound advice. I actually think that I'm learning a lot from you in this conversation.

**Abigail:** Yes, yes. Children. Parents learn a lot from their children, so listen to us.

**Stephanie:** That's very true. (Laughs)

**Abigail:** We have things to say. Just because we're young doesn't mean we don't know things.

**Stephanie:** That's very true.

**Abigail:** So, listen to us. Listen to everybody. Well, don't like listen to a random stranger on the side of the street. But listen to people like your parents, your siblings, your friends, those kind of things. Listen to what people have to say.

**Stephanie:** Awesome. And so, to wrap up, if you're a kid and another kid comes to you and tells you that they have something that they think is a secret, and it might be something about brain health, what do you think you should do? For example, if a kid came to you and said that they wanted to hurt themselves or hurt one of their siblings or something like that, what would you do? Or what should you do?

**Abigail:** Tell an adult. Or, like, tell them to tell an adult. And if they don't tell an adult, I'm going to tell an adult. Because, like, I don't want to invade on their privacy, but if they're going to hurt someone or themselves you need to tell someone. Give them time to tell themselves, and you tell [an adult] if they don't do it right away, make sense?

**Stephanie:** Yes, that makes a lot of sense. I think that's a very good answer. Well, thank you for sitting down and talking to me today. You had a lot of very mature responses to these questions, and I think this is going to help a lot of kids who maybe would be very confused to find themselves in this situation, and I hope your experiences can help them.

**Abigail:** If you're ever confused, if you're a child and you're confused, your parents have answers to most things, but sometimes nobody has the answer to the question you're asking yourself. So, what I do is I have a journal. I have a question journal, or that's what I call it, but some people call it a diary or whatever. And I just write down random questions. Sometimes I'll ask them at, like, dinner. I do this thing called Question of the Day when I ask everybody and they all answer. Or sometimes I don't ask them because it's not a thing that can be answered by a human or anything. It's just your mind is very confusing whether you have brain health or issues, or even just if you don't. You brain is confusing. It will always confuse you. Another thing, if you're confused and ask yourself what you're so confused about, and like if you find that, ask somebody and they will probably have the answer. If they don't, write it down, write a story, draw a picture. What are some other things?

**Stephanie:** Those are all great coping strategies. I know you like to play music.

**Abigail:** Yeah, I like music.

**Stephanie:** All right. Well thanks again for talking to me about this today.

**Abigail:** (whispering) Ask me another question.

**Stephanie:** (laughing) One more question. Okay.

**Abigail:** I normally don't like talking about myself, but this is kind of fun.

**Stephanie:** Okay, well let's do one more question today. Let's see. I think I asked most of the things that I had in mind. Is there any question that you have for me that you would like to ask? Or is there just any other general advice that you have for anyone?

**Abigail:** If you don't have a coping strategy, experiment with, like, different things in your room. Like reading. If you have a book, read. If you have a journal, draw. If you're allowed on your phone, or even watch TV. Try getting into a good TV show. That can, like, distract you. Reading, I really like reading because, okay I don't want to expose myself but I'm gonna do it anyway, so reading takes me into a different world. It's just like you get to be somebody else for a day. And that's why I like acting. It's like you don't have to feel feelings, I don't know. That sounds so weird, but like you can just be free for a day. And if you don't like the ending to a story you can change it in your own mind and say "This is how it ends." You can do that with life, too. Just be like, "This is not how it ends."

**Stephanie:** Okay.

**Abigail:** I like theater because, I don't know, when I'm acting I can just act like I've had everything's okay, even though it's not. I can just pretend, you know?

**Stephanie:** Sure.

**Abigail:** Music helps because you can just express yourself and some people will relate, some people won't, but that's okay because you'll find someone that you relate to. Like, you express yourself through music. You don't have to share it with the world, you can keep it to yourself, but you can share it to the world. It doesn't matter. Art. You can express pictures in your mind and place them down on a piece of paper, and that kind of stuff.

**Stephanie:** Yeah. There are going to be people, if I publish this book, who think that it's a very bad idea to share my kids' thoughts and feelings that way and to share Nicholas' experiences. What do you think about that philosophy? Do you think that it's a good idea or a bad idea to share this book?

**Abigail:** To share this book with their children?

**Stephanie:** The book is probably going to be more for adults and parents.

**Abigail:** Yeah, I get that cuz, like, you're an adult and you're writing it for them.

**Stephanie:** There are going to be a lot of people who think that talking about things like brain health should be private and that we shouldn't talk about it, because Nick's just a kid and he doesn't know what he's doing when he says that we should share them. What do you think about that?

**Abigail:** So, like, are you saying that parent doesn't want to tell their child that they have [brain health issues]...

**Stephanie:** No. There are going to be people who say, like they're probably going to say, "Oh, Stephanie Giese was very irresponsible when she wrote this book and how dare she share that stuff with the whole world because her son deserves more privacy than that." How do you feel about that?

**Abigail:** That's her decision that she gets to make. It's your decision. It's like your own decision. And, okay, so you don't have to scream it to the world that your child has brain health issues or whatever, but you can also tell a few people. And some ways to, like, tell people this are make sure they are trustworthy, and trust them enough to tell them this without them posting it all over social media and then starting this whole new thing that everyone's going to talk about for, like, a month and then everybody will eventually forget because that's how social media works. And make sure that person is mature enough to understand what it means, and make sure if they have questions about that— like some adults have questions about this stuff—like, try to answer them as best as possible. If you don't know something just say, "I don't know." Don't go into this whole thing about, like, "Oh, I don't know, BUT blah, blah." Like say you don't know. It's okay you don't know.

**Stephanie:** Do you, as a person who is in our family, do you have any problems with the book being shared, do you think? I know you haven't read it yet, but?

**Abigail:** Well, I don't intend to. No [offense to] you, but it's kind of a little old for me. Obviously, there's going to be some people in the world who hate it.

**Stephanie:** Sure.

**Abigail:** Everybody hates some things. There are just going to be the people out in the world who hate everything, like "I don't like the way you wrote this sentence. You used a comma instead of an 'and.'" Okay, so? But there are going to be some people who find this really helpful. Some people might like to understand what other people are going through because they have a family or know a family who has this issue. So, it can be helpful, and some people might just not like it. But you know what? With love, it comes with pain and hate and all that kind of stuff. But, you know, you just gotta forget the pain and the hate. You just gotta remember the love because the love is all that matters.

**Stephanie:** I think that's a great ending. All right. Thanks, Abby.

# In Dad's Words:
## Interview with Eddie

**Stephanie:** This is Stephanie and Eddie Giese on September 11, 2020 here to talk about all of the issues we're discussing in the book and get Eddie's perspective on them. How are you feeling about me writing this book?

**Eddie:** I feel pretty neutral, like it doesn't bother me at all. I think it's good for you to get all that out on paper, and I guess when I read through it, it just brought back a lot of memories and feelings and stuff like that. But it also helps me see how far we've come at this point. Hopefully things will continue to improve. But, yeah, pretty neutral overall.

**Stephanie:** All right, awesome. Can you comment on the accuracy of the stuff in the book?

**Eddie:** I think it's very accurate. I think there's some spots where you took a little creative liberty because it's hard to remember exactly what happened and some of the nuance, but overall it definitely gets the feeling across of what happened. Actually, I'm surprised at how much you remember, how much detail you remember that I didn't remember until you brought it up and explained it, and then I was like, "Oh, yeah. It did happen that way." So, yeah, it's good. Do you need a number, or?

**Stephanie:** No.

**Eddie:** Okay. I'm an engineer, so I like numbers.

**Stephanie:** (laughs) I know. How do you feel about Nicholas and his brain health as a dad?

**Eddie:** It's...he's challenging. He's very, very challenging. It's difficult for me because as a father I'm supposed to be, you know, a little bit more stern and still loving, but I'm supposed to be the discipline enforcer and the rule maker, abider, all that. So, it's difficult to have flexibility in that, and because sometimes if my job is to enforce a rule or whatever it creates a whole other situation. And so, I think in particular he has a hard time with me anyway, and I think that's probably the case for a lot of boys. [They] have a hard time with their dads, especially at his age because he's trying to be the male and, you know, his T levels are really high going through puberty and everything, so I bite my tongue a lot.

**Stephanie:** (laughs)

**Eddie:** Although it might not seem like it. It has definitely tried my patience over the years. It has made me a more understanding individual, not just within our family but outside of that. And more sensitive. My views on life and the world have changed a lot and a lot of that has to do with him and the effect that he's had on me.

**Stephanie:** Yeah, I feel the same way about a lot of that. Can you talk a little bit about a male perspective on therapy and treatment?

**Eddie:** Well, I do think there's this stigma. I mean it's not an easy thing for most men or even boys to talk about feelings, and it's often, "Man up, young man. Push it under the rug." Or whatever, to talk about your feelings. So, I think especially with men, there's definitely a stigma and a societal norm or pressure to not explore that and bring that out. I personally never really had a problem with it and I think it'd be nice if it was more normal for men to talk about that kind of stuff.

I think when you get to know somebody on a deeper level, men in particular since you asked, those things start to come out. But we never just sit around and talk about our feelings. It just doesn't happen. Like "Oh, I'm so upset by this and blah blah." That just, in the circle that I've been in at least, and I think that's pretty representative, it just doesn't happen. So, I am very supportive of therapy. I think it's a great idea, but I think it's tough. And until more guys make it normal, you know, you're not a sissy or whatever if you go see a therapist. You just have learned to talk about your feelings. I actually think that makes you more manly because you can identify an issue, face it head on, and deal with it, and just because it's mental health it doesn't mean it needs to be something to be ashamed of.

**Stephanie:** Awesome. So, what do you think that dads in particular could do to end the stigma of mental health in their own families, starting at home?

**Eddie:** Well, it's tough because I do think there's value in telling boys to man up sometimes and to be strong.

**Stephanie:** Can you elaborate on what you mean by that?

**Eddie:** (deep breath) Uh, it's hard to explain. It's kind of abstract.

**Stephanie:** Are you talking about like if they get a cut on their knee or if they're in, like, emotional situations?

**Eddie:** Well, sure. But yeah, emotional. I mean I think it's important to teach toughness in boys and girls because life is hard. It's never gonna be just a cakewalk and so if they just fold every time there's some kind of issue that faces them...

**Stephanie:** What do you mean by "toughness?" Do you mean like not crying?

**Eddie:** No.

**Stephanie:** Or do you mean something else?

**Eddie:** Like, not just folding up and running away from whatever problem or issue that faces them. That's what I mean.

**Stephanie:** Okay.

**Eddie:** Facing up to it, dealing with it, good or bad. Being brave and pushing through something even if you don't like it.

**Stephanie:** Okay.

**Eddie:** So, I do think that's important. And I think it's important to instill, but I also think that can't be the only thing. So, I guess if you were asking me for what advice, although I'm in no position to give any to other dads, it would be balance. Show them that it's okay to be vulnerable and express feelings, but also that they can be strong.

**Stephanie:** Awesome, I think that's a great answer.

**Eddie:** Well, good.

**Stephanie:** (laughs) Is there anything that you would like to add that you did not see included in the book or that you just think is important to make sure people know?

**Eddie:** Um (long pause) well, I guess one thing would be support is very important, but also if you're a person who's being in a supporting role, whether it's family or friends or acquaintances or whatever, colleagues, whatever it might be, just understand that the people who are going through it are still gonna feel isolated and lonely. No matter what support and time you put into them, money or other resources or whatever that might be, just understand that they're gonna feel isolated no matter what. And so, you just need to continue to be there, check in whatever, cuz that does matter and help. But there's no way to avoid it, it just feels like you're on an island and even if you're, like in our case, you know we have a strong relationship, supportive partners. If anything, it made us stronger and grew us closer together. But I can see how it breaks up marriages, absolutely. I think we're very fortunate that we were in a good spot before that happened, and so we were supportive of each other, but even then, even the two of us, I mean there were, you know, it's just hard.

**Stephanie:** Yeah.

**Eddie:** Certain aspects were really dark times and you just feel like you're alone and like nobody else gets it, even though there are other people that are going through it and you have support, and you have love, and you have a partner. It just still feels like you're in a dark cave or whatever by yourself. And sometimes you can't see a way out, and you just have to keep going and cliché "put one foot in front of the other," but that's it. Just keep doing your life.

I remember going to work one day after Nick had been taken up to the hospital and somebody had asked me, "What are you doing here, you shouldn't be here." And I'm like, "I can't be at home right now. I can't be alone with my thoughts. I just need to work and think about something else." And I know that you were at home, but you were doing something else too, because you can't. You just have to make a conscious decision at some point to just not submerge yourself in it either. I mean, it's all-consuming, but you have to distract yourself. So, it wasn't like I was choosing a different priority. I mean, my work was very understanding and they were like, "Take all the time you need. What can we do to help?" Um, but I was like, "What I need is just to be here, and treat me like you would normally treat me." It felt, I guess, it felt a lot like grief. Although we hadn't lost anybody, you know, in that sense, that's kinda what it felt like. And so, just like if you were dealing with grief through a loss, the only person that can really deal with that is you. Because you have to work through that.

**Stephanie:** Yeah. I know I noticed a pattern among my own friends where a lot of times people are afraid to say or do the wrong thing and they just kind of freeze and don't do anything.

**Eddie:** Well, it is tough to navigate. I think people who have been through that or something like that know what to say or what to do, but they might be just so exhausted from dealing with their own stuff that they can't put out that emotional energy. But I think you're right. I think some people just don't know what to say or do. It definitely comes from a good place, but they withhold and "Oh, we're thinking about you" or something. Which means something, but yeah.

**Stephanie:** I definitely started to appreciate the doers more and notice that's something I could improve myself when our friends go through hard times. 'Cuz the people who just didn't even ask and showed up, and were like, "I'm bringing you a pizza tonight" or whatever [were very helpful].

**Eddie:** Yeah, that probably made the big aspect [easier]. Or "Here's gift cards for gas" or "Here we're sending you $200." Or whatever. "Hey, we're gonna come up this weekend and you can take a nap or something."

**Stephanie:** Watch the kids, yeah.

**Eddie:** Watch the other kids or whatever it was. You know, there were so many different things, but yeah, you're right.

**Stephanie:** Yeah, the people who didn't need me to tell them what we needed, and didn't ask for permission, and were just like, "We are doing this" I really valued a lot during that time.

**Eddie:** Mmm-hmm.

**Stephanie:** Um, is there anything else that you wanted to add just from your perspective on our story?

**Eddie:** Mmm, I don't think I ever thought it would be like this. (laughs)

**Stephanie:** (laughs) I think all parents can say that in some capacity. But if you had known what you know now, would you do it again?

**Eddie:** That's a tough question because I feel like a horrible person if I say no. I don't honestly know. It's been really hard and, just even recently those thoughts have been in my head as to man what would it have been like, you know? But even then, you don't know. So, it's dumb to play that hypothetical game and it's not healthy, so.

**Stephanie:** Yeah.

**Eddie:** That's just something I'm just struggling with internally, but trying to push those thoughts and ideas outside of my head because it doesn't do any good to sit there and dwell on that.

**Stephanie:** Yeah.

**Eddie:** I mean, I'm a firm believer that everything happens for a reason and that God's pulling the strings on everything that happens in our life, whether it's for our own good or the greater good. I knew there would be stuff that we dealt with. I don't think I ever thought it would be like this. It showed me that we could do really hard things, though.

**Stephanie:** Yeah. For sure.

**Eddie:** It's just one day, maybe sometimes it was an hour, at a time you were just trying to do.

**Stephanie:** Yeah. Sometimes I don't think I would make any different decisions, but I do wish that I could go back with the knowledge that we gained and tell [myself] about the resources and stuff.

**Eddie:** Yeah, yeah that's a good way to look at it.

**Stephanie:** Because I think that we would do it better if we knew what we know now.

**Eddie:** Yeah, I think that's a good point. And because of that it might never have come to what it came to. So maybe that's more what I feel about with my "I don't know" answer? Maybe it's more of a I wish I would've done certain things differently. You know?

**Stephanie:** I think that's one of the reasons why the book is an important thing to create, because when we were going through it there just weren't any resources like this from the perspective of parents or...

**Eddie:** Well, and if there were they were not easy to find.

**Stephanie:** Yeah.

**Eddie:** I mean, and just with like every state being completely different, and then the situation with healthcare in this country it's like, "Well, you can get that in one state, but you have to have Medicaid to get it." Which is just dumb. Like, why is it so hard to get to mental health services? If you have or if you don't have Medicaid, why should that matter? That's stupid. It's just really dumb.

**Stephanie:** Yeah.

**Eddie:** I mean apart from, like a psychiatrist and you know, a therapist, but some of the more intensive stuff. Like why? I just have such a problem with the fact that we're profiting off people being sick. Because every person has something wrong. There's no perfect person, whether it's a physical or a mental illness, and how much money people are making on that is just disgusting to me. But even still, and it's a little bit different, but just the access to things.

**Stephanie:** Yeah.

**Eddie:** It's so hard. There were things that we didn't even learn about until we were...like the mobile crisis.

**Stephanie:** Mmm-hmm.

**Eddie:** We didn't even know that was a thing until we were like

**Stephanie** (laughs) Using them? Yeah.

**Eddie:** We were, this was the second year of issues, which was the biggest one, and we were like, I don't know, three quarters of the way into the mess? And then we found out about it? And it was like, "What? This was an option all along?"

**Stephanie:** Yeah.

**Eddie:** I mean, they wouldn't come out if, you know, he was being violent. But if we could at least get him calmed down to a point where you know we could have brought them, that would have been so much less of a traumatic experience for him and for us because we would have just been home. There would have been no going to the ER and sitting there for hours and you have to do the whole screening, and we didn't even know about that forever. It would be nice if there was just, like, a website for each state.

**Stephanie:** Yeah.

**Eddie:** Or each county, or whatever it is, where there's differences that's just like, "Here's all the resources and things that you need. Just here." But instead it was like, "Oh, I gotta go to this person to find out about this thing." And we didn't know that, like, partial placement was a thing until we were like way knee-deep, chest deep in it.

**Stephanie:** Even once we found out about it, they said we couldn't access the one near our house because we didn't have Medicaid for him. At the time.

**Eddie:** Whatever it is. So, I don't know. That would have been helpful for sure. Like, it'd be super if the states could do that themselves. Or like a non-profit or something. Just gather all the resources.

**Stephanie:** Yeah

**Eddie:** And I know that some states have lines that you can call where they probably would give you that information, but I feel like they wouldn't give you all of the information. I want a directory of everything where I can just go up "Oh, Early Intervention and the Intermediate Unit stuff, and oh here's MH-IDD, and here's some lists of therapists, but check with your insurance provider. Here's a list of psychiatrists, check with your insurance provider. Here are kids' psychiatric hospitals, here are adolescent, here are adult." Everything. It would be nice if it was just in one place. Like a one-stop place. Because when you're in the thick of it you aren't thinking about that kind of stuff clearly. You're trying to deal with the situation at hand.

**Stephanie:** Yeah.

**Eddie:** It would be nice if that existed, but I don't think it does. I mean, maybe some states have something like that, but...

**Stephanie:** (scoffs) None of the states we lived in.

**Eddie:** Pennsylvania sure didn't.

**Stephanie:** No, they didn't. Um, is there anything else you want to add?

**Eddie:** (long pause, shrugs)

**Stephanie:** No? All right, well thank you for talking to me. I think it's really important to get dads' perspectives in these kinds of situations.

**Eddie:** Yeah, it was tough to balance, you know, having to provide in a way that I was still, you know, performing at work to make sure things were okay.

**Stephanie:** Yeah.

**Eddie:** And all the costs that were associated with even just traveling up there to go see him. The medical expenses and all that stuff, that was a lot of pressure. Additional pressure above what was already happening.

**Stephanie:** I know, and I think it's important to acknowledge that we are among the most fortunate people in those kinds of situations because you had a job that offered paid time off, and a flexible schedule, and we had transportation and the ability to travel to go visit him.

**Eddie:** Yeah, that was when we would go visit him, which was not every time, especially after he had been in there many times for a long time, it just became really impractical to do that because it was like a two-hour drive.

**Stephanie:** Well, also it created issues for him cuz sometimes seeing their parents and stuff can cause more issues for them in treatment.

**Eddie:** Sure. Well, and the weather, whatever, cuz you know, it was in the winter.

**Stephanie:** Yeah.

**Eddie:** But, like, you know, on visitation days when we would go up and there would be, you know, twenty-some kids in his wing or whatever, his unit, and we would go up and there would be like two parents. I'm sure a lot of that was economic. They might have been coming from far away and just couldn't do it. You know they had to work and had other kids or whatever. So, it's tough. I don't know. I don't think there's a right answer for any of it, or a right way to do any of it. But that's what maybe makes it kind of hard.

**Stephanie:** I think just maybe kind of shining a light and having people understand how the process works helps a lot because a lot of the people making the decisions don't have experience with going through the process, and just being able to understand just how it feels as a family when you're going through it might be helpful.

**Eddie:** Mm-hmm. That's a fair point.

**Stephanie:** Well, thank you for talking to me about this.

**Eddie:** You're welcome.

# Resources

Dial the number 2-1-1 in the U.S. to be connected to mental health or community support in your local area. Calls are confidential.

The National Suicide Prevention Lifeline is 1-800-273-8255.

Visit crisistextline.org or text the word HOME to 741741 in the U.S. or Canada to be immediately connected to a crisis counselor for free.

The National Federation of Families is an organization that serves children with emotional, behavioral, or mental health needs and their families. Visit their website at ffcmh.org.

Visit mentalhealth.gov to learn how to access immediate help and locate services in your area.

The Substance Abuse and Mental Health Services Administration (SAMHSA) has a section on their website that can help you locate treatment options. Visit www.samhsa.gov/find-treatment.

# Coping Strategies

*The following strategies have been helpful for Nicholas. They are provided here for informational purposes only.*

**Controlled Breathing:** Inhale deeply through your nose, counting to five. Hold your breath and count to six. Slowly exhale through your mouth while you count to seven. Repeat several times.

**Five Senses:** Focus on what is happening at this moment. What do you see? A sofa, a blanket, a television. What do you hear? A bird. A dripping faucet. A radio. What do you smell, taste, or feel right here, right now?

**Press and Squeeze:** Start at your feet and press them into the floor. Clench your toes, hold, and release them. Slowly move up your body. Press your legs down into your chair. Squeeze your muscles, focusing on one area of your body at a time. Hold, then release. Keep moving up through your body until you reach the top of your head.

**Journal or Draw:** Keep a notebook just for your own private thoughts. When things are overwhelming, write or draw a picture about how you are feeling.

**Stop, Think, and Plan:** Before making impulsive decisions, try to think of a stop sign. Pause and take a moment to think about the consequences of what you are about to do. Make a plan that keeps everyone safe and won't get you in trouble.

**Talk Therapy**: Speak with a licensed professional counselor.

**Bibliotherapy and Cinema Therapy:** Read a book or watch a movie in which the characters go through a similar experience to the one you are living, or create a story of your own. Reflect on how you feel and how you can apply the lessons from the book or movie to your life.

**Nature:** Get outside. Take a walk, swing, draw with sidewalk chalk, or blow bubbles.

**Exercise:** Jumping on a trampoline, playing a sport, jumping rope, or riding a bike can help.

**Eat Well:** Try to eat at the same time each day so you won't forget. Keep healthy foods and snacks in your home, and be sure to drink lots of water. It is hard to make good choices when we are hungry or thirsty.

**Rest:** Set a bedtime and stick to it whenever you can. Sleep is important for brain health.

**Medication:** Do not be afraid to ask a doctor if medication might be a good choice for you.

# Acknowledgments

First and foremost, a huge thank you to my family for trusting me to share the most intimate details of our lives and for your patience during the process. Eddie, thank you for being you, but also for the extra parenting and household tasks you undertook so I could write, and especially for the times you booked me hotel rooms and sent me away in solitude to spend my days banging my hands (and sometimes my head) onto the keyboard. Nicholas, your story will touch so many lives and I am proud of you beyond measure for having the strength and the confidence to ask me to share it. I hope I have done it the justice it deserves. I tried my very best. Abigail, Penelope, Ana, and Donny, you have endured so much and I am constantly in awe of your grace, empathy, and compassion. I love you all. Forever and longer.

To my mother, Teresa Wilkins, for stepping straight into our chaos and never being afraid to get your hands dirty, for your skills as a copy editor, and for rising to meet the needs of a community desperate for more qualified mental health professionals. You are astonishing.

To my in-laws, Ed and Cindy Giese, my father and stepmother, Harry and Helen Wilkins, and our siblings Charlotte Beckmeyer, Harry "Trey" Wilkins, and Bobby Giese, we appreciate all of the love and practical support you showed along the way.

To all of the educators, health professionals, social workers, clergy, and friends who have offered help, advice, listening ears, and open hearts, your role in healing our family cannot be overstated. Thank you.

To the women on the internet who saved my sanity and quite possibly my life, all of my eternal gratitude and love. You know who you are. I wouldn't be here without you.

To the readers who have supported our family and shared our lives through my website *Binkies and Briefcases* since 2010, we appreciate you and are so happy to have you in our community and our corner.

Finally, to Matthew Glass, the best writing partner I could hope to have, thank you for patiently wading through piles of half-formed ideas, dramatic emails, phone calls, many misplaced commas, and even more misspelled words until a cohesive story began to show itself. It was a long five years, and I will never be able to thank you enough for sticking with me until the end. You were right. I did have a book in me. And we got it out.

# About the Author

Stephanie Giese is a mother of five and a children's advocate currently living in Tampa, Florida. She holds a master's degree in the field of education and has served as a public school teacher in the states of Maryland, Pennsylvania, and Florida. Her work can be seen in various outlets online and in print, as well as on her personal website *Binkies and Briefcases*. Stephanie's essays are featured in the parenting anthologies *Will Work for Apples*, *You Have Lipstick on Your Teeth*, and the *New York Times* best-selling *I Just Want to Pee Alone*. She has written for *Central Penn Parent* and *SMART Magazine* in York, Pennsylvania. Her work can also be seen online on websites such as HuffPost, The Blaze, and Good Housekeeping. She has previously been named a BlogHer Voice of the Year, and in 2014 was called one of HuffPost's "most viral bloggers of the decade." When she isn't writing, Stephanie enjoys binging '90's television shows, eating takeout, and reading just about anything, but she is especially fond of the works of Judy Blume, Bo Burnham, and John Mulaney.

# References

*Attachment-Focused Parenting: Effective Strategies to Care for Children* by Daniel A. Hughes. W.W. Norton & Company, 2009.

*Childhood and Adult Trauma Experiences of Incarcerated Persons and Their Relationship to Adult Behavioral Health Problems and Treatment* by Nancy Wolff and Jing Shi, 2012
https://www.ncbi.nlm.nih.gov/pmc/articles/PMC3386595

*Early Mortality and Primary Causes of Death in Mothers of Children with Intellectual Disability or Autism Spectrum Disorder: A Retrospective Cohort Study.* Edited by Katsuaki Suzuki, 2014
https://www.ncbi.nlm.nih.gov/pmc/articles/PMC4275172/

*The Fathers Are Coming Home* by Margaret Wise Brown. Margaret K. McElderry Books, 2010.

*I'll Always Come Back* by Steve Metzger. Scholastic, 2002.

*It Hurts When I Poop! A Story for Children Who Are Scared to Use the Potty.* By Howard J. Bennett. Magination Press, 2007.

*Llama Llama Misses Mama* by Anna Dewdney. Viking Books for Young Readers, 2009.

*Parents of Children with and without Intellectual Disability:*

*Couple Relationships and Individual Well-Being* D. Norlin and M. Broberg, 2012.
https://onlinelibrary.wiley.com/doi/abs/10.1111/j.1365-2788.2012.01564.x

*Play Therapy: The Groundbreaking Book That Has Become A Vital Tool in the Growth and Development of Children* by Virginia M. Axline Ballantine Books, 1981

Made in United States
North Haven, CT
11 March 2022

17027022R00248